D0540615

FURTHER REMINISCENCES

1864–1894

BY THE SAME AUTHOR

EARLY REMINISCENCES
1834–1864
DEVONSHIRE CHARACTERS
CORNISH CHARACTERS
THE LAND OF TECK

THE BODLEY HEAD

S. BARING-GOULD
From a Photograph

FURTHER REMINISCENCES
1864-1894
BY S. BARING-GOULD

Plenus rimarum sum, hac atque illac perfluo
TERENCE, *Eun.* I. 2

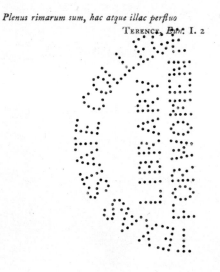

TEXAS STATE COLLEGE LIBRARY FOR WOMEN

NEW YORK
E. P. DUTTON AND COMPANY
PUBLISHERS

First Published in 1925

Made and printed in Great Britain at
The Mayflower Press, Plymouth. William Brendon & Son, Ltd.

PREFACE

THIS book is the continuation of my *Early Reminiscences*. As Paul Scarron says in *Le Roman Comique* : " Si le lecteur bénévole est scandalisé de toutes les badineries qu'il a vues jusqu'ici dans mon récit, il sera fort bien de n'en lire pas davantage ; car, en conscience, il n'y verra pas d'autres choses, et si, par ce qu'il a déjà vu, il a de la peine à se douter de ce qu'il verra, peut-être que j'en suis logé là aussi bien que lui ; qu'un chapitre attire l'autre, et que je fais dans mon livre comme ceux qui mettent la bride sur le col de leurs chevaux, et les laissent aller sur leur bonne foi. Peut-être aussi que j'ai un dessin arrêté, j'instruirai en divertissant."

86598

CONTENTS

CHAPTER   PAGE

 I. Horbury-Brig, 1864–66   1

 II. Dalton i' t' Muck, 1867–71 18

 III. A Honeymoon Tour, 1868 28

 IV. Mersea, 1871–72 37

 V. Belgium, Germany and the Tyrol, 1871–73 or
  1872 ? 51

 VI. The Eifel and the Algau Alps, 1874–75 . . 63

 VII. The Gould Family and Lew Trenchard, 1874–75 73

 VIII. Freiburg, 1877 83

 IX. Lew Trenchard, 1881 100

 X. Archbishop Temple, 1882–85 115

 XI. Devonshire Lore, 1882–85 121

 XII. The Montafun Thal, 1885 146

 XIII. Bohemia, 1886 157

 XIV. The Riesengebirge and Dresden, 1886 . . . 170

 XV. Folk Songs, 1887–88 184

 XVI. Genoa and Rome, 1889 216

 XVII. Rome Revisited, 1890 233

 XVIII. Dartmoor, 1891 243

 XIX. Les Eyzies, 1892 253

 XX. Squab-pie, 1894 264

 Index 279

ILLUSTRATIONS

S. BARING-GOULD	*Frontispiece*	
REV. JOHN SHARP	*To face page*	4
GRACE BARING-GOULD	,, ,,	26
THE MARSHES, MERSEA	,, ,,	38
THE SALTINGS, MERSEA	,, ,,	50
THE DOWER HOUSE	,, ,,	76
SIR EDWARD GOULD	,, ,,	82
FREIBURG IN BADEN	,, ,,	90
REV. CHARLES BARING-GOULD	,, ,,	100
RIGHT REV. R. BICKERSTETH	,, ,,	118
S. BARING-GOULD	,, ,,	138
CHURCH OF MARIA SCHMELTZ, MARTEL THAL	*page*	154
DEATH BOARDS AT CHAM	,,	163
REV. J. M. GATRILL	*To face page*	164
ROBERT HARD	,, ,,	190
JAMES GOULD	,, ,,	220
HUT CIRCLES ON DARTMOOR	,, ,,	250
THE VIATICUM TO THE DYING	,, ,,	266

FURTHER REMINISCENCES

1864-1894

FURTHER REMINISCENCES
1864-94

CHAPTER I

HORBURY-BRIG
1864-66

I WAS ordained by the Bishop of Ripon upon Whit Sunday, 1864, a memorable day in my life ; and the following day went to Horbury to enter on my curacy.

Horbury is a township near Wakefield, from which it is distant three miles. Formerly, it was a mere chapelry in the parish of Wakefield, but it is now independent of its mother, has a large church of its own, and two filial churches as well. That latter phase, however, is subsequent to my time. The town, if so it may be called, occupies a ridge of high ground, above the River Calder, the name of which is Scandinavian, and signifies the Cold-River. At the present day it would qualify as the Warm or Lukewarm river, on account of the amount of hot waste water injected into it from the factories.

At the time when I went thither, when my clerical life was initiated, in 1864, Horbury was in the condition of one who had ceased to be a boy, but had not as yet attained to manhood. It was in the hobbledehoy period of existence. No longer a large village, it had not then attained the size and acquired the dignity that would entitle it to be called a town.

Horbury stands upon a height composed of sandstone, that flakes into slabs, and which overlies the coal-measures ; accordingly a portion of the population is composed of colliers.

The valley of the Calder is deep in rubble brought down from the western hills that divide Yorkshire from Lancashire. In

B

this valley, and on the slope of the sandstone hill, were situated manufactories of yarn, of cloth and of devil's dust or shoddy. A few more lie on the further side of Horbury on the road to Wakefield, and also in the township of Ossett to the west.

The manufacture of shoddy consists in the tearing to pieces of old cloth, and reducing it to dust. This dust is disposed of to the cloth manufacturers, and is dribbled into the material that is woven during the process of textile work. The adulteration may be overdone. Whilst I was at Horbury, a large order for blankets came from New York, and the order when executed was consigned to its destination. On discharge at New York, all the blankets had to be carried away in wheelbarrows, resolved into their original constituents, dust, with a limited amount of fibre to retain the particles in place. The demand for old worn-out coats, waistcoats and trousers, however tattered and torn, to supply the shoddy mills was great. Whether, since I was in Horbury, it has been discovered that adulteration, if excessive, is inexpedient, and this discovery has led to rectification in the process of cloth weaving, I am unable to say. I write of matters about sixty years ago.

I generally meet with shoddy now in the sermons of clergy who neither read nor think.

On the further side of the Calder dale the character of the country is totally different : there is clay there with brick works ; but the population is for the most part agricultural and the intelligence of the people is below that of the inhabitants of the manufacturing districts.

To the east the height declines gradually towards the station of Horbury Junction. On the way thither is California, a spring of water so charged with gas that, if a match be applied to it, the gas bubbles explode in flame. The water of this spring is so soft that it wants " no-but a kettle " to hold it to make strong tea, though no leaves have been infused.

I have given a very graphic description of Horbury and the Calder vale in my novel, *The Pennycomequicks*, and I will not here repeat what is there said.

The factories are gaunt brick structures, standing in their " folds " or yards, and many of the cottages of the artisans open into these folds.

A pretty sight it is, on Monday morning, to see the troops of lasses going to the mills, in their clean white pinafores, arms bare, and over their heads scarlet, or pink, or blue kerchiefs tied under the chin. Many a joke passes between these lasses and the lads bound to the factories on their several ways. In the evening the "buzzer" having sounded to "loose" work, the lads and lasses swarm out on their way to their respective homes, carrying in hand the bright tin can in which their midday meal had been contained, filled in the morning, empty to the last crumb in the evening. The white pinafore has lost some of its purity, and by Saturday evening has become besmirched and dirty.

Later I picked up a pretty ballad, from an itinerant blacksmith who went by the name of Ginger Jack. Although a Devonshire man, he had wandered over a large portion of Great Britain and Wales, and had collected a wondrous store of ballads with their tunes. I presume that the following was gathered in Yorkshire, but I do not know. Ginger Jack professed not to be able to recall where he learned it. I may add that this wandering blacksmith had made the acquaintance of the inside of several of our jails, on the charge of wife and children desertion. The melody of the song is as fresh as the words.

"I saw a sweet lassie trip over the lea,
Her eyes were as loadstones attracting of me.
Her cheeks were the roses that Cupid lurks in,
With a bonny blue kerchief tied under her chin.

'O where are you going, my fair pretty maid?
O whither so swift through the dewdrops?' I said.
'I go to my mother, kind sir, for to spin,'
O the bonny blue kerchief tied under her chin!

To kiss her sweet lips then I sought to begin.
'O, nay sir!' she said, 'ere a kiss you would win,
Pray show me a ring, tho' of gold the most thin.'
O slyest blue kerchief tied under the chin.

'Why wear a blue kerchief, sweet lassie?' I said.
'Because the blue colour is not one to fade.
As a sailor's blue jacket who fights for the King,
So's my bonny blue kerchief tied under the chin.

The love that I value is certain to last,
Not fading and changing, but ever set fast.
That only the colour my love, sir, to win.'
So good-bye from the kerchief tied under the chin." [1]

I may add that whilst at Horbury I collected several folk-songs, carols and folk-tales.

The parish church of Horbury stands in the middle of the townlet. It was erected by a Mr. Carr, an architect, at his own expense, in the eighteenth century, and possesses a respectable tower and spire. Internally it has no aisles, and is apsidal at each end. This construction has its disadvantage, for every sound produced at the west end rings in the ears of the clergy within the altar-rails. Thus, when a mother, sitting under the organ loft at the further extremity of the church, admonishes her son : " Blow your nose, and don't snuffle ! " the priest at the altar receives this injunction in a distinct whisper, as though thus personally rebuked.

The vicarage was on the north side of the church, which cut off the sun from all the windows on the south side. It possessed a small walled garden to the east, the grass, the shrubs and the flowers, so begrimed with soot as to dirty the fingers that touched them. There was an old mulberry tree in it, but the fruit tasted of smoke.

Mr. John Sharp, the vicar, was unmarried, a peculiarly fine specimen of one of the old Tractarian movement, courteous, cultured, and tender-hearted. It always struck me that in appearance he resembled an Italian priest of the highest type. Although he was a ready extempore preacher, he was not eloquent, nor was he original in what he said. I must have heard over one hundred of his sermons, but cannot recall that I ever acquired an *idea* from them. But if not a great preacher, he was a most assiduous visitor, and the people were warmly attached to him. He was nominated to the Vicarage of Horbury by his father, who was Vicar of Wakefield in 1834.[2] He was quite a young man, but he had very definite Church views. His great-grandfather was Archbishop Sharp of York, a notable Churchman in the reign of Queen Anne, who laboured along with Archbishop Wake

---

[1] Published with the original music in my *Songs of the West*, Methuen & Co., 1891.   [2] Born 1810, retired 1899, died 1903.

REV. JOHN SHARP
From a Photograph

of Canterbury to effect an union between the Gallican and the Anglican Churches. When John Sharp became vicar, he found the interior of the parish church pewed up from the one end to the other. The " horse-boxes " were of various sizes, and were turned in diverse directions. They were possessed by the " respectables " of the parish, the mill-owners, the doctors, the lawyers, and the retired gentlefolks ; and none of these were assiduous in church attendance. They might or might not put in an appearance in the morning, but never in the evening, when they were too seriously and vigorously engaged upon their dinners or suppers. As to the factory hands, no provision had been made for them.

Accordingly, the first attempt at innovation made by Mr. Sharp was to get rid of the pews. He had been left a small income by his father. This he expended in legal and other expenses in attaining his purpose. Happily none of the pew-holders had considered it necessary or expedient to obtain " faculties " for their pews ; nevertheless they managed to obstruct him in various ways as suggested by the lawyers, in the expectation of exhausting his finances or his patience. However, he persisted. The horse-boxes were swept away, and replaced by open benches. Then, and not till then, ensued an influx of the factory hands, middle-aged and young, and the vicar found himself surrounded by a band of zealous young men ready to help in the choir, in the savings bank and in the various benefit clubs that he had instituted. It was noticed, and not forgotten, that disaster had come upon all those who had been the vicar's most strenuous and persistent opponents. Although the struggle over the pews had occurred thirty years before I came to Horbury, this fact was still recorded, and among those who had resisted his efforts with the greatest vehemence not one remained in the place.

There was something peculiar in my first arrival at Horbury.

I had left Ripon by a morning train and arrived in due time at Horbury main station, having changed trains at Wakefield, where I had my lunch.

On reaching Horbury Station I found that the place provided no cabs, and possessed no omnibus. No porter was available for my portmanteau. So I shouldered it and walked up the hill towards the houses surmounted by the spire. I heard a brass band playing, and soon fell in with a procession of men. On inquiry I ascertained that this was the School Festival. So I deposited my portmanteau in a little shop, and joined the procession. What caused me some surprise was the halting, and partial dissolution of the procession at the door of the public-house. But I understood that the instrumentalists, what with the ascent of the hill with the sun on their backs, and their exertion upon horns and pipes and drums, needed refreshment, and called for pots of beer. I could appreciate as well the sympathy exhibited by the processionists, in that they as well called for pots of beer, to show brotherhood with the orchestra.

When, after a while, refreshed and reinvigorated, the band reformed and after a brazen flourish, blew lustily " See the Conquering Hero comes ! " I concluded that this was a delicate allusion to myself, who along with another man brought up the tail of the procession. But when the band and all who followed it passed the church and vicarage, without entering or noticing either, I began to entertain suspicions, and, turning to the man with whom I walked, I inquired as to the nature of the school in which he was, as he had confided to me, a teacher. Then only did I learn that this was a Dissenting demonstration. I dropped from the tail, flew back, got my portmanteau, and stole very crestfallen into the house of the Rev. John Sharp, where I was heartily laughed at for my novel entry upon my duties.

I, myself, being a Devonshire man, and familiar with the minds, habits of thought, and prejudices of the agricultural and artisan class of my native county, found myself transported into a surrounding of people of a totally different mental and social complexion, and it took me some time to orientate myself towards them. I recall the shock given to me, in the very first cottage I entered. A mother was engaged at the stove over some cooking. Her infant was seated in a tall child's chair with a knife in its hand, smearing a piece of bread with treacle. I suppose that my sudden entrance startled it, for it fell headlong upon the stone floor out of the chair. It was not seriously hurt. I remonstrated with the mother at furnishing the child with a knife, and putting it on a tall chair unstrapped in. " The poor child might have fallen on the knife and have transfixed itself." " Eh ! so she might," said she composedly, " but she wouldn't ha' done it again." That was the way in which a Yorkshire woman taught me to mind my own business. We remained very good friends, and when I was married she made me a wedding present of a nutmeg-grater.

The dialect and expressions employed were to me at first puzzling. A little girl meeting me in the street stopped me and, looking up in my face, inquired : " When is the next potation ? " It was explained to me that " potation " meant a public tea.

A funeral feast was a great function. The table was spread with plum-cake, " parkin " or pepper cake, and jugs of ale. Along with the cake were served junks of cheese. If there were, as often was the case, apple-pie, then cheese was eaten in large slices with the apple.

After a while, during which I acted simply as curate of Horbury, my proper sphere was delimited for me by the vicar. This proper sphere was at Horbury-Brig, beyond the station and a mile and a half from the parish church. I was to work among the people who had been wholly neglected, even by the Dissenters, and to do what I could to raise money for the building of a school-chapel there.

Horbury-Brig was a very different place in the 'sixties from what it is now. By means of a canal that drained off most of the water of the Calder, it had become a lively *entrepôt* for coal, and there was great demand for house accommodation. Consequently I had a mighty difficulty in obtaining a *pied à terre* there. Eventually I secured a very small cottage, one in a row, and consisting of a single room on the ground-floor, with a very small back-kitchen. This room was styled " t' house," and it was kitchen and parlour. Out of it was taken a staircase that led to a single bedroom above, and under the stairs was the coal-closet.

The " house " I appropriated for a night school, and the bedroom over it I converted into a chapel.

I began with night school every evening in the winter, and with service every Sunday evening in the chapel. I had to stand on a stool before the chimney-piece, on which stood a cross and a pair of candlesticks. I wore no surplice, only a cassock. Very soon a congregation was formed, that grew till it not only filled the upper room, but occupied the stairs as well, and the kitchen below. Hymns were performed somewhat laggingly, as the singing had to bump down the stairs, fill the kitchen, and one strain of the tune after another came up irregularly through the chinks in the floor, to interfere with the smoothness and sequence of the melody as sung above. The notes from the stairs also jostled.

Staunch friends were made among the mill-hands, and I experienced the utmost kindness from them. I went to tea in one of their cottages every Sunday evening. My helpers were two nice young women, named Rushworth, somewhat superior to the rest ; they also worked in the mills. I was helped as well by an old muffin-man, who had been a Romanist, but had settled very happily into the Church of England. He helped to teach the boys. At intervals a waft of tobacco smoke passed through the room. I found that the old man had his pipe in his pocket, and that every now and then he drew it forth and refreshed himself with a whiff.

There was some opposition at first from the rowdy element, but that died away, and all went on smoothly. I had an excellent assistant, though not a teacher, in a stout, bald-headed wool-comber named Scholey, who would stand no nonsense, and if any roughs approached my door during school hours he would sally forth, crack a couple of walnuts in his fist, and shout like the bellow of a bull : " If you don't take care and be peaceable, I'll crack your heads as I do these here nuts." He said to me at the outstart : " Let's have no back reckonings." What he meant was : " Begin as you propose to continue, and do not retreat from a position once assumed."

There was a tun of a woman with a blazing red face, named Cardwell, who kept a little shop. The key of my cottage was left with her.

One Saturday I was in a revolutionary condition in my insides, and I had to go down to the Brig to carry on the Savings Bank there for an hour. Seeing how unwell I was, my fellow-curate, Davies, gave me a couple of pilules from his homœopathic chest. Thus fortified I went on my way, and called at Mrs. Cardwell's for the key. She saw that I was unwell and bleached, so said : " Bless your heart ! I have a fine medicine for English cholera. Take some of that." So she administered a dose. Then I went to serve at the Savings Bank. On my return to surrender the

key, she wore a look of concern, " Lord ! " said she, " whatever
have I done ? I'm so sorry. I mistook the bottle, and gave you
a cow-drench. Now I've found the proper stuff. Have a dose
of that." I did so.

When I arrived at the Vicarage, I told Mr. Sharp that I was
concerned for the morrow, which would be one of hard work
for me ; and expressed my wish that I could have what is called
a " chalk mixture."

" Well," he observed, " I believe that I have half a bottle
upstairs, that has been lying by on the top of my cupboard for
the last twelve years, and I do not know whether at present it is
good for anything. You can but try it." Try it I did. I drained
the bottle.

After supper that evening a longing came over me for hot
spiced beer, and I asked the cook to brew some for me. Davies,
the curate, was indignant. " You'll be dead to-morrow," he
protested, " and then Sharp will send me down to that confounded
Brig." But, to the amazement of Davies and Sharp, and of
myself also, I was well next day. What cured me ; whether the
globules, or the cow-drench, or the " right stuff," or the twelve-
year-old chalk mixture, or the spiced ale, to this present day I
am not able to decide.

Sometimes at night when the weather was stormy, and the
rain plashed down, instead of climbing the hill to reach the
Vicarage where I lodged, I slept in the cottage, on a folding bed
I kept there.

Then I could hear in the early morning, while it was still dark,
the patter of the wooden clogs worn by the mill-girls as they
came from Netherton or Ossett, to their early work at the mills.

Every night after the school " loosed " the scholars expected
me to tell them a story. As one says, who still lives, and loves
to record old reminiscences, " The boys and girls used to get on
Baring-Gould's coat-laps to keep him prisoner, and sing out in
chorus, ' You mun tell us a tale afore you go.' Then he would
begin, ' Once upon a time,' and he made it up as he went along,
and it was always something that suited us." Another says :
" Baring-Gould often stayed with us for tea on Sundays and wet
week-days. Sometimes he would tell us about Iceland and its
geysers, its wonderful scenery and interesting people. You see,

he'd been there, and in many other countries as well, and he used to tell us all about them."

My connexion with the parish church gradually grew less and less as I became more engrossed in my work at "the Brig."

There were about seven hundred people in my district, but across the bridge over the Calder there were more in the parish of Thornhill, two miles distant from the parish church, forming two hamlets, Upperton and Netherton. The rector was a man of the old school, a port-wine drinking, easy-going man, very good company at the dinner table if you were not nice as to the quality of his anecdotes and jests ; doing nothing whatever for the spiritual welfare of his people ; doing nothing because he did not know how to do anything, and not at all desirous of doing anything that would give him trouble.

I had great assistance from a gentleman who lived half-way between Horbury and the Brig, Fred Knowles, who played the little American organ, and helped in school and practice. Without him I should have been without my right hand. He died a few years after I left Horbury. The Lord remember him for his services, at the Last Day.

Almost every Sunday, as already said, I had tea with some one or other of the cottagers, all engaged in the factories, warm-hearted, kindly people, who could not do enough for one. It was a puzzle to me to explain their existence—utterly untouched by religious influences till the Mission was founded, and then unfolding as a closed flower to the sun's rays, and welcoming its warmth. The neglect in which they had been left was not due to remissness on the part of Mr. Sharp, but to the extent of his parish and the density of the population. He himself was a man of advanced age, and for long he could maintain but a single curate. But he had a number of zealous young men who helped him as much as they could in club and choir and savings bank, and some of the mill-lasses were excellent.

The cottage soon proved too small for our requirements, and I had to collect money by appeals in the *Church Times* and to my friends and relations. A singular subscription came to me, of half a sovereign, from a man in the mills who never went to church. Not till some time after did I learn how it came to me. He had been engaged with another in fighting their respective dogs on Sunday morning, for a prize of ten shillings, and when he got it : " It shall go to the Brig Mission," said he, and gave it me.

Of the factories at Horbury Bridge, one was in Chancery, one belonged to the Dissenters, a third had been recently built, which the owner had strained his resources to the utmost to erect, and supply with machinery, and a fourth was burnt down whilst I was founding my Mission. We consequently found difficulty in obtaining money sufficient to build a school-chapel, though I received generous help from some of the Horbury people : and the vicar, the Rev. John Sharp, also pleaded for the Mission among his many friends and admirers. Mr. Knowles, already mentioned, was owner of a stone quarry, and he generously offered to supply from it, free of cost, sufficient building stone for the construction of a school-chapel. For the foundations we were obliged to employ large slabs of sandstone laid upon the gravel and sand that formed the basis of the Calder vale, and on which several of the factories had been erected. It was a precarious foundation, and some of the smoke chimneys of the manufactories leaned considerably. The school-chapel was opened, free of debt, on S. Katherine's Day, 1865. In later years, after I had left, a large church, dedicated to S. John the Divine, was built, also a day school, and my structure was retained as a parish room.

As already intimated, the Vicar of Horbury was no great, though he was a ready and voluble, preacher. However, he had curates who could *teach ;* and their teaching was valuable, and lasting in effect. I will but mention two of them. The first was Anthony Cass. He was a man of strong character, and very definite in his views ; he knew how to impart what he had to say in such a manner as to grave an impression on the hearts and minds of his hearers. He was also a man of considerable presence. He was further, by birth and parentage, a Yorkshireman, so that he knew the ins and outs of the minds of the West Riding people. He was well aware in what they were strong, as well as in what they were weak.

One very rare and peculiar faculty he possessed ; and that was, when in conversation with anyone, and the subject did not interest him, he would suddenly become aware of what was actually passing in the mind of his interlocutor, and would abruptly interrupt the flow of common-place talk with the exclamation : " You are thinking of—this or that—(mentioning it), and not of the subject of conversation." The faculty or gift was no advantage to him, as it frightened many of those with whom he was acquainted. But this was due to his indiscretion. He should have been reticent, and not have revealed the fact that he could read the minds of those with whom he was in converse. I have known others possessed of the same gift, more or less, but they have been discreet or reserved. I feel convinced that to some extent dogs possess the same faculty.

Another curate was named Davies, a Welshman. He was a sound, practical individual, a good theologian, and had much influence, which he exercised over the factory lasses. He was not a good preacher, but he was a wise guide of souls, and as such was much esteemed.

He had his fads ; one of these was a belief in homœopathy, in which I had not a grain of faith. He was somewhat frail in health, stooped, and had a shuffling gait, and hesitation in his speech. In contrast with the vicar, Mr. Cass and myself, who all three were clean-shaven, Davies wore a considerable red beard and moustache, and sandy hair that grew in a tangle, and however much brushed would not lie smooth. He was after a while presented to the living of Onehouse in Suffolk, a rectory ; and I believe that he owed his nomination to the squire, a connexion of whom Davies married upon leaving Horbury. It is one of the misfortunes of the Church of England that the right men are frequently put into the wrong situations. Davies, unfortunately, was planted for the rest of his life in a situation quite other from one which by nature, by capacity, and by liking he was qualified to fill with success. For one thing, he was not of an optimistic nature, and work among the Suffolk rustics did not serve to cheer him after his experience among the quick-witted, straightforward, breezy and generous Yorkshire people. When a man loses heart, he spells failure.

I paid him a visit after he had been a few years in his rectory. The house was surrounded by a moat that was a breeding-place for mosquitoes, and his parlour had been invaded and occupied by a colony of red ants, that he endeavoured to expel by powdering

the floor with cayenne pepper.   I think that eventually the ants
retired to other quarters, but human visitors were unable to
remain more than a minute in the parlour, owing to the cayenne
pepper entering their eyes and nostrils.   Eventually Davies died,
as far as I could judge, of a broken heart.   There are, and have
been, and will be many such men, full of fervour, zeal, and a
hunger after souls, who are exposed to discouragement and dis-
appointment through lack of responsiveness.   You cannot go on
for years in succession playing upon a musical instrument in
which the strings are unstrung, or broken, so that no music is
evoked.   But there are many who, like Davies, are calculated to
do good work in a town, who have done so, and would continue
so to do, but who, on translation to a country pastorate, feel
discouragement within a year or two, and abandon all effort,
give up visiting, and in place of cultivating the spiritual nature
of their parishoners, a slow work, devote their energies to the
growth of daffodils, French-beans, and choice apples.

Pope had said " Dulness is sacred in a sound divine."   But
the Palmerston-Shaftesbury bishops were neither " sound " nor
were they " divines."   They were good men acting up to their
lights, but these lights were no more illuminating than are floating
wicks in oil as night-lights.

Lord Palmerston was himself neither a moral nor a religious
man.   In such matters as concerned Christianity and the Church,
he was a veritable Gallio.   His great object in the nomination of
bishops was to select characterless men, but plausible ; and having
nominated, to address them as Bombastes did his troops :

" Begone, brave army, and don't kick up a row."

Usually he took the advice of Lord Shaftesbury, who had an
awkward squad shambling at his heels.   In one of his letters he
likened himself to Falstaff leading his disreputable recruits
through Coventry.   " The vilains march wide betwixt the legs
as if they had gyves on."   But he had none but this fawning
feeble crew out of whom to choose.

The Bishop of Ripon did not interfere with Mr. Sharp.   The
latter was vastly popular among such people as Lord Wharncliffe,
the Gaskells, and some of the wealthiest manufacturers in the
West Riding.   He had no difficulty in raising money for any
object he liked, notably for his House of Mercy, a large and

stately structure in extensive grounds, under the management of a Sisterhood, presided over by Miss Goodenough, a cousin of his, daughter of Commander Goodenough. I do not recall her name in religion. She was a very capable Mother Superior as long as she had health and strength.

Lord Shaftesbury died October 1, 1885. His son, who succeeded him, was of a different cast, and was deeply in debt. His creditors seized Cranbourne, and the magnificent timber in the park was advertised for sale. The auctioneer was on the spot, and crowds of timber-merchants and spectators arrived to see the devastation of a glorious park of noble trees. However, just as the sale was about to commence, a messenger arrived from the post office fluttering an orange envelope. The auctioneer tore it open and read that the sale would not take place. Lord Shaftesbury had shot himself, April 13, 1886. He had been Earl in possession little over six months. I heard this from a timber-merchant who was present, and who came to purchase some beech trees from me.

A curious instance of superstition occurred whilst I was at Horbury-Brig. A man had been drowned in the Calder, and his body had not been recovered. It was not known where he had fallen in. So the people got a newly baked loaf, stuck a candle in it, lighted this, and set it afloat on the water, and where it rested stationary, there they dragged and, singularly enough, at this place brought up the body.

The people firmly believed in the Padfoot (foo-it), a monstrous supernatural dog with goggle eyes, that was supposed to haunt a lane between the Brig and Ossett. One evening I had been at the Brig and was returning to Horbury. The weather was stormy, and the wind caught my umbrella and wrenched it from my hands, and I lost it in the darkness. The umbrella had a white bone handle.

Several lasses returning to the Brig from Ossett saw a hulking black object restlessly moving in the lane, took fright and fled back to Ossett to make their way home by a circuitous road through Horbury.

That same night in the small hours, a man was returning to Ossett from the Brig, when, to his dismay, he saw a large dark object blocking the path, and having, as he supposed, a white nose. The object wriggled, danced from one side to the other, and would not let him pass. He thought it was a large dog, so he addressed it : " Eh, lad ! thou'lt let me gang my way—there's a good dog, good dog ! "

The object made a move towards him, he took to his heels, and ran to the public-house at the Brig, into which he burst, exclaiming in breathless panic : " I say, the Padfuit is in th' lane."

The taverner sallied forth with lantern up the lane—and found—my umbrella.

One night some of the Horbury-Brig girls were returning from an entertainment at Ossett when they heard a male voice in a field on the other side of the hedge raised in expostulation. So they halted to listen.

Now it happened that this field had been sown with beans, and the owner had erected a "flay-crow," as a scare-crow is termed in Yorkshire, as a protection against birds. As it fell out, a tramp had been imbibing somewhat freely at the Brig tavern, and had made his way up the Ossett lane. Not having money in his pocket, he turned into the field on his right in quest of a shed in which he might sleep ; when, to his dismay, he saw before him the flay-crow with arms extended, and the full moon rising behind it. Down he fell in drunken terror, thinking he saw the Devil come to fetch him, and he was addressing the object when the girls overheard him : " Na' then, Mr. Beelzebub, I know thou art a gentleman. We are both gentlemen. I see you be one, for you've drawed on your clothes when you've come to Horbury. Down below 'tis hot and you don't want any—but above it's cold—and for decency sake you put 'em on. Now you behave like a gentleman to me. I shouldn't mind warmin' my fingers and toes at hell-fire, but I don't want to be throwed on like a bushel of coals. I've served you in many ways. You mind and treat me civilly also."

The lasses, vastly tickled, united in one loud howl behind the fallen tramp. This so scared him that, tumbling over on hands and knees, he crawled up to the scare-crow and clung to the central stake for protection.

I heard the whole story on the next evening from the girls, only broken by fits of laughter.

A fellow I knew was going to Wakefield by night, and I said, laughingly, to him : " Mind you are not robbed at the Sike." " Eh ! " was his reply. " It 'ud tak' two to rob me—one to put t' brass into my pocket, and t'other to tak' it out."

There was a butcher at Horbury, a very worthy man, named James Walker. He got married, and went for his honeymoon to Bolton Abbey. On his return to Horbury, he said to his wife : " Noo, lass, get thee into t' scales."

After some hesitation she complied. Then he pulled out his pencil, made a calculation and said : " Eh, lass ! thou'rt the dearest piece o' meat I ever bought. Thou hast cost me 10¾d. a pound."

I had a white kitten and I stained it pink with one of Judson's dyes. Its mother repudiated it, set up her back, and hissed and spat whenever the kitten approached. The pink cat provoked considerable controversy in Horbury, but James Walker beat it down.

" I be sewer eno' you lass or you lad was a sight pinker once than the kitten : but you're gotten dirty since. Wait a bit. That kitten ain't a twelve-month old, and will get another sort colour in time. You took a sight longer to lose your roses."

James Walker possessed an old-fashioned barometer in a wooden case, 2 ft. 6 in. long. At a rainy time the glass persisted in standing at " Fair," then mounted to " Set Fair " on a pouring wet day. This was too much for James' patience. He unhooked the barometer from the wall, carried it to the window, and, holding it up there, said : " Look out yond, lass ! Dost thou see t'rain streamin' down ? And thou sayest ' Set Fair ' ! I'll teach thee to tell lees ! " And he smashed the glass on the window-sill.

A woman in Horbury was dying. She said to her husband, " Ah, lad ! I wonder whatever the puir bairns will do after I be gone."

" Get along wi' thy dying, lass," replied he soothingly, " I'll mind t'bairns."

Another wife was thought to be at her last gasp. She summoned her husband to her bedside and bade him sit down. There being no chair handy, he seated himself on the bed, and, so as to dispose of his legs without incommoding her, sat with his back to her. She then addressed him solemnly : " Eh ! lad ! I be that sorry for thee. Thou'lt be so lone wi'out me. None to cook thy dinner, none to mend thy socks, none to sew on thy buttons. It duz weigh on my sperits." "Don't concern thyself about that," replied he. "I've already spoke to Marg'et Rhodes to take thy place, and she's quite agreeable."

"Thou hast!" exclaimed the expiring wife, starting up in bed and bringing the palm of her hand with a resounding smack on the man's bald head. "Then, I'll tell thee what, Joe, I won't dee." "Very well," answered the man, pulling out his kerchief and wiping his pate. "If thou'st made up thy mind not to dee, I'll speak to Marg'et, and put her off."

I left Horbury two years after this, and Marg'et was still waiting.

There was no pulpit; the addresses were made from the altar step. Dirty Dick was for a long time fumbling in the book for a text. At last he read out: "The wages of sin is death." He paused, and presently began: "Wages, you see, dearly beloved, is—well—wages, wages. Wages isn't a gift, it isn't a present, it's not a subscription, it's not a donation. It is—it is—well—well—wages. The wages, my text goes on to say, are of sin. Dearly beloved brethren, what is sin? It is a short word of three letters, s and i and n. And what does it mean? Sin is not Good Works, it's not Faith, it's not Hope, it's not Charity; it's not Righteousness; it's just the contrary to all this. It's—it's—it's just sin and nothing else. And the wages of sin is Death. Death is not life. It is not breathing, eating, drinking, thinking, reading, talking, it's——" And so on for twenty minutes. Not an idea in the whole outpour of twaddle. I leaned back in my stall, mopping my brow, I was so ashamed at the exhibition. But, curiously enough, I heard for weeks after about the "grand sermon Muster Collins preached. Eh! but he were a fine preacher and no mistake."

Viscountess Downe lived at Baldersby Park, beyond Topcliffe. After the death of Lord Downe, she married her cousin, a Mr. Lane. She was the daughter of Richard Bagot, Bishop of Bath and Wells. She was still a beautiful woman, with delicate features, full bright eyes and grey hair. My predecessor she had liked greatly, as he had consulted her on everything about the parish.

In Baldersby Church a clock was erected in the spandril of the arches opposite the pulpit and the Dawnay pew. So soon as the vicar mounted the pulpit, every Dawnay eye was directed upon the dial. The preacher was allowed only so many minutes for his allocution. Should he transgress the allotted term, there came to the Vicarage in the ensuing week no presents of game, salmon, grapes, apricots, etc. Lady Downe set the hymns on Saturday for the ensuing Sunday, but I do not think that she appointed to the preacher his texts. She desired to be consulted not only upon everything that went on in Baldersby, but also in Dalton, and my predecessor had studiously humoured this hobby of hers. She was, notwithstanding this dictatorship, a most kindly, generous, and religiously minded lady, and no sick person in any of the parishes over which she reigned lacked any comfort and alleviation that could be afforded them. She was indeed the Lady Bountiful, and liked to be so esteemed.

I found at Dalton much unreality. A man would come diligently to church, in hopes thereby of having a pigsty built for him, and my predecessor rather lent himself to favouritism. I saw the ill-effects, and rigidly abstained from any interference with the tenantry and her ladyship.

I do not think that Lady Downe cared for me. I was wont on invitation to dine and sleep at Baldersby, and we got on together fairly well, but she was not sorry to lose me. Mallison, the rector of Baldersby, told me that it was not possible to remain there in such proximity to the Park and retain his self-respect. He was heartily glad to leave. His predecessor, a very able man, who made his mark in the Church afterwards, had means of his own, and was determined not to be ridden by a woman. She forced him to leave. A considerable number of livings were in her gift during the minority of Lord Downe, and afterwards he put all presentations into her hands.

A singular instance of localization of a myth occurred near Dalton. There was a farm, called New Mills,[1] before which was a long mound, named The Giant's Grave, and the story told was precisely that of Ulysses and Polyphemus, only Jack was the hero and not Ulysses. The giant was buried under the barrow, and in the stable was preserved a blade, which was traditionally held to have been that with which Jack had blinded the ogre.

Some curious customs lingered on till just before my arrival at Dalton. It was customary to put a candle and a coin into the coffin of a dead person to light him or her on the way to Paradise, and to pay the toll at the gate. One old woman was so interred while I was there. I heard of no other case at the time. On Christmas Eve it was still usual for the local grocer to send green wax candles to his customers, originally intended doubtless for the lantern that was carried to the Midnight Mass. On Christmas Eve also a bowl of furmity was eaten—boiled wheat

---

[1] New Mills is 1½ miles S.S.W. of Sessay Station. The present incumbent of Dalton writes 26 May, 1919, that the story is still told, and the grave is shown.

with currants. Parkin or Pepper cake was eaten at All Souls'-tide. When a child was born, those who came to see it brought it a present of a sixpence, an egg and some salt. We were much surprised when the villagers came to see my first-born, Mary, all bringing these contributions. At a wedding, the bride had many yards of coloured ribbon which were cut up, and the young men raced for them. This was a redemption of the garters that were formerly striven for and plucked off the bride's legs.

I went once, and once only, when at Dalton, to a Ruridecanal meeting, and that at the particular request of the clergyman of Sowerby-by-Thirsk, at whose house the gathering was, as the subject to be discussed was Clerical Reading. In those days Ruridecanal meetings took place by rotation in the various parsonages in the circuit and each wound up with a dinner.

When the conference took place at which I was present, the Rural Dean rose to his feet and expressed the need there was for the clergy to be studious.

Then up stood an unctuous Evangelical and said : " We have one Book, one Book that contains all we need. If we go outside the covers of our Bible, we err and go wrong, etc., etc."

Another suggested the advisability of the use of commentaries.

" I allow a Scott's Commentary," said the first.

" And a Cornelius à Lapide," I suggested. No one at the meeting had heard of him or of it.

Then up rose another.

" I think," said he, " that a study of the monthly magazines may be of use. It puts one in touch with the great minds of the present day. For my part, I find great value in *Belgravia* and *Temple Bar*."

Then another stood up, and said : " I agree with the last speaker, but I would supplement the magazines with the daily papers. The police reports are especially valuable, as letting in light upon the spiritual condition of the—the—the masses."

Another struck an attitude, and said : " There is one book that has not been mentioned, a book that must be read, ay, and studied—the hearts of our parishioners."

This was perfectly true, but the man who said it was perhaps the last man in the world to study that book.

This meeting was enough for me. I did not attend another.

Nor were my impressions of the then Archbishop more favourable. Archbishop Thomson was born in 1819 at Whitehaven. He was the son of a draper and grandson of a Scottish Presbyterian minister, so that he had to depend on his wits to push his way. He won a scholarship at Queen's College, Oxford, and took a third class in *Lit. Hum.* in 1840, and in due time became a Fellow of his College. He was ordained in 1842, and in 1847 became Tutor of Queen's and Rector of All Souls', Langham Place.

He filled all the benefices in his gift with Low Churchmen, not that he had any Evangelical convictions, but that he could trust them. *Quieta non movere.*

He possessed an autocratic and masterful temper, such as was naturally bred in a man rapidly advanced from a breeches-maker's shop in a small provincial town to positions of great authority, first as Provost of his College, then as Bishop of Gloucester, and finally as Archbishop of York ; and, wherever he was, he managed to quarrel with those who would not eat humble pie. At Queen's he quarrelled with the Fellows over a petty point of precedence in the Common Room, and as he could not carry his point he sulked, and thenceforth never went there with the rest. At York he fell out with the Dean, a man of birth and courteous manners. He presented a very stately figure in the evenings when he wore his purple velvet coat, purple silk apron, and stockings of the same colour, with large silver buckles in his shoes. He looked like one of the prelates of the old régime in France or one of the Episcopal Electors on the Rhine, and every inch as secular and unspiritual as they.

Whilst I was at Dalton, a mitigated scandal circulated. At one time the bishops unblushingly presented their sons, sons-in-law and kinsmen to the best livings in their gift. But the appointment of Mr. Cheese, son-in-law of Bishop Villiers, to the rich living of Haughton-le-Skerne, worth £1300 per annum, had provoked a cartoon in *Punch*. A poor, needy parson is by a table, whereon stands a Stilton cheese, and the Bishop is decanting over it a bottle of port, labelled £1300, and saying : " I am exceedingly sorry, dear brother in the Church, but, you see, I have not a drop for you, I have poured it all into my *Cheese*."

This taught the bishops caution. Now William Ebor had some one, I cannot recall whether a relation or a toady, whom he was desirous of rewarding with a good living. So he arranged with a brother prelate in one of the Southern dioceses, to present his man to a fat living then vacant, he himself undertaking, in return, to give a satisfactory living in his hands to a son-in-law of the bishop who would so kindly accommodate him.

Before my marriage I had in the house an elderly widow as my housekeeper, and a Mr. Mills, who went by the name of Brother Augustine, a bequest from my predecessor, an account of whom I have given elsewhere.[1]

But on my marriage both left, and for a little while we were without a domestic, and my wife had to do the cooking. I sat on a chair planted upon the kitchen table and read aloud Motley's *Revolt of the Netherlands* whilst she prepared the meals.

One day I was about to go into Thirsk, when my wife said to me : " I wish you would order some meat, there is none in the house."

I dare say she told me of what description it was to be, and how much as to quantity, but all that I forgot. I was busy at the time thinking out my book on *The Origin and Development of Religious Beliefs*. When I arrived at Thirsk I remembered no more than that I was to order some meat. So I went to the butcher and ordered some.

" Of what sort ? " he asked.

I considered. " Really, I do not know ; beef, I suppose."

" What joint ? "

" I do not know. Round of beef is said to be very good."

" How many pounds ? I suppose that you want a good piece ? Will forty pounds do ? "

" I dare say ; I have no doubt," without giving it a thought.

That evening, as I was busy writing, I heard an exclamation from the kitchen, and my wife burst in on me with a face of alarm, crying : " What have you done ? "

" What, my dear ? "

" Come and see."

I went into the kitchen, and saw the butcher's man labouring under a vast mass of beef, which he was glad to deposit on the

---

[1] *In a Quiet Village*, Isbister, 1900.

floor ; after which he proceeded to wipe his brow with the sleeve of his blue smock.

We were but three in the house, my wife, myself and a servant. That round of beef lasted us for weeks. We ate and ate till we came to loathe it as the Israelites loathed the manna. We had it sliced, cold, hashed, as toad-in-the-hole, as mince, as Bubble-and-Squeak—but could not finish it, till in despair I got in the choristers and set them on to it, and they completed the destruction of that Forty-pound Round of Beef.

A curious incident occurred whilst I was at Dalton. The surgeon at Topcliffe was a Mr. Carter Mitchel, whom I knew very well. He was called in to see the wife of a well-to-do farmer, named T——. He was a quiet, inoffensive man, but his wife was a mischievous woman, the terror of the neighbourhood, a strong and venomous dissenter, and one who invented and circulated the most abominable stories about any persons towards whom she bore a grudge.

Mitchel, having been called in to see her, was on his way for a drive in his dog-cart, with his wife and brother-in-law, and they had taken their long-haired terrier with them.

Mitchel drove up to the house and descended at the door, leaving his wife and her brother with the horse and trap. He was shown up to the sick-room and saw at a glance that the woman was dying. He sent instantly for the husband, and as this latter entered the room his wife expired. Next minute Mr. Mitchel descended the stairs and left the house, when he found his wife and brother-in-law in great agitation. The dog had been playing with a shaving of wood under the conveyance, when, a minute or two before, it had started, backed into the side of the road, its hair standing on end, and eyes starting out of its head, precisely as if it had seen some awful object that had scared it out of its wits. A moment later, the dog rushed off down the drive, uttering the wildest yelps and howls. Mr. Mitchel at once drove home, got a gun, and went back in search of the dog. He could not mistake the direction in which to go, as the yelps and howls continued. He finally discovered the beast crouched in a hedge, foaming at the mouth, with distended eyes and hair erect, reeking with sweat. He fired and killed it. Mr. Mitchel drove at once to Dalton and told us the circumstances.

I am conscious of an impression that horses and dogs possess a faculty of seeing things that are hidden from our eyes.

My grandmother was wont twice in the year, at Lady Day and Michaelmas, to send a covered waggon to Exeter to bring to Lew House the groceries needed for the half-year. The distance is thirty-three miles and the road is the old paved highway leading from Isca Dumnoniorum (Exeter) to the Tamar and thence into Cornwall. At one point upon this ancient road, the hills fold in on both sides and contract the valley to little more than a way for the Lew Water, which here consists of two branches. Here from the Roman period existed a bridge, of which all that remains is the name Point, i.e. *pont*. The high-road is commanded by two camps, one prehistoric, of vast size; and the other Saxon. This was the site of the great battle of Gavulford, fought by Egbert against the Britons, and the defeat of the latter previous to their complete rout at Hingesdon in 823.

The driver of the waggon was William Pengelly, who remained in the service of the family to his death at an advanced age. He has repeatedly told me how that on one occasion as he was driving the empty waggon on its way to Exeter, upon reaching Point, the two sturdy cart horses came to an abrupt standstill, and, although lashed with the whip, refused to proceed. Pengelly got out of the conveyance, and taking the lantern in hand, for the hour was early, about 4 a.m. and still dark, he examined the road, but could observe nothing unusual. The horses were standing, with their heads down, apparently staring at something, and were shivering with fear.

Pengelly now administered the whip to their sides with full force, whereupon, simultaneously, both horses made a leap, as if purposing to overcome some obstacle, and tore along the highway as fast as they could gallop, with the waggon bouncing at their heels. They were only stopped by a steep rise in the road, and when the driver caught them up, and recovered command over them, they were bathed in sweat, and were still shivering as with terror. What had caused their panic, Pengelly told me he could never learn.

It is quite possible that a keen sense of smell may be the cause of alarm or dislike to a horse, as in the case of proximity to a donkey or a goat, and that what repels and alarms the brute is

GRACE BARING-GOULD

not anything that it perceives with its eyes. But this explanation will not apply to dogs, which are occasionally affected with panic in a dining or bedroom.

The surgeon at Dalton was an old-fashioned, ignorant practitioner, with white hair, a very red face and watery eyes. When summoned to a case he would shake his head and say : " Bad, very bad, my man, it is a lucky thing that you have called me in. I, alone, can pull you through. But—but—I fear you have left it too long. Had you sent for me last week I could have saved you."

My father now allowed me £150 per annum, so that I had in all £300 ; but the expenses of the church, heating, lighting and of the choir fell on me, as the offertories were small. There was not a single person of means above the farmer class in the parish. The farmers were indifferent to religion and rarely came to church. Neither did they to chapel. There was a remarkable difference in this particular between the people of the West Riding and those of the East ; or, perhaps I may put it thus, between the manufacturing and the agricultural population.

CHAPTER III

A HONEYMOON TOUR
1868

ON May 25, 1868, I married Miss Grace Taylor, of Horbury. We decided to spend our honeymoon abroad and arrived at Interlaken on Whitsun Eve. The little church of Unterseen has its chancel cut off from the nave by a stone wall. The latter is given up to the Protestants, the choir is reserved for Catholic worship. We went to Mass there at 9 a.m. There was a little harmonium, but none to play it, so that the service was not sung. The congregation was reverent and devout. The priest preached a good sermon on " My peace I leave with you, My peace I give unto you." He pointed out the advantage of peace in the land, where was neither outer warfare nor inward broils. Then peace in the household, where husband and wife were united in love, and the children in obedience. Finally, the blessing of peace in the soul where reigns the love of God, and the will is subject to the Divine will. Not very original, perhaps, but very good. I preached the sermon at Dalton on my return, and I have preached it since at Lew. But here comes in something remarkable. Many years afterwards, I was at Brussels when the new dean who had been appointed to S. Gudule preached his initial sermon. It was a Sunday after Trinity, not Whit Sunday. He gave out his text : " My peace I leave with you, My peace I give unto you." It was the same sermon, with only this difference, that it was delivered in French by a dean, and that at Unterseen had been delivered by a poor curate in German. Obviously in the seminaries throughout Latin Christendom the candidates for Orders must be given skeleton addresses which they commit to memory, and amplify as they find expedient. It is customary in Romanist Churches for the

28

clergy to leave the choir and sit together, occupying a pew opposite the pulpit from which harangues the preacher for the day. How they must weary of this order, knowing exactly what he is about to say. It is bad enough in the English Church, where Sunday after Sunday one has to listen to pious twaddle, without in it one original, one vivifying thought.

On Whit Sunday evening we walked up to see the grotto of S. Beatus, the apostle of this district. He came from Ireland or Britain in the seventh century, and made his home in a cave in the face of a precipice above the lake of Thun. A more lovely walk cannot be conceived. The path scrambled along the edge of cliffs overhanging the still green lake, which reflected the glow of the evening in the sky overhead. Tufts of pinks clung to the rock, and bunches of campanula dangled their blue bells at dizzy heights over the still water. Yellow cistus, golden potentilla, and spires of blue salvia made glorious harmonies of colour in the little dales that sank in grassy slopes to tiny coves, where nestled brown cottages and where, in one creek, a gaily painted boat was moored. The cave of the saint was screened by a fir wood, clinging to the rock ledges. Its wide entrance was formerly walled up, so as to leave only a door and window. But as this had constituted a chapel, to which the pious resorted once a year, when Mass was said, at the Reformation the Bernese authorities sent soldiers to destroy the chapel, overturn the altar, and with their pikes drive back the peasants when they ventured to approach. In 1868, when I was there, the cave was only visited by a few sight-seers ; but since then an hotel has been erected on the spot, where much ale is drunk, and green and yellow Chartreuse are sipped, but no prayers are poured forth.

At Lungern, on the nearest point of the Canton of Ob-walden, where the Catholic faith still maintains its ground, loving hearts have built a little chapel dedicated to S. Beatus, and this is now visited by great crowds, who love to honour the memory of their apostle on the ninth of May, when a sermon is preached by one of the Capuchin friars of Sarnen.

The sun set as I sat at the door of the hermit's cave ; and as I walked back to Interlaken, its orange fires fell and touched with flame every white and heaven-aspiring peak ; and the spotless Jungfrau sat amidst a glorious company of mountain

forms, each with its flaming brow ; the sight called up a thought
of the events of that first Whit Sunday, when :

> " The fires that rushed on Sinai down
> In sudden torrents dread,
> Now gently light, a glorious crown
> On every saintly head."

I am not going to add an account of our tour.   Suffice it
that we went to Lucerne, to Meyringen, over the Grimsel, and
into the Valais.   And here I will insert one of my letters to my
old friend Gatrill.

" We walked down the Valais, and spent a night at Münster,
where was an interesting old German carved wood reredos,
painted and gilt-winged, and in very bad repair.   Climbing up to
a little chapel on a height I found a box of tickets promising
indulgences for so many years to any who would say a number
of *aves*, and pull a ticket out of a lottery box.   Some poor
creatures got only six months, some as many as fifty years—
according to the number drawn.   I forget which Pope it was
who granted these indulgences.

" At Sierre we stayed for the Sunday, and attended Mass in
the parish church.   The singing was wretched, the sermon
poor stuff, and the congregation shockingly dirty."

In the evening I climbed the mountain behind Sierre, through
vineyards, and past them to much higher ground where was a little
village or hamlet with a very poor church.   I had a chat with
the curé, who was sitting outside his house sipping wine and
smoking.   He had a very red nose.

" Ah !   Herr Pfarrer ! " said I.   " It is a long pull up the
mountain side with a bottle of wine, I fear."

" *Eine Flasche, mein Gott !* that would never suffice.   I
must have a barrel.   And these accursed peasants will not bring
me up a barrel for the love of heaven ; they ask payment.   It is
bad living up here, but what can one do ?   It is banishment to
Siberia."

" But the Bishop !—surely he will not continue you here ? "

He shook his head and tapped his red nose.   " Till this pales
—here I stay."

" And have you many cretins in your flock ? "

" They are all cretins, idiots ; not a man, woman, or child with sense enough to bring me up a keg of good wine, without taking toll of it on the way, and then asking of me a fee for bringing it."

The landlord at Sierre afterwards told me that the clergy who drank in the valley were sent up to cures near the snow to make it difficult for them to obtain wine. There were stages in altitude. The first for the moderate tippler. Two thousand feet higher for the immoderate drinkers ; then some six or eight thousand feet for those who had had a touch of delirium tremens.[1]

An amusing incident occurred while I was at Sion. The town is built on two pinnacles of rock starting out of the Rhone Valley, crowned severally by the old cathedral and convent, and by the episcopal castle. The modern cathedral is in the lower town, and to it I went on SS. Peter and Paul's Day, June 29. The chancellor of the diocese, a short, stout and very ugly man, preached.

I was sitting directly in front of the pulpit. He discoursed on Papal Infallibility. The sermon was decidedly clever, but would not have been relished by an Ultramontane, because he based the claim on expediency, and not on a Divine Commission. He said that it was absolutely necessary in all organized societies that there should be an ultimate authority to which all disputants could refer. In a family when there arose a dispute reference was made to the father, and his decision was without appeal. In a Commune when controversy arose both parties addressed themselves to the mayor, and his decision was final. When there was a cantonal quarrel the matter went to Berne, and the judgment of the Federal Assembly was beyond appeal. So in the Church, etc. Then he went on to the doctrine of the Immaculate Conception There might have been, perhaps there had been, doubts expressed as to this dogma, and such doubts were permissible till final judgment had been pronounced thereon, though in all ages the Fathers of the Church had been unanimous in declaring that OUR LADY conceived without sin : thus S. AUGUSTINE, S. GREGORY, and S. BERNARD. I raised my eyebrows slightly, perhaps involuntarily, shook my head, for I knew that it had been disputed, and that the doctrine

[1] An admirable sketch of one of these Pfarrers is in Ganghofer's *Hochwurden Herr Pfarrer*, 1882.

had never been ventilated by the two former. Instantly the
preacher's eye caught mine, and a twinkle came into it. He
abruptly changed his subject. " But," proceeded he, " what, we
may ask, is the ultimate court of appeal for Protestants ? The
Bible. But on what authority do they receive the bundle of books
that goes to make up the Bible ? Let us take up the case of the
Anglicans. I open the English Bible. What do I see next the
title-page ? ' The most high and mighty Prince JAMES '—on
the authority of a Scotchman ! " Very ready, very adroit, but
unscrupulous. He knew, as well as did I, that this was a
dedication, not an authorization. Next day, in the afternoon, I
was walking up to Evolena, when I encountered a descending
drift of priests coming from a clerical meeting. Among them
was the CHANCELLOR ; I took off my hat, so did he. After
passing each other I turned to look. He had turned also, and was
holding his sides, laughing, his jolly red face flashing with triumph.
And I laughed also. It was the meeting of the two augurs.

From Martigny we journeyed down the valley to S. Maurice.
The town is squeezed in between the limestone mountain
precipice and the Rhone. The abbey is the oldest Christian
foundation among the Alps, dating from the sixth century, and
the tower in its lower parts may belong to that period. The
church was much damaged by fire in the seventeenth century.
Nothing can be worse than its modern restoration. The piers
and walls are painted with vulgar carpet patterns. There is,
however, a good painting of the founder, S. Sigismund, by
Deschwanden ; it is stronger in character than most of his work.
" The greater the sinner, the greater the saint," seems to have
been a doctrine before the times of Wesley. Sigismund was a
great scoundrel. His first wife was Austrogotha or Amalberga,
the daughter of Theodoric the Great, King of Italy, by whom
he had a son named Sigeric. On her death he married her maid.
The lad, Sigeric, bore his stepmother no warm love, and seeing
her one day decked out in the garments of his own mother, burst
forth into the angry exclamation, " Your mistress' clothes ill-
become the back of her servant." This was never forgotten by
his stepmother, and she schemed his death from that time
forward. She gradually worked upon the feelings of her husband,
awakening his fear of the ambition of Theodoric, and then

pretended to discover a plot of the King of Italy to dethrone Sigismund and set up Sigeric in his place. In a fit of fury the Burgundian king ordered the death of his son. A thong was slipped by two young men round the neck of Sigeric as he slept, and the prince was strangled. No sooner was the crime committed than the most agonizing remorse took possession of the king, and he hastened to Agaunum (now S. Maurice), and if he did not found the abbey, he at all events richly endowed it. He spent his time in a cave in the cliff, whence escaped a trickle of water. It is said that he prayed that God would punish him in this world rather than in the next. The prayer was heard. The storm that was to overwhelm him was already gathering. Clotildis, wife of Clovis I, King of the Franks, was a daughter of Chilperic, King of Burgundy, who had been put to death with his wife and two sons by Gundebald, the father of Sigismund. Blood revenge was a sacred duty among the Franks. So Clotildis instigated her sons to take up arms against Sigismund. He was made prisoner with his wife and her sons, and carried as captive to Orleans. Gundemar, the brother of Sigismund, collected an army and recovered Burgundy. The next year, 524, Chlodomer, son of Clotildis, marched against him ; but before starting on the expedition he flung Sigismund, his wife and sons into a well saying, " I am not going to leave my enemy behind my back." So Sigismund figures as a saint and martyr. In good faith, saints must have been rare in the sixth century, when the Church was compelled to canonize such rotten apples as Sigismund ! and Clotildis as well !

We climbed the steep path cut in the face of the rock at S. Maurice to Sigismund's cave, in front of which on a narrow terrace is a tiny chapel and hermitage, the latter occupied by a peasant, in courtesy styled hermit, but who wears no distinctive habit, not even a long-tailed coat to hide the fact that he has sat out the seat of his trousers. Him we found a nice and sensible man, very pleased to gather a bouquet of the larkspur growing in his tiny garden, and to present it to my wife. He was expecting an accession of pilgrims on the morrow, and so descended with me to the town in order to buy a score of mugs for the holy water flowing from S. Sigismund's spring, of which they would desire to drink.

D

expanded of the same material, which broke before the lectures began. We received electric shocks, and looked into mirrors that distorted our faces either perpendicularly into long haggard objects, or laterally into bloated monsters. I endeavoured to get my wife to go down in the diving-bell, but she declined, not thinking that such a descent would be either amusing or instructive. At half-past twelve we had our lunch, but oh! what lunches were provided at the Pantechnicon! sandwiches, dry as boards, leathery old fowl, and wine on its way to transmutation into vinegar.

Then we looked at our hair magnified into gas-tubes, and were shown, if the glass were applied to the skin, that it came away covered with perspiration.

At four o'clock came a lecture on guns and pistols. That concluded, a bell rang, and we saw a series of dissolving views representing the experiences of Alice in Wonderland. Next ensued a lecture on the magnet; and whether anything further in the way of instruction was to follow, I know not, for my wife urged departure. She had had enough for the day.

"What next?" I asked.

"Amusement uncoupled with instruction," said she; so we went to the Princess's Theatre in the evening and saw the play of *Leah*, in which Miss Bateman acted.

"I hope," said my wife, as we entered the train to take us to the North, "I do most sincerely hope that at Dalton I may be fed with only egg-spoonfuls of instruction, and be given amusement in soup ladles."

"My dear," said I, "you shall be fed as your constitution requires."

Alas! There was not much amusement to be obtained in Dalton-i'-t'-Muck.

"You must be satisfied with what you can get, and profit by even that which is driest," said I.

"Like the sandwiches at the Pantechnicon," she observed.

CHAPTER IV

MERSEA
1871–72

WHILST I was at Dalton I wrote *The Origin and Development of Religious Belief*, as already mentioned. I also wrote *The Silver Store*. Longmans published it; and when the edition was exhausted they declined to issue a second, so I gave the book to Skeffingtons to do with it what they liked, and since then it has gone into four or five editions. I am no poet, but I can jingle rhymes, and the sole merit of the verses that make up the volume lies in the Talmudic and mediæval legends that I have run into metre and rattled out in rhyme.

On January 11, 1871, I received from Mr. Gladstone the offer of East Mersea Rectory.

I had become cramped at Dalton. My second daughter, Margaret, was born in August, 1870. In the red-brick house we occupied there were three bedrooms, one of which was occupied by the servant. Lady Downe declined to enlarge the house, so that we were in considerable straits.

Dr. Schweinfürth informs us that in Central Africa the natives erect domed huts of clay and straw on posts, with a vent hole at the top and a single door at the side. Into this structure all the babies are put at close of day, and are shut in for the night, so that their squeals in no way reach and affect the repose of their parents, who resume charge of the infants in the morning. We have not arrived at that pitch of comfort in England, but I considered the advisability of buying a van, into which I might myself retire for the night and leave the house to the mother, the babes and the maid. Nurse we had none. There was nowhere

37

where she could be stowed. Consequently the offer of East Mersea was a veritable relief to my perplexity.

I accepted East Mersea, and went thither on March 21, 1871. I remained rector till 1881, in all, ten years. I cannot say that I either liked the place or became attached to the people. I had been accustomed to the genial, out-spoken and intelligent Yorkshire folk, and, of course, I knew the kind-hearted, impulsive Devonians, but the Essex peasants were dull, shy, reserved and suspicious. I never managed to understand them, nor they to understand me. There must have been at one time an infusion of Danish blood, as Mersea was made headquarters of the Danes when invading East Anglia, but there remained no trace of Scandinavian vigour or romance in the people.

Mersea is an island about three miles long between the mouths of the Blackwater and the Colne. Between it and the mainland to the north is a causeway that is overflowed at high tides. The island is divided into two parishes, East and West Mersea. At the latter, during the Roman occupation of Britain, was the residence of the Count of the Saxon shore. It has a " hard," or gravelly stretch, where boats can be drawn up and where is a copious spring of water that is, however, overflowed by high tides. East Mersea also possesses a " hard," a very scanty one, but thence alone can a person cross in a boat over the estuary of the Colne to Brightlingsea, where was a station to a branch line that conveyed a passenger to Colchester.

The island is extended seaward by mud flats for a mile, over which the tide flows. Towards the island the clay has been dug out so as to form a sea-wall on the land side, leaving a channel between the fields and the flats, and this channel is filled with decaying marine vegetable and animal matter, producing an intolerable stench that pervades the air when the tide goes out and forms a breeding place for myriads of mosquitoes. Between Mersea and the mainland is a dismal tract of marsh, with dykes and a channel or run of mud and water—a famous district for wild-fowl shooting and for the catching of ague.

At a former period wild-fowl shooting was largely practised by the islanders, who had their punts painted grey. In these shallow boats they lay for many hours at night, and contracted both ague and rheumatism. My impression was that generations

THE MARSHES, MERSEA

afflicted with these complaints, acquired in the marshes, had lowered the physique and the mental development of the islanders. When the east wind blew the wild ducks and geese came in flocks near the coast, where they were surrounded and shot. Herons frequented the marshes in considerable numbers. Gulls were not numerous, as there were no breeding places in rocks along the coast.

An industry exercised by the women and children of West Mersea was the collecting of winkles off the flats for the London market. In order to enable them to walk on the wet clay they wore flat boards cut into ovals under their soles, and braced tightly over the instep and about the ankles. Walking or gliding on these, they stooped to collect the molluscs into a basket held in the left hand. Woe to such as slipped and fell! The adhesive clay held him or her fast by the arms.

There was little of interest in the island except a huge tumulus, called Grim's hoe, which, since my time, has been explored and has revealed a glass vessel of the Roman period. At West Mersea the church and churchyard cover the remains of a Roman villa, and portions of mosaic are often turned up when the graves are excavated.

At the east end of the island on comparatively high ground are the remains of a camp which had been erected by the Parliamentary soldiery so as to command the mouth of the Colne, in 1648, and several cannon were planted there, forming a battery. The place was well chosen, for below it is a spring of pure water. Hard by there was formerly a cottage, which had almost totally disappeared, but the site was said to be haunted by a female figure. The only person whilst I was at Mersea who had seen her was Mrs. Baker, of whom anon, and then only when she was in her cups. No one in Mersea save she, on her return from the " Dog and Pheasant," ventured by the mysterious well and the site of the cottage under the old earthworks. I was not able to recover any further tradition of this woman, save that she had been killed whilst the soldiers of the Parliament were in the fort ; but why was not known, or at all events told.

The apparition admits of a very prosaic explanation. The warm air charged with moisture, wafted up from the sea that flows in summer over the sun-heated mud flats, was condensed into a column of vapour above the chill pool of the well, and wavered in the breeze, ever dissolving and reforming. A slight stretch of imagination converted this pillar of vapour into a spectral woman.

The formation of Mersea Island to me was an occasion for interesting speculation. It appeared to be a moraine of the glacial period when the Gog-Magogs were actual mountains. The island consisted of detritus lying upon the bed of old London clay. The springs in it can have been fed only by the rain falling on the surface, that worked its way in a tortuous manner till it met the underlying London clay, when it broke out in sources near the edge of the marshes or the beach.

Some curious circumstances connected with the Siege of Colchester are related by François Raguenet in his *Histoire d'Olivier Cromwel*, Paris, 1691 ; which he took from the Manuscript Memoirs of M. de Brosse, a French Protestant Doctor of the Faculty of Paris, who was in England at the time. " C'est du même endroit, que j'ay emprunté plusieurs circonstances de l'intrigue de Cromwel avec la femme du Major Lamberth, de la vérité de laquelle je ne doute nullement, parceque j'en trouve des traces dans presque tous les ouvrages dont je viens de faire la liste."

According to De Brosse, Cromwell kept Mrs. Lambert as his mistress, and to get rid of the husband sent him to command the Parliamentary forces in the North. But Mrs. Lambert transferred her affections to the Earl of Holland, who, after having been in the Parliamentary army, went over to the service of the king. Still, however, she kept up her intrigue with Cromwell, in order to extort from him military secrets, but he, having discovered her double game, supplied her with false information. This comes out with reference to the Siege of Colchester.

De Brosse further relates how that Fairfax, having been unable to reduce the town, sent to London for the son of Lord Capel, who was in command in Colchester, and negotiated a meeting between the lines, when he presented the boy, who was aged seventeen, stripped to his waist, to the father, and threatened to shoot him unless Lord Capel capitulated. The lad urged his father to do his duty regardless of himself, and Lord Capel bade his son go and suffer in defence of his God and his King. Eventually Fairfax sent back the lad unmolested to London.

Mersea was very inaccessible. It was nine miles from Colchester, and the road, as there was no stone wherewith to metal it, was excruciatingly bad in winter. The great distances from the villages on the mainland made calling difficult ; and as far as I could see there were not many persons of value, as readers and thinkers, with whom to make friends. Add to that the causeway and its being occasionally overwhelmed by the tide. Our nearest neighbour was Mr. Musselwhite, Vicar of West Mersea, a kindly man, but not possessed of many interests or of much information.

The most intelligent of the farmers was Cant, a strong Dissenter. There were two others a little above the average, and the rest were addicted to eating and drinking and little else. Curiously enough several of them were unmarried. That did not conduce to refinement of manner.

There was, seaward of the church, a sort of landing-stage built ; and a channel had been excavated in the clay flat so that a vessel of small draught could be brought up to it. This was for the purpose of bringing coal in barges to the island, and " London muck," that is to say, the sweepings of the London streets, which was largely used as a manure for the fields, and then the stench was horrible. Another dressing employed was one of sprats. On such occasion gulls arrived in great flocks, and boys were employed to scare them away with rattles, horns and drums. The smell when a field was fertilized with sprats was not enjoyable ; but the odour was superior to that of London muck. From the landing-stage the barges carried away hay and straw, piled up high on deck, for London. When the mosquitoes were out in autumn they swarmed about the trees, that looked as if they were on fire and smoking. We had always to drive the pests out of the bedrooms in the evening by burning laurel leaves on red-hot coals.

The floor of the channel for the barges was gravel, and in this channel we were wont to bathe. One summer evening by moonlight my wife and a friend were bathing in this channel and had gone out a considerable distance when a boat came coasting along, and the crew suddenly seeing two white draped, diving and up-springing female figures at a distance from land, sped away as fast as they could row, to tell in Brightlingsea how they had seen a couple of mermaids. Mrs. Baker, of whom mention has already been made, came to the Rectory full of the news. " Nonsense," said my wife. " What they saw was Miss Deason and myself bathing." " No ! nothing of the sort," said Mrs. Baker, " the men asserted that the mermaids had fish's tails, they could swear to the fact. And as neither you nor Miss Deason wind up below the waist with scaly terminations, you see, Ma'am, it could not possibly have been yourselves."

The church was moated on all sides but the south, and was constructed of *streenite*, nodules of indurated clay dug out of the mud, like the lumps one encounters in badly boiled porridge ; but, unless plastered over, these clots are liable to scale off in wet weather. The whole church, which was in second and third pointed styles, had unquestionably been so protected from the day of its construction, but the plaster had flaked from the tower and left it in a condition of degradation. The interior of the nave and north aisle was boxed up with deal pews. The chancel had been fitted by my predecessor, Hayter, with an oak altartable, furnished with brass cross, candlesticks and flower vases, and with stalls. A simple, rudimentary screen of deal with quatrefoils backed with red flannel had been erected, bearing the inscription " Holy, Holy, Holy."

There was a harmonium, wheezy and uncertain in its temper, in the chancel, played by our governess, Miss Biggs, who could pick out a simple tune, but add no embellishments. The first Sunday I was at the church the wind was blowing strongly, and when I gave out the hymn the cowl to the stove flue began its musical gyrations. The principal farmer's wife, Mrs. Cockrell, living at the Hall, blanched, but gave a sigh of relief when Miss Biggs began to prance on the pedals and touched some notes, more or less correctly, on the harmonium. Mrs. Cockrell told me afterwards that when the cowl groaned and squeaked she thought it was the tuning up of the old orchestra, which she feared I had introduced after its dismissal by Mr. Hayter in favour of the American organ.

The pews formed quite an interesting picture gallery, as the fisher boys, when they attended Divine worship, occupied themselves in drawing ships upon the sides of the pews. Occasionally the illustrations assumed a more personal character. Attempts had been made to take the portrait of my predecessor, and when I left there remained pictorial efforts to represent me, my nose being given undue prominence.

There were no resident gentry on the island. The squiress, Mrs. George Round, did not visit the place, to my knowledge, in all the ten years I was at Mersea. Previous to Mr. Hayter, who had been rector for fourteen years, the parson had been an old fellow, more of a farmer than anything else, who served three churches, giving one service only at East Mersea on the Sunday.

A neighbour on the mainland had daughters whom he was desperately desirous of disposing of in marriage, and was warmly seconded by the damsels themselves. His time was spent in husband-hunting among the officers in Colchester. He drove a high waggonette with a pair of big horses harnessed into it. In the body of the conveyance sat his four tall, stiff-backed daughters, on the *Braut-schau*. Lord Dufferin had a native servant who was asked one day how his master had shot. " Famously," was the reply ; " only God was very merciful to the birds." And so it was with this gentleman. He hunted vigorously, but Heaven was very merciful to the officers.

I had no adult son, game for these Maypoles, so we were called on once only and then dropped as unprofitable.

We had, however, on the further side of the Colne estuary, the Rev. A. Pertwee, unmarried, a vigorous and devoted parish priest, greatly loved by his people ; but to reach him was not easy, entailing a row, and when one arrived at the Vicarage, two miles from Brightlingsea " hard," there were ten chances to one that he was out parishing.

To reach Brightlingsea we had to descend a mile and a half to the " hard," where lived a man named Baker with his wife in an old hulk drawn up on the shingle and there anchored. Baker or his wife rowed one across, and when the tide was out, carried the passenger pick-a-back through the mud. We went often to Baker's boat and had tea with him. Whilst tea was brewing he would set a pail of shrimps before us, on the deck, and bid us fall to until the tea was ready in the cabin. Baker himself was a sober man, but his wife was often tipsy. When she returned late from Brightlingsea, overcome with liquor,

Baker had hauled up the ladder. He emptied a pail of water over her head, as she stood shouting below for admittance, and left her to scold, swear and shiver till he considered her to be sufficiently sober to be admitted. Mrs. Baker wore an old red military coat over her back, shoulders and arms. I used her in my story *Mehalah*.

Elijah Rebow in that same novel was sketched from a leading Dissenter at West Mersea, who had rented the glebe of a previous non-resident rector.

When Mr. Musselwhite came to West Mersea he took the glebe away from Elijah Rebow, who had hitherto rented it at a sum far below its value, purposing to farm it himself. The church-warden earnestly entreated the vicar to insure his harvest recently gathered in. Musselwhite drove into Colchester, after seeing that his ricks were thatched. On his way he passed the churchwarden's house. The man called to him : " Have you insured ? "

" No."

" Then do so at once, to full value."

Musselwhite arrived in Colchester a quarter of an hour before the office closed. He went in precisely five minutes before it shut and insured for the total amount.

As he drove home in the evening, he saw his churchwarden awaiting him, standing at the garden gate.

" Have you insured ? "

" Yes."

" To full value ? "

" Yes."

" That is well. Your ricks are on fire."

So they were. It was a curious case, the ricks had been insured five minutes before the match had been applied to them by the man, as an act of revenge for not being allowed to retain the glebe. The insurance office tried hard to obtain evidence against Elijah Rebow, but failed. He was too subtle to be caught. He had chosen a time for setting fire to the ricks when no one was about, and all residents in West Mersea were too much afraid of the man to give evidence against him, even if they had seen him strike a light and apply the match. There was not a person in the island who was not convinced that Elijah had fired the ricks.

An amusing incident occurred whilst we were at Mersea.

S. Paul's is a small modern church at the bottom of the hill upon which Colchester is built, and is near the railway station. The parishioners are all lower middle-class persons, and the church-warden was the station-master. The perpetual curate was the Rev. W. H. E. R. Jervis. The magnates of Colchester knew him not, nor did the incumbents of the other churches invite him to their tables. Their wives were especially sniffy towards Mrs. Jervis. I preached occasionally in S. Paul's to a congregation of railway porters, small tradesmen and artisans. The clergy of Colchester kept aloof from Jervis and did not demean themselves so far as to invite him to occupy their pulpits.

But all of a sudden the aspect of affairs changed. Mr. Jervis, of the four Christian names, put in his claim to the Viscountship of S. Vincent. If the marriage of his grandmother to the first Lord S. Vincent could be established he had an undoubted right to the title. His lawyers offered three hundred pounds for an authenticated copy of the marriage entry. A clergyman in Hampshire demanded the reward, and forwarded a duly certified copy from the parish register.

At once Jervis assumed the title of Viscount S. Vincent, and his wife figured as Viscountess ; as such they had their cards lettered. Down the hill in streams came the carriages of the aristocracy of Colchester, the horses and carriages blazing with armorial bearings, and the faces of those issuing from the carriages beamed with smiles, and their lips gushed with protestations of affection. The clergy also regretted their previous aloofness and begged his lordship to preach in their churches. The ultra-Protestants were the most urgent.

A fortnight later it was discovered that the entry in the register had been forged, and the parson who had forged it, in place of receiving three hundred pounds, got a term of imprisonment. At once my lord and my lady dropped back into plain Mr. and Mrs. Jervis, and were regarded by the great folk, and such as imagined themselves to be great, as hot coppers, not to be touched. The town clergy no longer recognized Mr. Jervis when they passed him in the street, and their wives plucked back their skirts to avoid contact with Mrs. Jervis should they encounter her in Tabrum and Jones's grocery shop, or in that of the fishmonger.

An interesting and perplexing feature of the fringe of the Essex

marshes is the existence on it, at irregular intervals, of " Red Hills,"
mounds of various heights and dimensions composed of burnt
clay. Where they occur in ground that is under cultivation, they
have been ploughed down, but their former presence is revealed
by the brick-red colour of the soil around ; and as they fertilize,
the farmers are glad enough to level them. Nevertheless, a good
many remain intact. I dug into one or two, but found nothing
indicative of the period of their erection. A prevalent notion is
that they had something to do with salt works, but no traces of
salt pans have been discovered in connexion with them. Possibly
they belong to various periods. Dr. Schweinfürt informs us
that in marshy districts of Central Africa similar mounds of burnt
clay are reared to form the base of the hovels, as they serve
as a protection against ague and marsh fevers. In my opinion
the Essex Red Hills were cast up for a like purpose, and sustained
the huts of those who fished and caught wild fowl in the marshes.
That some may go back to a prehistoric period is possible enough,
for near one I recovered two magnificent polished chert celts,
some of the finest I have seen. They are now in the Colchester
Museum. I cannot, however, say that the Red Hill near which
they were found belonged to their period.

My parish clerk, Ellis by name, was a frequenter of the tavern,
the " Dog and Pheasant," adjoining his own cottage. His ideal
of a rector was Foster, who had preceded Mr. Hayter, and who,
as already intimated, gave but a single service on Sunday, and
then mounted his horse and rode full gallop to some church on
the mainland, to earn a guinea by taking the service there.
" Ah ! " said Ellis, " he wor the passon for us, as we liked. He
grew wery good taters, and he left us gloriously alone."

On Christmas Day, when I gave out the Proper Psalms, the
clerk shouted : " All wrong, 'tis the twenty-fifth day." He was
in liquor. Sometimes he would walk about the nave with a cane
in his hand and whack the fisher boys and school children, if he
found them inattentive and whispering. He was the survival of
the old dog-nawper, the official employed to drive the dogs out of
church and the sleep out of the heads of the congregation. The
old dog-nawping implement was a rod with a blue knob at the
end. I heard of a case where the squire, who was a very zealous
churchman, told the clerk who, like Ellis, acted as dog-nawper,

that he would give him half a crown for every sleeper he awakened during the sermon, hoping thereby to keep the clerk wakeful. One Sunday the weather was sultry. The squire had eaten an abundant lunch and had imbibed a corresponding amount of ale. In the afternoon, during the sermon, the squire began to nod. The clerk had his eye on him and saw the occasional bob of the head, bald and smooth as a billiard ball. So he stepped out of his desk with the nawping staff in hand, walked up to the manorial pew, and as the bald head rose above the side, whack upon it came the blue knob, so loudly as to resound through the church, and with such startling effect that the squire was fully awake in a moment and was staring indignantly at the clerk, who thrust his hand over the pew door and said : " Half a crown if you please, sir ! "

The children of the parish were uncouth, and some of the parents were very poor. It was usual for these latter to buy discarded military uniforms and cut them to the sizes required. Very often small boys had their feet protruding out of soldiers' trousers that had been cut above the knee. Boys and girls wore military red coats fitting more or less badly. When we had a school-treat one day in the autumn, my wife noticed a girl scantily dressed, her garment hanging about her in a manner that in no way disguised her person. Distressed at this, she said to the girl : " Hannah ! you have not much clothes on, and the weather is cold."

" Oh ! " replied the maiden, aged about fifteen, " I've got my frock, and then comes Oi." Literally she wore nothing save a thin cotton dress.

The Essex dialect is markedly vulgar. The letter *v* is sounded as *w*. The clerk would read the verse in the psalm : " I vowed a vow," as " I wowed a wow " ; and one was informed that wines grew well against the wooden walls of the cottages. The letter *i* becomes *oi*. A violet is pronounced woiolet, and a line is a loin. The Essex folk are fond of picking up a big word and mispronouncing it. A woman asked me one day whether I had observed the elephant over her house on the preceding evening. She meant the element, when there had been an Aurora Borealis. The peasants have some peculiar words : a drizzle is described as " tiffling toightly." Water-weed is called " mardlins "; a hart's-tongue fern is " snakes' wittles " (victuals) ; and blackberries are " bummelkites."

Haymakers and harvesters rush to the road to arrest a passer-by, and demand " a largess." I am not sure whether the Essex folk are troubled with deep feelings. I called on a man who had a minute farm, to sympathize with him on the loss of a cow. " Ah !" said he, " I've had much trouble, wery sewere trouble ; there have been carried out of my premises three wives, two cows and four pigs, them last with swine fever. Wives," said he, wiping his nose, " you've only to hold up your hand and whistle, and a score applicants for the sitiwation will come about you. Wives," he added, again wiping his nose with his fingers, " is wery cheap ; but pigs is costly, and cows is plaguy ruinous."

East Mersea Hall was an old house close to the church. It had undoubtedly at one time been the manor house, but it had fallen into the condition of a farm, and was occupied by a Mr. Cockrell —a descendant of a Coquerelle, a Huguenot settler after the Revocation of the Edict of Nantes. His wife was a sweet and superior person, who more than once did us a good service. In spring at Mersea we found that the skin of the children's faces became rough, peeled off and left sores. We sent for the local doctor, who dosed them with pills, purges and draughts of various colours and flavours, all nasty, and all in vain. My wife mentioned the fact to Mrs. Cockrell, who said at once : " Oh, it is nothing but the east wind. When that blows I always rub my children's faces over when sending them out with cold cream or glycerine."

We adopted this method, paid the surgeon's bill, and did not send for him again, as happily Mrs. C.'s remedy proved efficacious.

Mrs. Cockrell told me that her favourite reading consisted in books of travel in Switzerland, and that the yearning of her heart was to see snowy mountains, but that she was well aware this yearning could never be satisfied. Not the remotest prospect opened before her of ever leaving Mersea and seeing a mountain, even if not snow-clad.

I smiled and said : " God never implants a desire in the soul to be disappointed. I have seen the snowy Alps from the Schänzli above Berne ; but I have seen more splendid landscapes here."

" How so ? We are in a dead watery flat."

" We are given an uninterrupted horizon to the south and east. And never elsewhere have I had that. And never elsewhere have I seen such superb cloud scenery, great domes of snow, silver *nevées*, gulfs of shadowy blue ; in a word, Alpine scenery far more sublime than any in Switzerland."

" But it is so transitory."

" You look on the Alps and they are always the same in form. Here you have a rapid change of scene from one splendour to another."

" I never thought of that."

" God grants compensations only to those who look for them."

" Then I shall look for them in the clouds, and fall in love with them."

There was one phenomenon at Mersea to which I never could accustom myself as to something inevitable and that must be endured, and that phenomenon was the piping of the wind. There never was on that coast complete stillness of air. In our best bedroom, that had one window facing south and another facing east, the wind was ever audible. When a visitor came to stay with us, I had to warn him or her to endure the bitter sound that ceased not day or night, summer or winter. The cry was especially audible when the fire was lighted in the grate. I was wont to prepare my guest for it by telling him or her not to be uneasy if the souls of drowned sailors who had found a watery grave in the Northern ocean were to be heard sobbing all night long because of their inability to reach the fire so as to dry their soaked garments and thaw their chilled limbs. My guests always thanked me for the information, but advised me not to be over-communicative with my knowledge. At Lew the house is so sheltered that we are not distressed with wailings of the wind, but on stormy nights we have to endure the roar of the gale in the Scotch pines and oaks to the North, that resembles the breaking of the surf on the Cornish coast at Bude.

THE SOULS ON THE WIND

" The wind blows cold on waste and wold,
    It bloweth night and day,
  The souls go by 'twixt earth and sky
    Incessant,—know no stay.

E

They fly in clouds, and flap their shrouds
  When full the moon doth sail.
At dead of night, when quenched all light
  We hear them sigh and wail.

And many a soul, with angry howl,
  Doth rattle at the door,
Or rave and rout, with dance and shout,
  Around the granite tor.
I hear a soul i' th' chimney growl,
  That's sodden with the rain,
To wring the wet from winding-sheet,
  To see the fire were fain.

In gentle breeze, 'mid tender trees
  Souls whisper as they pass,
And secrets breathe beneath the eaves
  Or whistle in the grass.
My life I spend, and have no end
  To turmoil, stir and strain
And must it be eternally
  I cannot rest attain ? "

THE SALTINGS, MERSEA

CHAPTER V

BELGIUM, GERMANY AND THE TYROL
1871–73 or 1872 ?

MY friend, the Rev. J. M. Gatrill, was a curate in Leeds, and in 1871 he wrote me that he was to be given a three weeks' holiday. I at once proposed that we should go together to Belgium. He agreed. I was disappointed to find him listless and unappreciative. He told me that he had been overworked during Lent, and was fagged out ; that in order to enjoy buildings, scenery, paintings and costume, what he needed was a week of rest, lying in the sun, and not even thinking of anything. Then he would recover zest for foreign travel.

At Dinant, on the Meuse, he was silent and sulky, and bade me walk on one side of the river, he on the other. He did not want to talk, or to be bothered with my chatter. I walked all the way to Bouvignes, and climbed to the ruined castle, concerning which such tragic tales are told. When I returned to Dinant I found Gatrill in a totally different mood, chirpy, communicative, and with a twinkle in his eye. " My dear fellow ! " I exclaimed, " what has produced this revulsion in you ? " Pointing to an empty bottle on the sideboard, he said : " I have had a siphon."

Bell in his *Wayside Pictures* says of Belgium, that the visitor is driven to take interest in works of art, for there is nothing else to attract him—miles of road between double rows of poplars, one poplar just like its *vis-à-vis*, or its neighbour, miles of canal, fields on fields of mangel-wurzel, turnip crops and potatoes, and miles on miles of dead, dull flat. This is true of all save the upper Meuse. But this fact has produced a new school of painting ; and the school draws its inspiration from the delightful bits of

51

street architecture that are to be found everywhere, and peoples the canvas with figures in late mediæval costume.

I made the acquaintance at Antwerp of Edouard Tyck, a young artist of this school, and bought two of his paintings. Afterwards he came to visit me in England, and, at his request, I took him to Windsor. He had expected to see a mediæval and regal residence with many towers, all capped with extinguishers, having in front great galleries sustained on richly carved corbels, large bay windows, cloisters with twisted columns, and reticulated vaults. His face fell, and, turning to me, he said sadly : " Your English architects never had *Imagination*."

He assured me that an artist with any merit could gain a living in Belgium. Large pictures do not sell, but cabinet paintings are in demand. " When a Frenchman has made some money," said he, " then he says, ' I will go to Paris and to the café-chantants.' When a German has money to spare, he says, ' I will go with my Frau to a watering-place, and eat sausages and drink lager beer till I have to call for a *Kellner* to help me out of my chair.' When an Englishman has cash at his command, he says, ' Now I will travel.' But when a Belgian has a sum at his disposal, be he grocer or fishmonger, he says, ' Now I will buy a picture.' "

Edouard Tyck informed me that to the north of Bruges, outside the walls, is an old abandoned cemetery. The graves are actually small walled vaults, whitewashed and covered with slabs of stone, many of which are broken. The interesting feature of these graves is that at the east end of each is a fresco painting on the wall representing some religious subject. Such are occasionally rude, but also occasionally possess some artistic merit. He accordingly employed himself in copying the best.

To effect this, on a certain day he had descended into one of these vaults, that are hardly over six feet below the surface, and hoped to finish his drawing before twilight set in. Presently he heard two Germans conversing outside, whereof one was a woman, elderly, apparently, and obese.

" Ach ! Gott in Himmel ! here is another. I wonder, if we peered in, whether we would be so fortunate as to see the skeleton."

" Bah, Rosalie ! one skeleton is like another. It is the *fat* that differentiates individuals, that affords comeliness and personality. What would you or I be, walking in our bones ? It is our fat that makes us what we are."

Next moment the light was cut off from Tyck, as two heads appeared, blocking the gap by which the ray entered.

The artist at once lifted his voice, and intoned : " De profundis clamavi ad Te Domine. Domine exaudi vocem meam."

The heads were instantaneously withdrawn, and the light once more entered the tomb. The woman uttered a scream and the man a Potz donnerwetter. Both took to their heels. Tyck, on clambering out of the vault, saw them running in the direction of the town. Presently the woman halted, and exclaimed : " Ach, mein Mann ! mein Regenschirm hab' ich verloren ! " And she turned. But as she saw Tyck's body extricating itself from the tomb, she shrieked out : " He is coming after us ! Run, mein Schatz, run ! "

The artist allowed the lost umbrella to lie on the slab where it had fallen ; but he considered it doubtful whether the couple would muster up sufficient courage to revisit the cemetery on the morrow in broad daylight to recover it.

A point that strikes a visitor to Belgium for the first time is the complexity of the races forming the population. The Belgian nation is made up of Flemings and Walloons. The former are of the Teutonic stock akin to the Dutch, grave, self-possessed, stolid. The Walloon is Celtic, light, frivolous, volatile, akin to the Gaul.

The two races have different views of life, different tastes, and different modes of thought. Naturally the Fleming inclines to fraternize with the Germans, and as naturally the Walloon is drawn towards the French. Nevertheless they entertain a common interest in the preservation of their independence ; and this subdues the external expression of their differences. They concur in desiring an independent nationality, because they dread absorption, the Fleming by Germany and the Walloon by France.

Liége, Namur, Hainault are Walloon ; East and West Flanders and Antwerp are Flemish. Brabant is in the centre, containing the capital, mainly Flemish, but with an infusion of Walloon ; and the population of Brussels has lost the characteristic good qualities of each of its ingredients.

Germany, at the time of which I am writing, was an empire of ill-consorted and ill-compacted units that had been shattered by the Napoleonic wars, and had been put together again after a fashion by the Treaty of Vienna. But the fragments did not cohere. The petty duchies and principalities had their little courts as rallying centres, but such were mere nests of intrigue and of mean ambition, as well sketched by Marlitt. The old ecclesiastical principalities had lost their courts, and were devoid of vital interests in the welfare of the whole community. The Jew had spun his web everywhere, he had monopolized the law, and had become the great regrater of all the industries in the land, and in so doing had killed its self-respect and initiative. He appeared to have mastered all the vital nerves of the nation, so as to reduce it to a lump upon which he could feed at his leisure.

There was much to be observed and collected in various quarters. Much in the habits, speech and folk-lore of the people traceable to primeval mythology and organization. German arts had never reached the delicacy and refinement acquired in Italy, but in force had far surpassed them. Art in the land had been killed by the Thirty Years' War and buried by Napoleon. But its fragments were strewn broadcast over the land. In architecture it had developed an individuality of style of surpassing charm at the time when French Middle Pointed languished into Flamboyant, and English stiffened into Perpendicular.

That which was so noteworthy in the German spirit up to the Thirty Years' War was its forcefulness. In whatever direction it thrust, in painting, poetry, music, sculpture, architecture or theology, it was characterized by determination, courage and confidence. There was in it none of the tentativeness of the Italian, French and English genius, but a bold assurance which carried it beyond all its compeers.

In the winter of 1872–3 I had suffered from bronchitis and rheumatism, and needed a change of climate and of scene. I had, moreover, accepted an offer to compile a work on the *Lives of the Saints*, which might supersede that of Alban Butler, which had been composed for the purpose of edification and with little regard to historic truth. I was well aware that the task was certain to entail great labour and severe criticism. I knew that some of those who had been enshrined in martyrologies had as

little claim to be considered as historical personages as Cinderella
and Goody Twoshoes ; and as slender justification for their
elevation to the calendars of the Saints. My work was to be
comprised in fifteen volumes, one to be delivered every half year
till the hagiology was completed.

Before starting on my work I resolved to rest for a few weeks
in one of those quiet nooks where at Whitsuntide the air was
redolent with the fragrance of the flowering grape, and the
atmosphere throughout the year breathed simple and unques-
tioning piety.

Würzburg was to me a pleasant memory of early childhood ;
accordingly my wife and I betook ourselves there in the spring of
1873, by way of Dovercourt, Rotterdam and Cologne.

Würzburg was anciently the see of a prince-bishop who from
the time of the Ottos was also Duke of Franconia, and who had
the privilege when he said Mass to have his Grand Marshal
precede him, carrying the sword of the Duchy point uppermost,
and to stand by him at the altar till the consecration, when he
sheathed it and thenceforth carried it point downwards.

The prince-bishops formerly lived in the castle on a height
that commands the town, and is on the further side of the Main ;
but Bishop Schönborn in the rococo period began a stately palace
with gardens in the town. I remembered well how that one of
the rooms in this palace was lined with mirrors, so that in it one
could see oneself reflected *ad infinitum*. Another chamber was
that of the *carrousel*, a merry-go-round ; one of the mounts was a
purple-velvet carriage with mitre in gold above, in which coach
the bishop would ride on a rainy day, or after a merry dinner,
his guests and chamberlains astride on wooden horses, and all
aiming, as they twirled about, at targets, either with pistols or
with foils. When last I visited Würzburg, the *carrousel* was no
longer shown. I presume it was considered too scandalous a
revelation of the vanities and luxury of former prelates. If these
wealthy bishops had confined their activities to building palaces
for themselves, or as did one in erecting the noble Julius Hospital,
it would have been well. But unhappily they took it into their
heads to spoil the city churches by altering them from Gothic
into Classic edifices. One, happily, was spared, the Liebfrau
Kirche, built of red sandstone and with an open lace-like spire.

Formerly when a new prebendary or canon had been appointed, he had to submit to strokes over the back and shoulders from rods wielded by the other members of the chapter. The purpose was to prevent the admission of a prince into a prebend. It was judged that, not even to receive a benefice worth £350 per annum would a member of a reigning house submit to a whipping, and that although residence was not required for more than one month out of the twelve. Many of the canons formerly held prebends as well in other cathedrals.

Looking out from our hotel window upon the market-place, full of buyers and sellers on the Saturday, we saw it transformed in an instant into a flower-bed. A slight shower had come on, whereupon the market-women spread their umbrellas, of all colours of the rainbow and ornamented with wreaths of flowers printed on the cotton. These umbrellas are of a great size, and in place of whalebone stretchers have canes, and the handles are of ornamental brass.

At our hotel I was so happy as to make acquaintance with the Stein wine that is produced only at Würzburg. The place and its neighbourhood are famous for the abundance and excellence of the wines there produced, but of all the Stein wine is the best.

I was very much struck on the Sunday with the vernacular hymns sung by the immense, closely packed congregation, mostly of men, in the Liebfrau Kirche. I will here give an account of the German vernacular hymns as used in the Catholic Church, because thereby I may do somewhat to correct the popular opinion that Martin Luther was the first to create German vernacular *Kirchen Gesang*.

When the Teutonic tribes were converted, to the Latins their language seemed barbarous, and their many dialects bewildering. The German voices shocked them as coarse and ill-modulated. Paulus Diaconus says : " The discordant voices of the Germans produced only notes which resembled the rumble of a loaded waggon descending a hill."

By degrees the Teutons learned modulation from the Latins, but in Divine Service they had no vocal part save in bawling out the Kyrie Eleison, and in order to prolong the enjoyment of hearing their own voices they spun out the notes to a great length, shouted it after the sermon, and howled it during a procession. It was not long, however, that this unintelligible mode of singing suited them, and words were added, forming a hymn that always concluded with the words " Kyrie Eleison." Thence came the German word *Leisen* for songs. In the statutes of Salzburg, 799, occurs the order : " The people must learn to sing Kyrie Eleison, not in the same uncultivated fashion as heretofore, but better."

Christmas hymns appear in the eleventh century, and in the twelfth many occurred.

The Provost Gerhoch von Reichersberg, who died in 1169, wrote : " All people sing the praises of the Saviour in hymns in their own tongue ; but this is especially the case with the Germans, whose language is above all suited for melodious songs."

A great number of the Latin liturgical hymns were translated into German by a Saltzburg monk in the fourteenth century. Another who did the same was Henry von Laufenburg in the sixteenth century, who added new to the traditional folk-hymns. This man was Dean of Freiburg in Breisgau in 1545.

With the invention of printing, the press was employed continuously in the production of vernacular hymn-books. Some, indeed, were of mixed character, partly in Latin and partly in German, as " In dulci jubilo, und singet und seid froh."

It is quite a mistake to suppose that Luther was the father of the vernacular German hymn. He himself made no claim to that title. He said that " he had the Songs of the Ancients," which he inserted in his Gesangbuch, " as a witness to what pious Christians lived before our day." And Melancthon, in his Apology for the Augsburg Confession, said, " This usage has always been held praiseworthy in the Church ; and, although in some places more, some places less, of German song has been customary, yet in all churches the people have had their part in singing in German, consequently this is no novelty."

But there had been a dread entertained lest the people should transform the Mass into a vernacular service. Accordingly in the Synod of Eichstädt, 1446, it was forbidden to cut short the Latin canticles in High Mass, and interpose German hymns. The Council of Basle in 1435 forbade the crowding of the Service of Mass with folk-hymns to the drowning of the liturgical

told me that his was a deplorable case. He could not retain a situation. " Why not ? " I inquired. " In a foolish mood," he answered, " I one day had Adam and Eve tattooed on my arm, and as my arm is exposed when kneading the dough, I set all the other men laughing when they see Adam and Eve." " Was it before or after the Fall ? " I asked. " Before, of course ; and then the master baker dismisses me." " Mein lieber Freund," said I, " the matter is easily rectified. Tattoo them fig-leaves, or, better still coats of skins, and so you will have them presented to the eyes of your comrades, as *after the Fall*." " Potz donnerwetter ! " exclaimed the baker-boy, " I never thought of that expedient. You have saved me, and made my fortune, and now I shall be able to marry Mariandel—who would not have me with Adam and Eve imprinted on my flesh as before the Fall," and he broke out into singing :

> " Mariandel ist so schön,
> Mariandel gibt mir All's,
> Und wenn ich sie erblicken kann,
> So fall' ich ihr um der Hals."

" Ach Gott ! " he rambled on, " our Pfarrer is always crying out against the Fall, but the Fall will do a good thing for me : it will help me to Mariandel."

" O felix culpa," said I, quoting S. Bernard.

On our way from Munich we made a short stay at Pertisau on the Aachen-see. We found the fields there dense with heart's-ease, so thick as to scent the air. Walking in the woods we came suddenly on a statue of a Tyrolese peasantess, life-size, in black bodice, white linen sleeves, and blue skirt, a straw hat on her head, holding a sickle in her hand. Her great eyes stared one in the face, as much as to say, " What has brought you here ? Down on your knees and invoke me." For this was a representation of S. Nothburga, born at Rottenburg in the Inn valley, in 1265, a very popular saint in these parts, whose skeleton we saw in the church of Eben which we passed. In front of the figure was a kneeling stool and a bench on which some children had placed a mug full of forget-me-nots.

The story goes that, when at Eben in service, one Saturday afternoon at harvest time the church bell tinkled for Vespers, marking the beginning of Sunday, and Nothburga laid down her sickle. The farmer urged her to continue the work, but she refused, and catching her sickle, flung it into the air. There it hung suspended, shining like silver in the darkening evening sky, opposite to the setting sun. And when the Tyrolese child looks up at dusk, and sees the silver sickle of the new moon over the mountain tops, he thinks it is Nothburga's implement, just as he believes the spots in the full moon to be the Sabbath-breaker and his faggot. Obviously this is a pagan myth which has attached itself to a Christian saint.

Nothburga's body was taken up in 1718, and a new church was erected as a shrine for her remains. It contains a rococo high-altar piece, immediately above which is a large glass case like a sentry-box at the centre of the reredos. In it stands the skeleton, dressed sumptuously in red velvet, spangles and blue satin bows. The grinning skull is crowned with a wreath of artificial flowers bearing tinsel leaves ; the bony right hand holds a silver sickle. Anything more horrible can hardly be conceived. Pilgrimages are made to this shrine annually on September 14.

We descended the hill to Jenbach and crossed the Inn to Brixlegg. There we found that the people were engaged in a religious feud over an advertised Passion Play. The man who previously had personated the Christus was ill and could not perform his part. Accordingly, a professional actor was engaged from Munich. To this the clergy were vehemently opposed, and endeavoured to suspend the Play. But those who looked to reap a harvest of money out of the performance persisted, so that the people were divided into two factions, and the devout would not attend ; whereby the sale of tickets suffered exceedingly.

The Play was well carried out, but the jarring element manifested itself, and the audience was mainly composed of young peasants from the neighbouring villages who were not inspired with much reverence. There was smoking and sausage eating between the scenes. At the appearance of Judas Iscariot there ensued loud shouts of *Fuchs ! Fuchs !* on account of his red head and beard. When all was over it was rather startling to see Mary Magdalene at a table in the garden of the inn drinking beer with Pontius Pilate, S. Peter and S. John, knocking glasses and singing out *Prosit*, as she drank ; and Judas and the Virgin Mother engaged in devouring *Wienerschnitzel* and cracking jokes with one another.

Here we met Mrs. Frith, the wife of the great artist, the Hogarth of the nineteenth century, and her daughter. Mrs. Frith told me that for figure drawing the Munich school is unsurpassed, but for colouring a student must go to Paris.

I need say nothing of the Dolomites which have been so admirably described by Messrs. Churchill and Babington.

We walked over the Tre Croce Pass into the Pusterthal. We stayed a day and night at Brunecken, where was a very clean, comfortable inn kept by a noble family, whose portraits of generals and prelates lined the staircase and the *salle à manger*. We were waited on at table by the two daughters of our host, pretty refined-looking girls, happily not in the ugly costume adopted by the women of the Pusterthal in and about Brunecken.

It was not possible for me to have more than a brief holiday, three weeks, or a month at most.

On our return to Mersea I began my *Lives of the Saints* for the publisher, Hodges, who undertook to pay me £50 for each volume. Unhappily he became bankrupt and I never was fully paid for my labour and application.

CHAPTER VI

THE EIFEL AND THE ALGAU ALPS
1874-75

IN 1874 I went with my friend Gatrill to visit the Eifel. We went first to Trèves, a city full of historic interest. We walked out to the Amphitheatre: the wild pink roses were in full bloom and made me think of the massacre of the gallant Treveri there under Constantine. When the wild beasts that had been turned on them were glutted with blood and refused to continue their work Constantine ordered the surviving captives to kill one another. This they refused to do, and in preference fell on their own swords. I wondered whether the wild roses had tipped their petals in the blood of these noble martyrs for the cause of their people and country.

The cathedral is of special interest. It was the palace of Helena, mother of Constantine. This building she surrendered that it might be converted into a church. What rubbish at Colchester, to think that Helena was a daughter of old King Cole, " that merry old soul, who called for his fiddlers three." She was an hostelress at Drepantum, which Constantine afterwards named Helenopolis. She was doubtless a comely girl, who became the mistress of Constantius Chlorus, and so the mother of Constantine. But she was a strong character, and a noble woman, and has left her mark on the Church. The cathedral in its nave shows clear indications of the old Roman palace. The crossing of the transepts was over the atrium and impluvium, and was open to the sky till mediæval times.

Gatrill and I walked down the Moselle. The river was too low at Trèves for the boat, and besides we preferred to walk. We went to Bertrich, a watering-place a little way up from the Moselle, all hotels and lodging houses. There we spent Sunday, or at

63

least the greater part of it. A thunderstorm broke over the Eifel in the afternoon, and as soon as it was passed we walked on to Gillenfeldt. The Eifel district is most interesting : it is all volcanic and is studded with craters ; in some lie dark lakes, in others, that are dry, nestle villages.

At Gillenfeldt on the Feast of SS. Peter and Paul there is usually a dance on a platform erected in the water over the lake. But owing to the rain it was this summer held in the village inn. We were utterly fagged, and though the dancers would fain have had us caper with them, we were unable to comply with their wishes, and retired to bed. The noise of the fiddles and tramp of feet, which continued until early morning, mingled with our dreams and interfered with sound slumber. Next day we went to the church to the celebration of SS. Peter and Paul and then walked on to Daun. There were craters everywhere. The Weinfelder Maar, said to be the loftiest in the district, is a perfect basin with a little church on the brink of the tarn. There are others quite as perfect and very curious. On the Eifel one feels as though on the surface of the moon, blistered with volcanic eruptions.

After dinner at Daun we walked to Manderscheid, where there are two old castles. A story attaches to one of these that when it was founded a child was buried beneath the foundation. About two years ago a portion of the wall fell and the skeleton of a child was found embedded in the cement. As Gatrill and I walked about Daun I was struck with the geological formation of the rocks, and said, " I am sure there is manganese about here." Then I called to mind that it was the Eifel manganese which killed our production of the metal at Lew. My grandfather and father had derived a good income from the manganese raised there. But the production in Germany was more abundant, labour cheaper, and all other expenses so much less than in England that it later failed to yield a remunerative return.

We slept at Manderscheid, and in the morning walked to the Mosenberg and back. It is a long hill of lava, with three peaks. After dinner we paid another visit to the ruined castles and then strolled back to our old quarters at Gillenfeldt.

I had a curious experience on the following day when, after passing through Lützerath, Driesch and Ellers, we made up our minds to halt at Münster Maifeld, a little inland from the Moselle. The day was very hot, and, overcome by the heat, Gatrill lagged behind. I walked on ahead in order to secure rooms in a quiet inn. When I reached the place I, too, felt the need of rest and refreshment. Accordingly I went into the first *cabaret* that I came to and ordered some wine. To understand what follows you must know that all Jesuits and priests who will not conform to the Falck laws have been expelled from Germany and forbidden to re-enter. There were several peasants drinking in the little public-house, and I noticed that they eyed me curiously. I was wearing a white canvas suit and had on a red tie. Presently one of the peasants came up to me, and saluted me. " So, Father S——, you have come back to us again ! " " How," said I, " I have never been here before." " Oh ! " said the man, " we know you very well ; you were in the Jesuit College here ; we recognized you at once." " But," said I, " I am an Englishman, and have just come from Trèves." " Oh yes," he answered with a smile, " when the Prussian government turned you out, you went to Coblenz, thence to Brussels, and from Brussels to Trèves, and now you are with us again." " Nothing of the sort," I said. " I am an Englishman taking a foreign tour." " Whence do you come ? from what part of England ? " " From Colchester." " Ah, ha ! " exclaimed the man, " I have been to school and learned geography, and I know there is no such place as Colchester in England, or, indeed, in the world." Just then I saw Gatrill's profile pass the window, so I started up, paid my shot and was leaving, when the hostess, who accompanied me to the door, touched my shoulder and said, " Glad to see you back; we will not inform the police."

How noticeable it is that a man's profession or calling stamps a mark upon his face ! I remember in Iceland meeting Dr. Dasent, and he said to me as we were talking of some person, " I can always recognize a banker by the nape of his neck." There is no mistaking a groom or coachman, the set of their jaws tells you what they are, and there is a look about the close-shut lips of a lawyer, which proclaims his profession at once.

Gatrill and I were once at Malines on the fête of S. Rombaud, the patron saint of the town. In the *place* a fair was in progress. The principal attraction was a booth wherein the bills announced

F

found that my fellow-travellers were not affected to anything like the same degree. They preferred Cologne. But the façade of Cologne does not move me.

Alack and a day ! We went bathing in a stream outside the town, and got sorely stung by mosquitoes, C—— especially. He was a very large man, stout and red-faced, and wore a scarlet Garibaldi flannel shirt, with collar turned down over his white canvas jacket.

When we arrived at Sonthofen, very hungry, we entered the little inn, and C—— called for the *Speise-Karte* before ordering lunch. It was, of course, in German. He sat studying it, his face blotched with mosquito stings, looking like an ogre, and then shouted, " *Ich will haben Kind-braten !*" The German characters *R* and *K* are only slightly differentiated, and he mistook *Rind-braten* (roast beef) for *Kind-braten* (roast child). The waitress reeled back, burst into convulsions of laughter, and plunged into a back parlour to call up host and hostess, with their children, to see the ogre roaring for his accustomed feast. I was reminded of a quiet demand made by my mother of a *Kellner* at Linz in Austria, many years ago, for " *ein Stückchen Kaiser* " (a slice of the emperor), for "*Käse* " (cheese). It sent the waiter staggering back in uncontrollable merriment against the wall.

We had to send K—— back to England ; Gatrill, with great self-denial, promised to see him safely home. The poor fellow, who had not been out of England before, was scared out of his wits, and in mortal fear of being left behind. He could enjoy nothing, admire nothing, not the lovely scenery, not the meadows waving with forget-me-nots, not the picturesque villages, not the glorious minster of Strassburg, not even the red-legged storks perched on their nests.

I heard an amusing story of a gentleman in one of the fast through trains to Vienna. He had travelled night and day from Birmingham and had not had an opportunity to change his shirt. He was alone in a carriage, and at a station which preceded a tunnel he asked the guard how long the tunnel was. " *Ein Stund* "—an hour, thought the Englishman, " that will give me time to change my shirt." So as the train moved he opened his portmanteau and drew forth a clean garment. Then he proceeded to strip ; but, alas ! *ein Stund* has a double meaning in German,

an " hour " or a " mile," and before the traveller had got into
his new shirt the train had whisked out of the tunnel and drawn
up at a station.   Without any warning the guard threw open the
door of the compartment in order to admit a lady and her two
daughters.   On both sides ensued a shock.   The station-master
was summoned, and a consultation held by guard and porters
to discuss what was to be done, whilst the nervous traveller was
vainly trying to fit a stud into its place and to get the linen
collar to lie around his neck.   It was with some difficulty that
he induced the officials to let the matter pass over, and not
detain him for improper exposure of his person.

We next went to Oberstdorf.   I do not think that the Algäu
Alps have been sufficiently appreciated in England.   No more
admirable spot for a visit during the summer can be found anywhere.   Oberstdorf lies in a hollow with five valleys radiating from
it, each full of interest and beauty, and the whole dominated by
the Mädele Gabel with its snows.   In the variety of excursions to
be made from it, Oberstdorf surpasses Partenkirchen and Gar-
misch.

At Oberstdorf we were given a feast of snails.   I cannot say
that " they eat better than they cut."   I tried one and that sufficed.
Yet there they were esteemed a luxury.

The edible snail, *Helix pomatia*, according to tradition, was
introduced into England by Sir Kenelm Digby as a cure for his
wife, who was in a decline.   But as it is found usually in the
neighbourhood of Roman settlements, it is more probable that
it owed its introduction from France, where it is a native, to the
masters of the world.   That snails were a favourite dish with the
Romans we know.   They had their *cochlearia*, in which the
gasteropods were reared as they are still in France and Southern
Germany.   These nurseries consist of a large enclosed place, with
a floor covered half a foot deep with herbs, in which the snails
fatten.   Fulvius Hirpinus was the first to discover the luxury, a
little before the civil wars broke out between Cæsar and Pompey.
The snails were pastured on bran sodden in wine.   If we could
credit Varro, they grew so large that the shells of some would hold
ten quarts !   The younger Pliny for his supper took one lettuce,
three snails, two eggs, a barley-cake, sweet wine, and snow.   In
Germany the edible snail is largely cultivated ; it is there called

and learn lessons from German independent architecture of the fifteenth century.

There is another feature of German Gothic that merits attention—the treatment of the spires or caps to the towers. We know but too well how wearisome becomes to our eyes the lack of variety in our square towers, with or without battlements and pinnacles, and the extinguisher spires more or less attenuated. The square parish church tower becomes a little less tedious when it is furnished with a side turret at one angle, carried up above the top of the tower ; and the spire is slightly relieved when it has a coronal of lights or sound-holes under gables. Our English spire-capped towers have grown like natural plants out of the soil, but the foreign type, such as at Antwerp, consists of one story set, box-like, on another.

A pleasant relief to the spire was afforded after the Renaissance, and exhibited itself in Strassburg and in the granite church towers of Brittany.

But still later a bold diversion was made in the bulbous caps, infinitely diversified and almost invariably according picturesqueness to a distant view of a town. These are not confined to Germany, but are most conspicuously developed there. The caps are made of metal sheets, slate cannot be used where there is much wind ; and in Germany are usually of copper or are painted red. What mean and miserable stuff are the church towers of Wren and his followers in London !

I suppose no English architect would venture on reproducing in our land one of the first-class bulbous spires. But were he to do so, after a pause of astonishment and adverse criticism from such as cling to old English traditions, there would ensue an outburst of gratulation that he had added picturesqueness to a town which had previously been devoid of it, in a word, had been characterless.

CHAPTER VII

THE GOULD FAMILY AND LEW TRENCHARD
1874–75

ABOUT 1874 and 1875, in addition to my hagiological labours, I worked at the wills in Somerset House, and extracted all the particulars I could find relative to the Gould family, so that I may here quite fittingly give some of the results of my researches, prefacing them with some remarks upon Lew Trenchard, with which it has for so long been connected.

The valley of the Lew Water runs due east and west between ranges of high land to the north and south, which rise to the height of 600 feet above the sea, and were capped originally with downs. That upon the north has been under cultivation since I can recollect it, but that to the south is moorland to the present day, overgrown with gorse and heather.

Lew Water is supplied by two confluent streams that meet at Coombe Bow. That from the south rises on Fernworthy moor, that on the north in the marshes of Sourton, in the watershed between the Bristol and the English Channels. The meeting was at the point where the hills closed in upon the main Roman paved way leading from Exeter by Okehampton to Launceston and Cornwall. The name of Point attached to the farm at the junction of the two streams indicates the fact that here was a stone bridge (Pons).

The southern confluent breaks through the ridge, and the height above is occupied by a vast prehistoric camp, now called Burleigh, but formerly Gavul-ford (the Forked Way), because at this place branched off a way to Lydford. Here in 823 (?) was fought a notable battle in which the Britons were repulsed and driven back across the Tamar. The farm below the camp, now in ruins, bore the name of Slaughter.

73

resided at Lew Mill in the so-called Dower House till her death in 1667.

Upon the dining-room granite mullioned window is cut the date 1664, but this is the date of the several additions and alterations made to the far earlier house. This unfortunate habitation of widows has gone through several changes. To the south is a broad gable, and under the apex was originally a granite doorway, and to the drawing-room on the right was a five or six light granite window, and above that was another of much the same width, but not so tall. In 1664 Edward Gould removed the doorway, placed the entrance on one side, and converted the space where had been the ancient entrance into a recess for containing bee-hives. His object was to put into this wing, under this gable, a commodious staircase. The original one of stone was in the thickness of the wall in the dining-room, very steep, narrow and inconvenient. In the next place he narrowed the wide drawing-room window, cast out the granite mullions and substituted others of oak for them. He closed up a window looking into the court at the back, and panelled the room throughout and gave it a very beautiful plaster ceiling.

There was a charming little room on the left hand of the entrance hall that had oak panelling a century earlier, as also a singularly rich Elizabethan ceiling. But alas ! when my grandfather converted the Dower House into five cottages, he destroyed the ceiling, tore out all the panelling except on one side, and converted this delightful ladies' bower into a back kitchen.

On the Restoration the circumstances of the family were in a prosperous condition. Nicholas Gould, the brother of the deceased Henry Gould, had been created a baronet in 1660, and his first cousins, James and Sir Edward Gould, the latter residing at Highgate, were merchants of large fortune, and the relationship to George Monk, Duke of Albemarle, was close.

About this time probably some repair was done to the Manor House ; but Edward died of the plague in Exeter in 1667, when administering his mother's will. His widow married Francis Edgcombe, Esq. He was succeeded by his son, Henry, born 1657, who probably resided at Lew House till his death in 1704. His widow married the Rev. John Ellis, and died a resident at the Dower House in 1749.

THE DOWER-HOUSE BEFORE RESTORATION

I most earnestly trust that neither my son nor my grandson will be induced to part with the Dower House, as that has been so much more the continuous residence of the family till the close of the seventeenth century. From 1718 the Manor House was fairly regularly occupied till 1736, when William Drake Gould inherited the Staverton estate, through decease of the eldest branch of the family, when he pulled down a portion of Lew House and went to reside at Pridhamsleigh in Staverton, leaving Lew House to his mother in 1796, since which date it has been the residence of her descendants by Margaret, her daughter and heiress, who married Charles Baring in 1767.

The story of Captain Edward Gould's trial for murder has been told by me in my *Devonshire Characters* under the heading of Dunning, Lord Ashburton.

Edward was the only son of William Drake Gould and of Margaret, his wife. He was born on December 27, 1740, at Pridhamsleigh, and he was aged twenty-seven when he inherited the Lew Trenchard and Staverton estates. He entered the army in the 15th Dragoon Regiment in 1760, but retired in 1764-5.

I have looked through piles of bills and bonds, extant at Sandridge, that reveal how heavily Edward Gould was indebted to Dunning, who knew all the ins and outs of the property, and was ready enough to lend on the security of these lands. Moreover, Captain Edward owed to Dunning a large sum for getting him off at the Exeter assizes when tried for murder. Edward's mother and his relative, Miss Joan Gould, of Rock, in Buckfastleigh, paid off a good many of his debts, but as fast as he was relieved, he managed to overload himself with fresh debts, and at length there ensued a final crash, 1777 ; when, by indenture dated May 14, Pridhamsleigh and many other holdings passed to John Dunning.

There still remained some lands in Widdecombe and Holne, not yet alienated, but these also were made over to Dunning on October 20, 1779, after which Edward had not an acre of land left on which to plant his foot, nor a house of his own to cover his head. Lew he had long ago mortgaged to his mother for ninety-nine years, so that he could not sell that. He lived at Shaldon, and died there on June 29, 1788. His last request was that he might be conveyed to Bath, to be buried in the abbey, beside the body of a married woman who had eloped with him in years gone by, and who had predeceased him. He left no will. There was no administration of his effects, for he left *nothing*.

John Dunning was the nephew of Margaret, "The Pearl in Gold right meetly set," the first wife of Edward Gould of Combe and Pridhamsleigh. She died without issue and was buried at Staverton on April 26, 1662. She was the daughter of Wilmot Dunning, widow, of Gnatham, in Walkhampton parish.

John Dunning, created Baron Ashburton in 1762, married Elizabeth, sister of Sir Francis Baring, Bart., and had by her a son, Robert Barré, second Lord Ashburton, born in 1781. His father died in 1783. In 1805, Robert Barré, Baron Ashburton, married Anne Selby Cunninghame, daughter of William Cunninghame of Lainshaw, Co. Ayre, and died without issue. He left all his estate to his wife's nephews for life. These were James Edmund, Lord Cranstown, and Charles Frederick.

Lord Cranstown died in 1869. By Robert Barré's will, after the death of his wife's nephews, the estates were to go to his wife's nieces, Margaret Elizabeth, who died unmarried, and Anna Maria Isabella Macleod, the last survivor to dispose of the property. Robert Bruce Æneas Macleod of Cadboll, Co. Cromarty, came into the property in 1784 ; he had issue, Roderick, born in 1786, who married the sixth daughter of Mr. Cunninghame, and the only one who had issue. The property was left so as not to go to any of her sons, but to her daughters. Her sons were Robert Bruce Æneas, who died about 1888, and Henry Dunning, who died in 1902. But they had no interest in the estates, which went to Margaret, a daughter of Baron Cranstown. This daughter married a Belgian, the Baron de Virte, who died in 1904. Then it passed to the third daughter of Elizabeth Macleod, who had married John Wilson of Seacroft, Yorkshire. She had three sons, Roderick John, who died without issue in 1883, whereupon the second son, David Bruce, inherited Seacroft ; and by a sliding clause, Arthur Henry, the third son, stepped into the position of the second son, and inherited all the Devonshire property that had once belonged to the Goulds, except Lew Trenchard. He is of Sandridge Park, and has an only daughter.

Pridhamsleigh House is now occupied by a farmer. It consists of a moderately sized mansion built so as to form three sides of a quadrangle and on a steep slope. It has gone through much renovation, and nearly all the fine oak in the grounds has been cut down. The hall has been turned into a wood-house, and the old back entrance has become the principal one. The glazing of the hall windows was quaint, and I have reproduced it in the lights of the ballroom at Lew. In the spacious kitchen is the old roasting jack in good working order. Beneath the house are extensive cellars for cider. The pigeonry is very interesting and perfect ; it is situated in the orchard. The sun-dial from Prid- hamsleigh, with on it the arms and E. G., 1696, I was allowed to remove and place over the porch at Lew.

During my researches into the collateral branch of the Gould family I had the great good fortune of making acquaintance with Mr. Edward Gould, of Earl's Colne, the last male representative of James Gould, Mayor of Exeter, a staunch royalist who saved the lead roof of the cathedral and the bells, when the Parliament was preparing to sell them, by himself purchasing them and leaving them *in situ*. In Exeter there were something like sixteen parish churches in addition to the cathedral, and it was a question with the Commissioners whether they should pull down the cathedral and sell the materials, or sell the sixteen churches. James Gould by his purchase rescued the cathedral, and it was used in place of two churches, a brick wall being erected at the screen, to divide the nave from the choir.[1] All that was pulled down was the cloister, because people walked and talked there to the annoyance of the preacher in the nave.

James Gould, Mayor of Exeter in 1648, was the brother of Henry Gould, of Lew Trenchard. " He was bred a merchant in the city of Exon," says Prince, in his *Worthies of Devon*, 1701, " where, by a diligent hand and the blessing of God, he grew rich." Here is a fuller account of his resolute loyalty from *The Answer of the Merchants Petitioners of Leghorne*, Lond. 1704, on behalf of Edward, the second son of this James of Exeter.

" Mr. Gould's friends conceive it a piece of Justice which he's bound in duty to pay to the memory of his deceased Father,

---

[1] One portion to serve for Presbyterian, the other for Independent predications.

James had two sons, James, in the Foot Guards, who was killed in the battle of Malplaquet, September 7, 1709 ; and Edward, who was heir to his uncle, Sir Edward Gould. He married Jane, daughter of Sir Francis Pemberton, of Much Hadam, Kent, Lord Chief Justice, who defended the Seven Bishops in the memorable Trial of 1688.

By Jane, Edward had a large family. His portrait was painted by Kneller.

Both James Gould the elder, James the merchant, and Sir Edward left considerable fortunes, but the accumulated money was not to be touched for thirty years.

Alas ! Edwin Thoroton Gould came in for the accumulations, married Lady Barbara Yelverton, only child and heiress of the Earl of Sussex ; ran through the Earl's property and that of his grandfather and great uncle, and died in Paris, unable to show his face in England, for fear of arrest. His son, Henry Edward, changed his name to Yelverton to inherit the barony of Grey de Ruthyn. The barony passed through a female heiress to the Hastings family, and is now held by the Earl of Loudoun.

Of all the fortunes left by Sir Edward Gould, and James Gould, the China merchant, little remains save the clay figure with a smirk on the face, modelled in China, that now stands on a shelf in my gallery.

SIR EDWARD GOULD, KT.
From a painting by Carlo Maratti

CHAPTER VIII

FREIBURG
1877

IN the year 1876 I went to Lew with my family. I had received distressful letters from my uncle imploring me to go down. The tenant to whom I had let Lew House was a Mr. X——, and he had proved most unsatisfactory. He himself was a poor bleached creature, like sea-kale but not so tall, and was in fragile health. His wife was a buxom woman. She filled the house with young men who drank, gambled, and flirted with her. When any of the party came to church, it was to behave with so great impropriety as to scandalize the congregation. Accordingly, I had to give Mr. X—— notice to quit, and, singularly enough, he died in the very last week of his tenancy. The servants carried away a good many things from the house. Amongst other articles were the contents of a drawer of uncut opals. The lock had been forced and the stones purloined.

Nor was this all. The innkeeper, a patriarchal-looking man, with snowy beard, had seduced the wife of the local saddler. So I had to displace him, and I put in his room his son, a very respectable man, with a nice capable wife. The saddler separated from his wife, left the place, and settled in London.

As may be understood, under the circumstances my uncle pressed me to go down to Lew for a while so as to quiet disorders ; accordingly I put my friend Gatrill in charge of my Essex parish.

On January 12, 1877, I began the restoration of Lew Church by the demolition of the deal pews, which I replaced with carved oak benches, old and new.

The altar was a deal box on legs, that contained my uncle's canonicals and the communion plate. Thus, every Sunday, preparation for Divine Service began with the yawning of the Lord's Table, and its disgorging surplice and stole. My uncle wore no hood. He had not proceeded beyond his B.A. degree at Cambridge. All I could then do was to provide a decent altar frontal, tight fitting, in place of the straggling and sweeping, as well as moth-eaten, blue baize tablecloth.

I returned to Mersea on May 6th.

In September I received an appalling letter from the Vicar of Staverton. The architect of the Dean and Chapter, Ewan Christian, had undertaken the " restoration " of the church. The ledger-stones had been torn up and thrown out into the graveyard, and our family vault was being filled up with concrete. All that remained to me of the Staverton estate were the bones and memorials of my ancestors. If I desired to save either or both, the vicar wrote, I must go down at once. This accordingly I did.

One day I was in the church. Just below the chancel step was the grave of Julian Rowe of Will, daughter of Edward Gould of Combe. She had died in 1696. A few days before I went to Staverton I had been in Somerset House reading her will. It was very long. The old lady seems to have forgotten no one related to her in any degree. To her son, John Rowe, she bequeathed her " brass chattle, press, chaire and bed, now in the parlour chamber at Will ; a grate pair of andirons, wedding-ring and striped carpet and brass andirons." To her grandson, John Rowe, son of the above, " My silver Salt. To grandaughter, Joan Rowe, a silver-gilt spoon marked J.R. ; to granddaughter, Julian Rowe, forty shillings. To son William a gould mourning ring. To grandson Roger Rowe a silver tankard and £20. To son James Rowe the largest silver-gilt bowle and mourning ring, marked M.G. To my daughter Julian one Sammy gown and scarlet broad-cloth petticoat with silver lace, and linen and beds from Wash . . . a silver caudle-cup and silver dish. To son Edward Rowe four Turkey chairs and looking-glass in the Hall-chamber at Will, four Turkey cusheons, and two silver bowles and one gilt, now at Wash. To sister Elizabeth Cloud a broad piece of gold seal with the Rowe arms."

As I stood holding Julian Rowe's skull in my hand, musing on the way in which the busy and kindly brain it had contained had thought of all whom she desired should remember her, one of the vicar's daughters rushed into the church fluttering an orange envelope. This contained an announcement that my wife at Mersea had given birth to a son.

" Then Julian shall be his name," said I.

As I write this, the same Julian Baring-Gould, born on the 5th of September, is returned from Sarawak, where he has been in the service of the rajahs for twenty-three years. Having accomplished his time he comes back to England with a pension.

On October 11, 1877, we all started for Freiburg in Baden. I had suffered considerably from aguish attacks and bronchitis. My friend Gatrill was at Mersea as my *locum tenens*. My second daughter, Margaret (Daisy), had been ill with bronchitis, and was so delicate that I was required to take or send her abroad, as the damp, marshy island of Mersea, and the bitter east winds in spring, were prejudicial to her health and might throw her into a decline. Curiously enough, in 1900, she married a Philip D. Rowe of Great Haye, so that the Rowe connexion was relinked.

In place of choosing a warm and relaxing place of exile, I resolved on making Freiburg im Breisgau my winter quarters, as dry and bracing, though cold. I had been advised that it was a better health resort than Vevay or Lausanne.

On reaching Freiburg I was struck with the gorgeous autumnal colouring of the Black Forest, the beech golden-yellow, the bird-cherries carmine, and the pines sombre green. I expressed my admiration to the waiter at the inn. " Freilich ! " said he, " our mountains are fossil rainbows."

I at once wrote to Sutton to send down six hundred bird-cherries to Lew, and gave orders that they should be planted in the woods. This proved a failure, as the leaves fell before the frosts came to touch and translate their colour. They have proved a greater satisfaction to the birds than to me.

An amazing sight at Freiburg was that of the market-women coming in from the country with perambulators, in which lay young pigs being taken to market to be sold. This was my first acquaintance with perambulators, which had not then made their way into England.

At Freiburg we made the acquaintance of Frau von Hillern, the distinguished authoress of *Die Geir-Wally* (The Vulture Maiden) and *Ein Arzt der Seele*, which I was engaged in translating, and which was published under the title of *Ernestine*. It is the story of a medical man who deliberately brings up a maiden without religion, and kills what natural religion he finds in her conscience. The tale describes the gradual awakening of the girl's soul to the truths of Christianity. Both are powerful stories. At Freiburg I was told that, actually, plot, characters and much of the working out of the tales were due to one of the professors of the University. This I set down as local gossip, and doubted it ; but her subsequent novels, such as *Sie kommt doch*, are coarse and disagreeable, and show no signs of the talent displayed in the two former.

Frau von Hillern was the daughter of Frau Birch-Pfeiffer, the dramatic authoress, whose plays are very delightful. Frl. Birch-Pfeiffer appeared once only on the stage at Mannheim, where Herr von Hillern saw her, and fell in love and married her. When I made her acquaintance she was elderly, grey-haired and lame, for she had been a keen rider, had fallen from her horse and so injured her thigh that she could not walk without a stick. She was anything but beautiful ; she had a wolf-like appearance, with very large jaws, and grey eyes under heavy brows. Herr von Hillern was a retired judge, living at Freiburg, and was Chamberlain to the Grand-duke. Frau von Hillern told me that the Grand-duke of Baden had said, after returning to his own land, from a visit to England : " Now, at last, I can eat in comfort, and put my knife into my mouth."

Frau von Hillern, at the time when we arrived in Freiburg, was furious, because a young German woman in the United States was walking for wagers and advertised herself as Miss von Hillern, whereas her real name was Schmidt. The ex-judge wrote to the German Ambassador at Washington to have a stop put to this assumption of his name. Nothing, however, could be done to prevent it, by American law ; so Frau von Hillern's wrath was directed against all things American.

No man in Germany is considered a gentleman *armiger* unless he has a *von* prefixed to his name, and he cannot assume gentility arbitrarily ; he must have the *von* granted to him by the Emperor, the King or his Prince. On this privilege being accorded the man assumes a coat-of-arms ; he does more, he seals his letters with a coronet of strawberry leaves, as though he were a duke.

But only where *von* precedes a territorial name does it possibly indicate nobility or gentility. Consequently all the von Müllers, von Webers, von Schmidts, von Schornsteinfegers are *parvenus*. But this distinction is not always true. The artist Schnorr entitled himself Schnorr von Carolstadt, because he had been born at Carlstadt, though his family had never possessed an acre of land in the township.

Acting in the theatre as prima donna was a Frau von Fels. She was a handsome Jewess. Herr von Fels was actually a Prince of Thurn and Taxis, but forfeited his title so as to marry her. I have told the story in the fifth chapter of my *Early Reminiscences*. She exacted from her husband that, whenever she acted, he should throw a bouquet on to the stage at her feet, and get his friends to do the same.

The English chaplain at Freiburg was a Mr. Lawrence. His eldest daughter was over five feet nine inches high and bony. One day, walking down the Kaiser Strasse, the principal street in the town, she noticed on the footway a couple of Prussian officers swaggering along with an insolent air and defiant. She reasonably expected that one of them would step into the roadway to allow a lady to pass. But not they. Their purpose was to force her to leave the pavement, cross the runnel of water, and step on to the cobbles of the street, or else they designed to crush her against the wall, as did Baalam's ass with the prophet.

She looked firmly at them, but they stared back undauntedly, and did not stir. Then she put her hands upon their epaulettes, gave them a twist, and sent one man round with his face to the wall, and the other off the footway into the runnel, and walked composedly between them.

The humiliation of these officers was so great—not because they had behaved like cads, but because they had been spun like tee-totums by an English girl, that both were forced to leave Freiburg for another regiment quartered in Lithuania.

At Freiburg was a Major Festing with his daughter, a pretty girl. He had come from Homburg. At table d'hôte, when he was seated for *déjeuner*, there entered two German officers with eyeglasses, who raked the table, and, one nudging the other, took their seats opposite to Festing and his daughter. During the meal their behaviour was offensive. The father's blood was up.

At dessert one of the officers began to crack nuts on the table. The English major called to the waiter and said : " *Kellner*, fetch me a coal-hammer."

" A coal-hammer, mein Herr, what for ? "

" A coal-hammer. I want to crack nuts with it on the dinner table."

Up sprang the principal officer. " Is this intended as an insult ? " he inquired fiercely.

" Not at all," replied Festing ; " I desire above all things to conform to the manners of polite society, wherever I find myself. When I am at Rome I do as Romans do. When I am among wolves—I howl."

The waiter was aghast. When the father and daughter rose to leave the Speisesaal, he said with a blank face to the former : " Do you know whom you have been addressing ? "

" I neither know nor care."

" It is Prince Wilhelm von Bismarck."

Count Herbert von Bismarck was pushing himself very unceremoniously into the room at a reception of Pope Pius IX and was told to stand back. Only a limited number were admitted to audience at a time.

" Are you aware whom you are repelling ? " asked the Count haughtily. " Know that I am a Bismarck."

" That," answered the chamberlain, " fully accounts for, but does not excuse, your bad manners."

One of Bismarck's sons got into money difficulties, and that not by any means for the first time ; I think it was Wilhelm. He went to his father about them, and desired relief. The Prince received him very coldly, and said : " I have no money for you, but "—opening his table drawer—" I will lend you a pistol."

I do not mean to intimate that there is absolute dearth of gentlemanly manners and feeling among the German, especially among the Prussian officers. Because Prince Bismarck was bearish in his conduct it was esteemed the right thing to assume an insolent manner. But it was forgotten that behind this brutality of behaviour lay a great genius. Every petty officer, without a grain of talent in him could easily, and did actually, copy the *Grobheit* of the great exemplar. It needed culture to suppress his inordinate self-conceit and self-assurance, and this was precisely what these men did not possess.

I shall now insert some letters written by me from Freiburg to my friend, Gatrill.

DREIKÖNIG STRASSE NO. 10,
FREIBURG i/B,
November 5, 1877.

MY DEAR G.,

First about this place. We have secured a flat just outside the town. Our landlord is a Dr. Schill, a geologist, who married his housekeeper, a handsome woman with an incipient goitre which she carefully conceals beneath an enormous brooch, a cameo with Venus on it. " Emma," the landlady, is a curiosity. She possesses, apparently, an inexhaustible variety of grand gowns, and we watch with interest the variations in her daily costume. The floral changes of the surface of the earth are great and successive. So are those of Frau Schill, I beg her pardon, Frau Doctor Schill—women in Germany take the official titles of their husbands. In the morning, glimpses are to be had of her in very dirty and tattered petticoats and bodice with soiled sleeves. She, with the doctor and two dogs, Popperli and Schücherli, occupy an annexe, a sort of rabbit-hutch built up against our house. She throws all the broken crockery, old newspapers and cabbage stalks into the garden before our doors. The garden is also a dumping-ground for wrecked chairs, torn window blinds and dishevelled mats. In vain in the morning do I try to tidy up before visitors call. By the end of the day the litter has again accumulated. I ventured to remonstrate, and sought for the most delicate terms in which to express my dislike of the litter. "Ach Gott ! " exclaimed the Frau Doctorin, " freilich, es ist eine Schweinerei." But she has made no attempt to clean up the piggery.

The furniture of the house suffers from many infirmities, the joints are weak, and the chair backs afflicted with lumbago. The cupboards have each lost a foot. The muslin curtains are tied back with bits of dirty pink ribbon that at one time served to adorn " Emma's " hair. One, I am convinced, is a discarded garter.

A few days ago the Celebration of All Saints and All Souls took place. On the Eve the people decorate the graves of their relatives, and on the afternoon of All Saints visit them and pray for the departed. The cemeteries have become flower-gardens, and folk rival each other in the originality and beauty of the floral decorations. The graves are adorned with solanum, primulas, the white feathery Michaelmas daisy, etc. Wreaths have been woven, festoons formed, and crosses fashioned out of leaves, flowers and berries. One garland I noticed of holly-berries wound round a crown of vivid green moss. Another is made of autumn leaves and grasses, picked out with scarlet poppies. A whole grave is bordered with mignonette and heart's-ease. A tomb of red sandstone has been edged with silver-leafed fever-few and rosebuds. On a well-weeded grass mound is written with the red berries of the mountain-ash " Ruhe-Sanft " ; on another, fashioned out of pansies, " Mütterchen denk an mich."

On a husband's grave stands a burning lamp with Michaelmas daisies forming a belt round it, and the words " Zum Wiedersehen." The crosses of babies bear white muslin weepers.

One sees many pretty and touching incidents. Three little children, the youngest aged five, were doing up their mother's last resting-place, and I could see by the headstone that she died in childbirth five years ago. The little creature that cost her mother's life was now laying on the turf in forget-me-nots (I fear artificial) *Vergiss mir nicht !*

Another group of little ones was beautifying the resting cradle of a baby brother. They had brought a large wreath and a cross in a go-cart, and the eldest boy was engaged in surrounding the mound with white pebbles, whilst the others were regaling themselves after their exertions by a meal off a raw turnip.

A father and his children were standing at the foot of his wife's grave. Each had brought a twisted wax taper, and had set it, lighted, on the mound, where the flames twinkled like stars in the midst of the clusters of flowers with which it had been covered. They had their hands folded and prayed in silence. Then the father produced a stone jar and sprinkled the grave thrice with the holy water it contained. He passed it on to his son who did the same. The sister repeated the action, and so it went on to the youngest child.

The cemeteries—there are two—are full of beautiful monu-

FREIBURG IN BADEN

ments. The old graveyard, now closed, has a curious chapel, over the porch of which are paintings of two gigantic skeletons ; one points to the clock and brandishes his scythe. The other is writhing in the toils of the undying worm. Within the porch is a Dance of Death. There are twelve subjects. Death fiddles a baby to sleep, and rocks its cradle. Death takes a pen from a schoolboy's hand when he has written O in his alphabet. Death takes the cross off a man's shoulder, and under the picture are the lines : " Death alone relieves the married man of the cross he has himself laid on his own back."

Some of the inscriptions on the tombstones are neat, and some touching. On an obelisk we read : " In Uprightness alone can I find Repose." On another monument a little boy is shown sleeping under an urn, from which a butterfly escapes. With one hand the child holds a snapped bough, bearing unripened fruit, with the other he is closing his ear to the sounds of the earth. Beneath is written merely : " He will wake presently ! "

The new cemetery is outside the town. Above the entrance gate is inscribed in letters of gold : " De Mortuis nil nisi bene."

A peasant who was a bit of a scholar and his mother came up. " What is the meaning of those words ? " asked the old woman. "They are Latin," replied the youth. " They mean: 'Von den Todten es bleibt nichts als Gebeine.' " (Of the dead nothing remains but the bones.) This will apply as well to the form in which the passage is usually given in England : " De Mortuis nil nisi bonum."

I get very enjoyable walks to villages in the neighbourhood. To-day I have been up to the ruined castle of Schneeburg, the seat of the noble family of Schnewlin, now extinct. Above it, parted by a valley, rises an extraordinary mountain of volcanic conglomerate, round and tree-covered to its summit. This is the scene of a Tannhäuser legend, the knight who went into the mountain being one of the Schnewlins of Schneeburg. The hill on which the ruined castle stands is covered with traveller's joy : the sun shining on the feathery seeds gave it a strange gauzy look.

We are not far from Zähringen, the cradle of the Grand-ducal House of Baden, but the ruin of the castle is so complete that it has lost all architectural features, although it retains its legendary import.

The story is this. The ancestor of the Dukes of Zähringen was a charcoal-burner in the Black Forest ; one day he made his pile of wood, covered it over with earth and stones, and lighted the heap. When all was burnt out and he cleared the spot, he found on it much molten silver. From that time he continued his charcoal burning, covering the pile with stones and earth, and was always successful in obtaining silver. By this means he accumulated a great treasure of the metal.

Now it fell out that at this time the Emperor had been cast from his throne by a rebellion, and he fled with his wife and children to the Kaiserstuhl chain of low mountains nearly opposite Freiburg, rising out of the basin of the Rhine. There he suffered much distress and shed many tears (Zähren). Thence he announced that he would give his daughter in marriage to any man who would help him to recover his throne, and that he would create him a Duke. The collier, hearing of this, visited the Kaiserstuhl range and promised the Emperor as much silver as would enable him to regain his lost position ; and made over to him the accumulations of precious metal. In reward for this the Kaiser married his daughter to the charcoal-burner, created him a Duke of Zähringen, and granted to him a tract of land in the Black Forest, as well as the silver-bearing mountains therein.

In commemoration of their origin the Dukes of Zähringen, ancestors of the House of Baden, bore as their crest a collier's cap, surmounted by a globe of silver ore.

The genuine history of the family is interesting. The first that is known in history was a certain Bezelin of Villingen, in the tenth century, Count of Thurgau, Brisgau and Ortenau. He obtained much land in Baden, and the acquisitions were enlarged under his son, Berthold I, Count of Zähringen, created in 1061 Duke of Carinthia and Marquess of Verona. He was, however, deposed in 1072, but his sons recovered most of his titles and territories. His youngest son, Hermann I, who died in 1074, became Marquess of Verona and regained part of Baden. The son of this Hermann, of the same name as his father, established himself in Baden and assumed the title of Margrave of Baden.

Berthold von Zähringen, the last of the direct line, died in 1218, and is buried in the cathedral. His is the only monument that remains. On All Souls' Day a taper burned before it. The people tell strange stories of him. He was a sort of Nebuchadnezzar, filled with pride and very cruel. At last one day he had a child roasted and brought to his table. After having tasted a mouthful of the *Kinderbraten* he went raving mad, melted up all the silver plate and money he had, made it into one great lump and rolled it into a cavern in the Rosskopf mountain, went in after it and disappeared from human sight. The rest of the story is a Black Forest version of Barbarossa with some variations. Turned to stone, he sits at a table, but once in the year the sound of the church bells of Zähringen penetrates to the heart of the mountain and he becomes flesh and blood again. He looks at the lump of silver, and counts his jewels spread before him. But directly the bells cease ringing, his feet, then his legs, then hands, heart, and head become stone once more.

In 1801 Baden was compelled by Napoleon to cede to France all the possessions on the left bank of the Rhine, and in return was given the bishopric of Constance, parts of the bishoprics of Basle, Spires and Strassburg, as well as numerous suppressed abbeys. Annexations followed, and the Duke of Zähringen by the grace of Napoleon became Grand-duke of Baden.

The population here is by no means pure German in appearance. The original settlers were Celts, and presumably Celtic remains have been found on the Schönberg. The majority of the people have dark hair and eyes. The land was invaded by the Cimbri and Teutons, whom Marius massacred on the field of Pourières. But they did not settle in Baden, only passed through it. A real invasion took place later, when it was occupied by the Suevi. In the third century it fell under the sway of the Allemanni, who were, I suspect, a horde of mixed breed, Swabians, Franks and Saxons. Although the Allemanni spoke German, their dialect was peculiarly bad and almost unintelligible. The poet of the people is Hebel, whose *Allemanische Gedichte* are delightful. They have had, however, to be rendered into literary German in order to be generally understood.

The men are certainly undersized. In the double transept of the cathedral, which was crammed with men on All Saints' Day at High Mass, I towered above their heads, and I failed to see a fair-haired man among them. I am exactly six feet high.

CHAPTER IX

LEW TRENCHARD
1881

MY uncle, the Rev. Charles Baring-Gould, died on February 15, 1881. He had suffered from bronchitis for fourteen years and had been incapacitated from the performance of his duties, which had been discharged more or less intelligently and capably by a succession of curates.

The doctors had recommended his spending winters at the most unsuitable places ; other than the bottom of a well. One was passed at Pau, the most relaxing spot in the South of Europe ; another at Teignmouth, the most relaxing watering-place on the south coast of Devon. In the winter of 1880–81 he caught a cold that brought on pleurisy, and when that had been reduced by blisters, he had not the strength to rally, and rapidly sank.

The dear old man in his coffin looked like the statue of a saint, his face had acquired a spiritual beauty by the touch of the Angel of Death.

He was a man in whom the softer Christian graces shone calmly and soothingly. No one ever heard a harsh word from his lips, nor would he pronounce judgment on any man. He had called my attention by letter to the scandals occasioned by the X—— family, in Lew House, and to that caused by the innkeeper and the saddler's wife, because urged to it by his wife, who was a woman of energy and vehemence of character. I have seen him at table, when she was expressing herself strongly, rise and quietly slip out of the room. His caution was perhaps too extreme, so that it was not possible to obtain from him a definite and decided opinion on a mooted point. He formed in this particular a marked contrast to my father, who came to a conclusion

THE REV. CHARLES BARING-GOULD

at once on any problem submitted to him ; and when once he had expressed his opinion, never swerved from it.

My uncle was undoubtedly in principle a High Churchman, and he was always definite in his teaching ; but I believe that his sermons were derived from the plain discourses of Newman and other Tractarians that had been published, and that there was in them nothing much of his own. The books he gave me as a boy were of a High Church tendency. He had been nominated to the Rectory by his father, whilst he was in Deacon's Orders, in 1832. He was then aged twenty-five, and had been a curate but a few months at Okehampton, with the Rev. Dr. Tanner, whose daughter, Marianne, he married. He never had the chance of seeing how Church matters were carried out on High Church lines. When the Bishop of Exeter ordered the use of the surplice in the pulpit, although Philpotts withdrew the order on account of the storm it provoked, my uncle adopted the surplice and never gave it up. He wore no hood ; he had taken a B.A. degree, but never went further. Neither did he wear a cassock. The parish surplice had a high collar up to the cheekbones, was elaborately goffered and very long.

He was buried on the 19th, a balmy, sunny day. In accordance with his own request he was not laid in the family vault, but in the earth, near his daughter Caroline.

As Lew House had been let, I was obliged to occupy the Rectory till Mr. Morshead's tenure expired. It was not, however, possible for me to live there with my family till it had been thoroughly overhauled and put in a sanitary condition. Much painting and many repairs had to be effected, as nothing had been executed in that direction for something like forty years.

I did not send to the Bishop of Exeter my presentation of myself to the living until June 29, and I was instituted by him personally on July 19.

It is usual to have one's recommendation signed by four incumbents in the diocese one is leaving, and to have these signatures countersigned by the bishop of that diocese. But this I did not do because I hardly knew, or was known by, more than two of the neighbouring Essex incumbents, owing to the desolate and watery tract intervening between Mersea and the mainland, nomination of William Doidge, gent., of Milton Abbott. The Doidges, by the way, possess the extraordinary coat-of-arms representing a woman's breast distilling milk. The family is still extant, but their ancient mansion was levelled with the dust by one of the Dukes of Bedford.

His successor was John Truscott, nominated by Henry Gould, gent., in 1692. Rector and squire were greatly estranged in their politics, and this estrangement was aggravated by an attachment springing up between Susannah Gould, daughter of the squire, and Peter, the son of the rector. The engagement was strongly opposed by her father and mother. Nevertheless, she was married to him. (March 19, 1727—to Peter Trustcott, gent., of Lew Trenchard). On her way back to Lew House, unattended, in her bridal dress, she fell dead of heart-complaint in the drive, and was buried, a virgin-bride, 23rd March. He did not die till April, 1758.

To my mind there can remain little doubt that the White Lady who is supposed to be the family ghost and to haunt the house and grounds, derives from Susannah Gould. In process of time the story of her unfortunate fate was forgotten, and Madam Margaret Gould, who died in 1795, so impressed the imagination of the villagers with her strong personality that she superseded Susannah in popular tradition.

The Scottish pines about Lew House and the woods were planted by Henry Gould as indicative of his Jacobitism, whereas the avenue of limes leading to the church porch owe their origin to the ecclesiastical and political proclivities of John Truscott.

The successor to Truscott was John Haviland, B.D., a very staunch Churchman, who was nominated to the living, 1735, by Arthur Tremayne, Esq.

We are now able to obtain some authentic information as to the condition of the parish from the returns made by the incumbents to the bishops at their visitations ; and as these are vastly characteristic of the times I give them from 1744 to 1786.

" John Haviland, B.D., Sept. 10, 1735, d. 1762.

" At the Visitation of 1744 there were 25 families in the parish, and 70 Communicants. One Sermon was preached on Sunday Morning. There was no parish-school, but the parents were expected to teach their children the Catechism at home, and the children were catechized as to their knowledge, and understanding of what they had been taught, upon Sunday afternoons. The Rector kept a Curate, Francis Welles, to whom he payed £30 per annum and allowed the surplice fees."

Observe the excellence of this system in contrast with that of the present day, when the parents are relieved of all moral obligation with regard to instruction in religious matters, which is transferred to the schoolmaster.

"John Vickary, 1762 ; d. 1786 ; was master of the Grammar School, Okehampton (dist. 11 miles) and where he was Chaplain to the Mayor and Corporation, and was bound to read prayers daily in S. James's Chapel at 7 a.m. and 5 p.m.

"He was also rector of Lydford, and vicar of Denbury, near Totnes.

"In 1764 there were only 11 families in the parish, and the communicants had fallen to 10. There was no dissenting meeting-house in the parish. The children were only catechized upon Whitsunday."

What was the occasion of the decline of the numbers in the parish is not stated. Vickary died in 1786, after a long non-resident incumbency of his three cures. Of Lew Trenchard he was an incumbent for twenty-four years.

"William Elford, 1786 to 1833.

"At the Visitation of 1831 there were 62 families in the parish. No Dissenters. The Rector resided in Tavistock (dist. 9 miles). Had had two paralytic seizures, was also troubled with piles, the stone, and gravel, 'and occasionally a great complaint in my stomach, also a double rupture. I perform duty myself. I am also Vicar of North Petherwin, where I have a curate for the sick, who resides, and receives £50.0.0 per annum. I am also rector of Coryton, where Mr. Wilsford receives £35.0.0 per annum. Divine service at Lew is at 10.30 a.m. and at 2 p.m. There is a Catechising in the Summer. The number of the Communicants is 16. The parsonage is in good repair.'"

The reason for the increase of the population was the opening
of manganese mines in the parish. Mr. Elford was instituted
to North Petherwin in 1796.

I have elsewhere told some anecdotes relative to Parson Elford.
He was wont to ride over from Tavistock to Lew on Saturday
evenings and spend the nights of Saturday and Sunday in Lew
House, where he was hospitably entertained by " Old Madam."
When the Bishop complained of his non-residence his excuse
was : " My Lord, how can I possibly be expected to live in a
parish in which there is no barber who could curl my wig ? "

He was compelled to keep a resident curate, a Mr. Caddy
Thomas, who had been a missionary in the Bahamas. I am not
sure that he had Communion more than four times in the year,
or that he ever concerned himself to catechize the children.

Now consider how intermittent had been teaching and Divine
worship in the church, and this during 350 years. No definite
instruction given as to the nature of the Church Catholic, none
as to the obligation of Divine worship, but a sort of sloppy
theology that contained nothing edifying where it was not posi-
tively heretical. At periods inundations of Calvinism or Luther-
anism, obscured all light and killed spiritual life. At one time we
had the arch-heretic, Romaine, as curate at Lew. The spirit, the
flame of zeal and worship flickered here and there in the Church,
with sudden and transient spurts of flame. It was there, and had
not been extinguished, that was something, and it was accordingly
capable of being fanned into flame. But this would have to be
done with caution, with patience, and with self-suppression. I
am convinced from what I saw in my childhood that Catholic
feeling and belief were very widely diffused among the clergy and
the cultivated laity ; but it was suppressed, labouring under
timorousness, and unable to make itself manifest through lack
of leadership. Indeed, this unsuspected rise of the Catholic
spirit against the attempt of William III, Tillotson, Tenison and
Burnett, under Jane and the Lower House of Convocation, was a
surprise to the Latitudinarians ; and the rally of the clergy of the
diocese of Exeter around their Bishop in a later synod was another
instance of the presence of this living Spirit still present in the
Church of England.

My uncle, the Rev. Charles Baring-Gould, was instituted to

the living in 1833. He was very young and inexperienced at the time, but thoroughly well-intentioned. He instituted a monthly celebration of the Holy Communion, and discarded the black gown.

I came to Lew parish in 1881, as already mentioned, and I had a work before me to execute for which I was not sure that I was competent.

There existed a certain amount of torpid religious feeling in the place, but it wanted quickening. Among the young people there was little or none. I felt that I had a work to do, not like that of Newman in England at large, but at Lew Trenchard, the small. But I knew from the outset, as I know now, that my capacities are limited, and that I should be utterly unfit for work in a larger sphere. I think it not at all improbable that both the Archbishop of York and Claughton of Rochester had inserted my name in the Episcopal " Black Book," for I had shown precious little deference to either. But, so far from this injuring me, it has availed in limiting my energies to my own parish. All I desired was to be let alone, and suffered unmolested to devote myself to the spiritual rousing of the people, the restoration of the church, and the making habitable and comfortable the houses on the estate, including my own.

The first of these objects must necessarily entail patience, and take time to show itself. I remember in the winter of 1840 standing beside the Rhine at Cologne, and watching the break-up of the ice which had covered it with so thick a panoply that carts had been driven across from Deutz. The first tokens of a change consisted of cries as of pain, when the floor of ice cracked, and there ensued the rending into floes, that leaped and revolved and crashed into one another, sending up spirts of water and splinters of ice. All was confusion, all contest ; only little by little did the surface of the river display itself, smooth and persistent in its onward course.

The whole of the period of the Church Revival was one of break-up of ice with the thaw produced by the Spirit of God breathing on the waters. Inevitably, without there would be fightings, and within fears. We have to be patient, and in patience possess our souls ; and the clumps of ice will go—they are going under already.

The second and the third objects I had set before me would afford sensible evidence of progress achieved. The labour of wakening and guiding of souls is necessarily hidden, and its manifestation is not with a flourish of trumpets.

The Parish Priest stands in need of both faith and patience. Moreover, to acquire patience he must learn self-mistrust, and exercise self-control. He must not expect the river of God to be freed from the ice that has covered and chilled it during four centuries, whilst he is looking on. If by his example and his teaching he can do something to dissipate the fog of ignorance and prejudice that has brooded over the English mind he must be content. With the advent of " the Wolves," as Bishop White called the Marian exiles, in the reign of Elizabeth, all conception of worship was extinguished.

I saw that we must rely on the sowing of definite faith in the hearts and minds of the children. With them would be the future of the parish.

In former days a certain amount of moral compulsion, probably involuntary, was exercised by the squire upon his tenants, requiring them to attend church. Spiritually I do not think that the influence of the parson availed much. He droned out a borrowed sermon that touched no hearts ; one that was pulled out of his pocket, and had not been heated by a fervent heart.

In 1817 a suit was brought at Bedford by a Dr. Free, Rector of Sutton, against Sir Montague Burgoyne, Bart., for not frequenting the parish church, where he was squire, to recover twenty pounds a month from Sir Montague, on account of absence from the manorial pew. This claim was based on an ancient and obsolete statute, unrepealed indeed, but rendered inoperative by the altered spirit of the age. The defendant was able to show that during many months there had been no service in the church, and that he had been ill during the rest of the time ; so that on the merits of the case he was accorded a verdict. It appeared that, to make assurance doubly sure, the Bishop's chaplain was in court, with the Bishop's written declaration that the defendant, if he had offended, had subsequently been reconciled to the Church. Had this declaration been presented after the verdict and before judgment had been given, no judgment could have been pronounced on the case.

Although the law had proved inoperative, it had left an impression on men's minds that parishioners were legally bound to attend Divine service in the church. The tenants came to Morning Prayer, not as a duty that they owed to God, not for any spiritual edification they expected to receive, but because it was expected of them by the landlord of the cottages they occupied.

But so soon as they learned that this obligation could not be enforced there was a falling off in attendance, and for spiritual teaching the labourers went to the Methodist Chapel, where appeal was made to their emotions, and that in terms they could understand. Not only was this the case, but they became proud of the liberty newly acquired and resolved to exercise it. I remember a washerwoman who was reprimanded by my mother for the slovenly way in which she returned the linen entrusted to her. "Oh!" said she defiantly, "if you don't like my washing, I shall go to chapel and leave the church."

The country parsons were well aware of the alienation of their poor parishioners, but they made no attempts to retain their impatient, and recover their errant sheep. They did not know how this was to be done. They lacked the necessary fervour. They were so Tillotsonized that they could preach only duty, and not Christ crucified. They were good men, worthy, clean in life, kindly to the poor, but woefully deficient in unction. It was the Evangelicals who broke through this formal inculcation of Honesty being the best Policy as the sum of Gospel teaching, and of Gospel promises, and who sought to reclaim the strayed sheep by copying Nonconformist methods, and teaching heretical doctrine.

A quotation from my diary in 1862 will show the spiritual deadness of the place that existed twenty years before my induction.

"Christmas Day. Alone, except for my little brother, in Lew House. The rats were celebrating Noël. They had a frolic last night, kept high festival, had a wild hunt. They scoured along the passages, they scampered between floor and ceiling, they danced a hornpipe in the storeroom and rollicked up and down the stairs. They kept me awake. Presently I

The Bishop was a fanatical teetotaller. At a meeting at Oke-hampton he stated : " That he had tried all his life to induce men to drink in moderation and had failed utterly." It was a hard cut when the reporters rendered this in the morning papers, " He had tried all his life to drink in moderation and had failed utterly."

It was amusing to observe how that whilst Temple was Bishop of Exeter the curates and vicars hoping for promotion adopted the blue ribbon and wore it conspicuously. No sooner was Temple moved to London than these ribbons vanished.

A greater contrast to Temple could hardly be found than was Bickersteth, his successor. It was a change from an east wind, rough and bracing, to one from the south, soft and relaxing.

Temple was a man of brains and learning, but lacking in polish. Bickersteth was a thorough gentleman, kindly hearted and tactful, but he was no scholar, nor was he possessed of any originality. When at Lew for a confirmation, and the ringers were giving him a peal, Bickersteth jumped up from table where he was lunch-ing to run to the tower, so as to thank the ringers : a thing that Temple would not have thought of doing.

The story was told of him, that when he was in London, he saw a little urchin vainly endeavouring to reach and pull a bell at the door of a stately mansion in the West End. " Let me help you, little man," said the Bishop kindly, and he proceeded to ring the bell.

" Cut along, old cock ! " shouted the boy ; " we shall have the police after us. I wanted to do it for a lark and to make the footman swear. It's a joy to make those fellows say, ' Damn.' Don't you relish it ? "

Bickersteth was a kind, amiable man, but very vain over his " poems," in which are no poetical ideas, and his hymnal that has been almost everywhere superseded. He wanted to alter my *Onward, Christian Soldiers*, in the line, " With the Cross of Jesus, going on before," into " With our Lord and Master going on before," or some twaddle like it. Also in the Children's Evening Hymn he wanted to wash the colour out of the lines " Guard the sailors tossing on the deep blue sea." But to this I would not consent. I greatly relish the bringing of a little colour into verses, however ordinary they may be. It is like the bit of sky that an

RIGHT REV. R. BICKERSTETH
Bishop of Ripon

artist introduces into a portrait. Bickersteth's one hymn that may survive is " Peace, perfect peace." This line was very appropriately inscribed on the tomb of a scold by the relieved widower.

I saw nothing of Bishop Ryle. He had the better of Anwyll, of All Saints', Plymouth. They met to discuss the procedure of the vicar, who promised to abandon certain things he had adopted in the church, as the dressing up of images in silks and velvets. Anwyll promised, but like a Welshman, did not keep his promise. Ryle (Herbert Robert) was appointed in 1900 and translated to Winchester in 1903, where he at once got across with his clergy by injudicious dictatorial acts. He resigned and became Dean of Westminster and sank into insignificance.

Earle, Archdeacon of Plymouth, afterwards Bishop of Marlborough and Dean of Exeter, possessed an unfortunate passion for destroying screens. He devastated his own church at West Allington, also that of Marlborough and that of South Huish. The destruction of that at Marlborough was most unfortunate. The church is large, and the screen was the only object of beauty in it, and served to bring the interior into proportion. When it had been removed the church had no more beauty and character than has the skeleton of a camel in the desert that has had all its flesh picked off by vultures.

Earle tried to induce the rector of Ogwell to destroy his. Mr. Pierce Taylor, however, before consenting to do this, wrote to Harry Hems, the wood-carver in Exeter, for his opinion what would be the cost of putting the screen in repair.

" Sir," answered Harry Hems, " if you destroy that screen, your name will be handed down to posterity with execration. Tell the archdeacon that the same will be his doom for having recommended such a piece of sacrilege."

That saved the Ogwell screen.

Talking of screens, at Ashburton the church was handed over to Street, the architect, who erected a screen, an absolute monstrosity. Enough fragments of the former screen were found to show what it had been, and yet Street insisted on putting in a cumbrous mass of oak of his own design, totally out of character with screen work in Devon. Oh ! these architects ! how I detest them for the mischief they have done. I should like to cut off their hands, or limit them to designing new churches and new mansions and hotels, but absolutely forbid them to touch and maul an ancient building. " I know their tricks and their ways," as said Jenny Wren in *Our Mutual Friend*.

There are bishops and bishops, as there are architects and architects. The old bishop who was elevated from a head mastership of a public school, possessed some experience as a ruler. He had little or no spiritual experiences, but he possessed dignity and showed that he knew what he was worth. The Low Church bishops, none of whom had been schoolmasters, and were not even scholars, thought themselves infinitely more capable than they were. A good many bishops whose parentage was of the middle-class at once developed " swollen heads," and exercised their authority arbitrarily and tactlessly. They were, and conducted themselves, like Mr. Dorrit when he emerged from the Marshalsea and came into his property. They were Dorrit in their strut, their posturing, their self-importance, and cultivation of parasites.

As I have been dealing with bishops, I may be allowed to give a couple of anecdotes of prelates.

Archbishop Tait was dining one evening at the house of the Duke of Westminster. During the meal his face became ghastly. Laying down his knife and fork by the plate, he said to himself in a suppressed voice : " It has come to pass at last as I feared. I have been dreading, expecting, a stroke."

" Console yourself, your Grace," said the Duchess of Sutherland, who sat beside him. " It is not *your* leg but *mine* that you have been pinching."

Here is a story of Dean Lefroy of Norwich. He gave a garden party upon the occasion of his golden wedding. A guest brought to it a French gentleman who was staying with him and introduced him to the Dean.

" Sir," said the Frenchman, making a profound bow, " I do not quite understand vat is a golden wedding."

The Dean put his hand on his wife's shoulder, patted it, and said : " This good lady and I have lived together for fifty years."

" Ah ! now I do understand," exclaimed the Frenchman, as his face lighted with intelligence, " so now you are at last about to marry her ! "

CHAPTER XI

DEVONSHIRE LORE
1882–85

I WILL now call up certain reminiscences connected with country life in Devon.

I cannot say for certain that the village *charivari* is at an end, and may not be resuscitated. With us it goes by the name of a " Stag Hunt."

In July, 1882, the son of the captain of the lime quarry married. He and his bride lived with the father till Michaelmas Day, when they had a promise of a cottage on Lew Down. There had been some scandal about the young wife, which I believe to have been totally unfounded, and based on her extravagance in dress alone. On January 20, 1883, I tore down a manuscript notice that was affixed to a corner building where advertisements were wont to be displayed. It ran to this effect :

" Lord Folkstaff's staghounds will meet next Wednesday, January 24th, at Lew Trenchard, at 7 p.m., by Invitation ; when good sport may be expected, as the Hounds will be hunted by the celebrated Huntsman, Old Tom."

So on the Wednesday night there was a stag hunt before the cottage of the young carpenter and his wife. A man dressed in a cowhide with horns ran, and was pursued by men and boys and " Old Tom " in a scarlet coat mounted on a cob; to an indescribable uproar of horns blown, kettles rattled, and vocal yells and barks. Finally the pretended stag was brought down on the doorstep of the cottage, and a bladder filled with blood was sliced and poured over the threshold. Old Tom meanwhile blew a continuous blast.

I remember a similar affair some years previous to this. My father was very angry and interfered, but that only made matters worse. On the present occasion I warned the policeman, but he said he could not interfere so long as no injury was done to person or property, and there was no trespass. A year or two before 1883 a case occurred of the same kind in the adjoining parish of Coryton, and Mr. Newman had the ringleaders up before the magistrates, but nothing could be done, as no illegal act had been committed. Another stag hunt took place on Lew Down in 1905 ; on which occasion real damage was done, such as consisted in the breaking of slates and the battering of the front door. The constable, who knew what was purposed, had deemed it expedient to go to the extreme limit of his beat, so as *not* to be on the spot. I found it impossible to obtain evidence as to who had done the damage.

The following notes were taken down by me in 1883 in the neighbouring village of Broadwoodwidger, a very remote and primitive place.

Mrs. Jackman, of the inn, aged forty years, told me that as a child she had repeatedly seen Jack o' Lanterns in Bradover Wood, between Broadwood and Stowford. She had been told that they danced over metal, whether in veins, or buried. Our servant, Eleanor Sibilla Horton, assured me that her father had seen Jack o' Lantern many times between Broadwood and Bratton. William Henry Shopland, of Bratton, said that he had never seen a genuine Jack o' Lantern, but he told this story :

"About twenty years ago, a man named William Hicks, who rented the glebe, lost his son John, a young man, just about harvest time.[1] Shortly after the burial his sister and two nieces of Hicks were gleaning one evening in the field, and, after they were gone, I along with some others who were harvesting near by saw a light dancing about just where these girls had been at work. It ran from place to place as though tracking their footsteps. The evening was fast closing in, and we saw it perfectly, as a blue candle flame. It moved up and down and finally settled on a mow. For three or four months after the light continued to be seen, frequenting the same field, by myself and several others. We often went out after dark and looked at it. As this was dry ground and cornland it could not have been Jack o' Lantern. We thought that young Hicks who had died was troubled in his mind about something, and that this was his spirit."

[1] Buried August 4, 1856, aged 20 years.

In connexion with this I will quote a letter from Mr. C. H. Laycock in Devon and Cornwall *Notes and Queries* for July, 1920.

" On February 26 last, after attending the Winter Council Meeting of the Devonshire Association at Exeter, I had the misfortune to miss the last train back to Moretonhampstead. So, as it was a fine evening and bright moonlight, I decided to walk the 12½ miles home from Exeter. I was amply rewarded for my exertion by witnessing a phenomenon which I have seen but once in my life before, and that not in the county of Devon, namely, a Jack o' Lantern, or, as the Dartmoor folk more usually term it, *Jacky-twoad*, which is probably a corruption of *Jack-with-a-Wad*.[1] It occurred about 8.30 p.m. As I was walking on the road near Stops Bridge, in the parish of Dunsford, I noticed a very bright light which appeared to be dancing or running about close to the ground in a low-lying water-meadow on the bank of the River Teign. At first I thought it must be a man or boy with a lantern or electric torch searching for a straying bullock, sheep or fowl. But, on closer inspection, I found that, although there was a certain amount of mist hanging over the river, the light from the moon was quite bright enough for me to see there was no sign of a human form anywhere near the spot from which the light emanated. I guessed at once what it was. And my supposition was more fully confirmed on my mentioning it to an old retired woodman at Lustleigh, when he informed me that many years ago his father was driving a waggon along the road from Dunsford to Christow one November in the early hours of the morning, when, to use his own words, ' he zeed wan o' thaize yar lights dappin' about on the road, an' he thought sure 'nuff zoom feller was 'avin' a geam wi' 'en, but try aul he cüd, he niver cüd'n catch en, so they told en he must ha' zeed a Jacky-twoad. ' "

I have mentioned other instances in my *Book of Dartmoor*.

At Buddle in Broadwood I made the acquaintance of a remarkably handsome old woman, Joanna Worden by name, with a nobly cut profile. When a girl, Mrs. Worden had been engaged to a young man, who had given her a coloured silk handkerchief for

[1] A " Wad " is in Devonshire a common term for a torch, particularly a blast of " vuzz " used in " swaling " (i.e. burning the furze), to convey the flame from one bush to another.

her neck and bosom, as a keepsake and pledge of love. He died. She married William Worden, the farmer at Buddle, and retained the kerchief till just before the wedding, when at night the deceased lover appeared in her room and demanded the kerchief. She said that it was her purpose to keep it to her dying day and to be buried with it tied about her throat and crossed over her bosom. To this, however, he would not consent. He told her that married to another she could not be until " loosed " from him, and " loosed " she could only be by restoring the love-token. This she promised to do on the ensuing night ; and she held out her hand to him, but it was the left hand, and this he refused to receive. So she drew her right hand out of the bed and extended it to him. This he clasped. Joanna told me that the touch was cold. Next day she drew the kerchief from out of her box and laid it under her pillow. At night the apparition reappeared. She extended the love-gift to him, he accepted it and disappeared. " An' if you was to dig he up," added Mrs. Worden, when she told me the story, " I reckon you'd find thickey kerchief in the corfin."

The good lady was not reticent on the matter. I heard the tale both from her own lips, as also from Mrs. Blagden, the vicar's wife. The extremely rude and early cross now erected in the churchyard at Broadwood came from Buddle. Joanna was buried June 24, 1889, aged seventy-one years.

The Wulf is a river that flows into the Thrustle from Broadwood. From time immemorial a spirit has been seen where the road crosses it, leading to Portgate, on the main highway from Okehampton to Launceston. Originally there was no bridge there, but a ford. The apparition was wont to be seen standing by the water, and when anyone wanted at night to traverse the river, the spirit lifted him or her in his arms and carried the passenger across. By day there was no need for his help, as there were stepping stones, but these were not always perceptible by night.

An old woman in Broadwood died in 1882, who was the last to be transported across the Wulf by the spirit.

The origin of this story is not far to seek. On the north wall of the nave of Broadwood Church had been a painting in distemper of S. Christopher crossing a river, carrying Our Lord as a child on his left arm, and in the distance might be seen a church on a height. Now there existed a sufficient resemblance between the river and the church on the higher ground in the picture and the Wulf and the parochial church, in fact, to lead the people to imagine the figure of a spectral Christopher at the ford.

In the lane leading to Wortham, from the highway half a mile out of Lifton, a spectral figure is supposed to be seen, and his name is Old Stripe. He has vastly long legs, and is usually seen striding across the lane from one hedge to the other. Several persons still alive in Lifton profess to have seen Old Stripe.

Shopland, of whom I have already made mention, told me that he and ten other men had resolved to watch over midnight in the tower of Broadwood Church to see the spirits, or the doubles, go by who would show who were to die within a twelvemonth. But all failed to keep the appointment save two, himself and one other. However, as midnight approached, his companion's courage gave way, and he deserted his post. This was too much for Shopland, and he also retreated from the church tower and yard. But as he looked behind him he saw some mysterious white object drawing itself along the roof ; he was too frightened to remain and find out what manner of creature this was.

Miss Hole, of North Tawton, informed me of a somewhat similar case that occurred at Broadwood Kelly. There the watchers did maintain sufficient courage to keep together in the church porch till after the stroke of midnight, when they all saw the figure of a well-known young man, a carpenter in the village, enter the graveyard gate and advance along the path towards the south porch. This was too much for them, and they fled in an opposite direction.

Very injudiciously they told their story in the village, and it reached the ears of the young carpenter, who took it so to heart, that he sickened and died before the ensuing S. Mark's Day, although the doctor could not discover that there was anything the matter with him.

Several of the parishes in my neighbourhood are supposed to be haunted by Church-grims or Bahr-ghests. I have dealt with the subject fully in my *Strange Survivals*. Marystowe possesses a black dog that haunts the churchyard, Coryton a white calf, another church, which I will not name for fear of giving offence, has a ghostly ass. There the churchwarden, a farmer, was wont to say : " The volk du talk o' a black hass as is seen in and about the church at night. I dun' know much about that, but I ha' seed 'n and ha' heard 'n bray scores and scores o' times. He frequents the pulpit."

Our church-grim is a white pig, or, as some say, two white pigs yoked together with a silver chain. I was dining one evening with Mr. Alister Grant, who tenanted the house I had built upon the Ramps. I was then residing at the Rectory as Mr. Morshead still occupied Lew House. About half-past-eleven I left the Ramps to return home, when, on opening the wicket gate, an animal appeared in the road. In the starlight I could discern that it was white and very much like a large pig. As I closed the wicket it manifested an extraordinary interest in my legs, against which it thrust its snout, and, on my walking with quickened pace up the high-road, it trotted after me. From the church to the old Rectory is a narrow lane, and down this lane I was pursued by the beast. The way was dark, overshadowed by trees. I could no longer see my pursuer, but could hear the tramp of his feet. Now this lane is regarded as specially haunted by the bahr-ghest. I candidly admit that my rapid walk resolved itself into a run, till I reached the gate leading into a field that has to be traversed before the Rectory is attained. I slipped through the gate and slammed it against my pursuer. It was a stray boar-pig that belonged to the quarry farm.

In 1914 a panic prevailed in the parish relative to the old road leading from the church to Lew Down, as during the winter nights a white beast was encountered in it by workmen returning home. My carpenter at the sawmill was so frightened that he preferred to seek his home by the very circuitous high-road. I believe that the white beast on this occasion was none other than a stray dog that, for its own ends—rabbit hunting—frequented the lane by night. If a man approached he ran to and snuffed at him to ascertain whether the individual were his master in quest of him.

A farmer in the adjoining parish of Stowford a few years ago, about 1911, had murrain among his cattle. He went to Exeter and consulted the White Witch in the parish of All Hallows-on-the-Walls, who told him that he must draw a circle with chalk on the ground in his field, and must throw a white cock high into the air. If it came down dead, the cattle would be cured; if, however, the bird flew away, the disease would remain and ravage his stock. The farmer called several men to his assistance, amongst others, my carpenter, who, by the way, is a member of our Church Council, and is in our choir. This man volunteered to throw the cock. It was done, and the bird fell dead within the magic circle. The murrain ceased. I asked my carpenter if it were a fact, and he assured me it was true.

I may here add an anecdote of the same man, though not connected with witchcraft. He had killed a pig that he had fattened, and his wife had prepared and salted the hams and sides of bacon. One day, to her confusion, she found that one of the hams was gone. She sent at once for the police; every inquiry was made. No one could surmise who the thief could be; and Anne —— concluded that it had been carried off by the pixies, when a disclosure ensued that explained the mystery. Her husband had fallen considerably in debt at "The Blue Lion," and to liquidate the score had given the ham to the taverner. Fearing his wife's recrimination he had not dared to confess the fact. He was as timorous of his wife's tongue as he was of the bahr-ghest's snout.

William Rich, a farmer at Town, in Broadwood, was very ill in the summer of 1882, with a complication of disorders, the chief of which was diptheria. Dr. Budd, of North Tawton, was called in to consult with Dr. Thompson, of Launceston. Both gave him up. Then his wife's relations sent for a posthumous child to be brought and breathe into his mouth. This was done several times in the week, and the man recovered completely. What is more, the child was none the worse for the experiment.

In 1879 Jonas Squire of Collisham Farm, Meavy, had sickness among his cattle. Accordingly he sacrificed a sheep, and burnt it to placate the " Good Folk " on the moor above his house, and the cattle recovered from that day. He told the vicar, the Rev. A. A. G. Grey, and had no idea that he had performed anything extraordinary.

A woman in a Devonshire parish was believed by the

the purpose rather than adopt the mechanical contrivance for removing the charred wick. Besides, these nippers point upwards to the ceiling, and, so as to employ them for curtailing the charred wick, the candle would have to be removed from the socket at the end of the arm, and be held horizontally ; a procedure certain to cause a discharge of molten tallow on the floor, perhaps on the apron of the wench snuffing the wick. As likely as not, moreover, the charred wick would fall on the floor and set fire to the straw or rushes there strewn.

The design of the nippers was different in purpose, if I am not mistaken. The German *Lichtspan* is a rude torch composed of a strip of burning beechwood held transversely in a rude contrivance. These were formerly common in the Black Forest, where I have seen them in use. Now the iron nippers were intended to hold in position a burning torch. The apparatus would serve two purposes, as employed in Devon, either to hold a rushlight or a torch.

The torches employed in this county and in Somersetshire were the stalks of the cow-parsnip dried, called by the people *limpen-skimps*. I think these must have been helped out with a little tallow, for when I employ them to light my pipe I find that they rapidly burn to a glowing core and then the flame goes out. Yet I have been informed that they were much employed on the ground floor in cottages and farmhouses that were paved with slate.

I possess as well a short iron nipper, fitted into a wooden handle, for carrying these torches about the house and preventing the burning of the fingers when the *limpenskimp* came to an end. The hand held it firmly between the block of oak into which the nipper is fixed and the curved handle that opens and closes the blades. The thumb passed over the curve and compressed the cow-parsnip stalk that flamed, so as to keep it secure in its place. Should a portion of the burnt cane fall on the floor the foot at once extinguished it.

The standard candlestick was intended, like the German *Lichtspan*-holder, to be stationary ; it was accommodated with a socket at the end of a movable arm, so as to hold a rushlight or a tallow dip, and also with the vertical nippers to support a torch.

Rough and ready were the methods adopted by our forefathers, especially in the cottage and the farmhouse.

The candles everywhere except in the drawing-room and on the dinner table were tallow dips. In every grocer's shop there used to hang bunches of these dips for sale ; not one is to be seen now. At the theatres a boy was retained, whose office it was periodically to snuff the footlights. Many and many a night have I had to snuff those by which my father was reading aloud.

A clever invention consisted of a plated tray to contain the snuffers, which were contrived like scissors, the burnt wick being retained in a box on the back of the apparatus. Oh ! the blessed time when composite candles came into use, and tallows went out ! The trays are now occasionally converted into holders of candied fruit, but no use has been found for the snuffers.

I possess a pair of very quaint candlesticks ; they have broad feet that support a rod furnished with a branch candle-holder and which have, in addition, a reflector behind, one of burnished steel, the other of polished brass.

I have no doubt but that the practice of either painting oak panelling white, or of tearing it down altogether and papering the walls, was due to the discomfort our forefathers felt when sitting in panelled rooms with poor lighting at night ; the dark oak absorbing the little illumination afforded by the candles. A lady, now long dead, told me of the terrors she endured as a bride in an old mansion on the north coast of Cornwall during her husband's absence, and how she sat in the middle of a with-drawing-room whose panelling was black oak, and tried to read or do needlework by a tallow candle. The rats raced behind the wood, and when she looked up to see why the light was so dim she saw a thief like a fungus growing out of the dock. Even if she substituted a wax candle for the " dip " it had a habit of sending down the side an overflow of wax that curled and spread and was commonly called a " Winding sheet," and was held to prognosticate death if it were directed against the terrified beholder. The first to observe a winding sheet pointing towards himself, silently without being observed, was wont to turn the candlestick and point the excrescence at another individual.

Formerly every year the village girls went out in parties collecting rushes for lights, and singing to a pretty melody :

> " Don't you go a rushing, Maids in May,
> Or you'll get a brushing, Maids I say.
> Don't you go a rushing
> Or you'll get a brushing,
> Gather up your rushes and then go away."

But like all lasses with whom I am acquainted they said one thing and did the contrary.

The rest of the song as I heard it must belong to some other lay.

> " I'll give you a chick that has no bone,
> I'll give you a cherry without a stone,
> I'll give you a ring that has no rim,
> I'll give you an oak that has no limb.

> When the chick is in the hatch, it has no bone,
> When the cherry is in the flower, it has no stone.
> When the ring is in the melting-pot it has no rim,
> When the oak is in the acorn, it has no limb."

We have in Lew House a couple of very tall brass candlesticks twenty inches high, with a " pusher," a contrivance for thrusting up the candle as it burns down to the socket. Their bases of solid brass are seven and a half inches in diameter. These candlesticks in former days were sometimes used as weapons.

In the Rutland Papers is an account of a quarrel between Lady Mohun and Mistress Brown, which began " with ill words and candlesticks." The matter was taken into the House of Lords where " it entertained the King mightily."

In the *Hutchinson Memoirs* (II, 288) the gallant Colonel, we are informed, " snatched up a candlestick and laid him (his adversary) over the chaps with it." Lady Standish wrote to Robert Kenyon, M.P., that " Lord Willoughby is almost as great a plague to me as he is to his wife and his maids, for my Lord fighting with my Lady's woman, she has broke his shins with a brass candlestick, and he is a cripple." Encounters with such weapons are of frequent mention in letters and diaries of the seventeenth century and much earlier.

There was also in the house a copper boot for boiling, or at all events heating, spiced ale, but it has disappeared.

One other curious "oddment" I may mention is an iron contrivance fitted with a wooden handle, that at the further end has a small cup of metal that is closed by a cover which can be turned down upon it. In the side of the cup is a small perforation. This is a contrivance for ascertaining the quality of gunpowder. The cup is filled with the explosive and the cover is brought down to close it. Then a light is applied to the hole in the cup. The gunpowder explodes and drives up the lid to an iron dial furnished with a hand pointing to a number, which indicates the quality and force of the powder. In our spare bedroom beside the fireplace is a cupboard cut in the granite for gunpowder, to keep it dry without the possibility of the flames or sparks igniting it.

I had built a pretty cottage, already referred to, on the Lime Quarry Ramps, and this I let to a Mrs. Bussell, whose son, F. W. Bussell, was at the time at Magdalen College, Oxford; but having passed a brilliant examination for his degree he was elected fellow of Brasenose, the fellows of Magdalen rather despising him for his eccentricities. When congratulated on his success, he dryly remarked : "Either the fellows of Magdalen or those of Brasenose have made a great mistake."

Bussell was a dandy, wore very showy ties, and had hot-house flowers sent him from London of the same colour as his ties, to wear in his button-hole. He sang falsetto, and was quite unconscious of the amusement he provoked when singing " Dinah-do." At a concert the audience was convulsed with laughter, and his mother would look about her with glances of fury at those who dared to feel amusement at " Freddy's " squawks.

He had taken his Mus. Bac. and was an accomplished musician ; but he said to me, "A good melody affords me no pleasure. What I love is a fugue or intricate piece of harmony ; it gives me as much gratification as working out a mathematical problem does a mathematician." He was of enormous advantage to me in collecting the folk-airs of Devon, and was ever good natured, obliging, and ready to help in the matter.

He possessed one or two peculiarities that may be noticed. He invented a conveyance, like a sentry-box on wheels, provided with a little table, book-shelf, writing materials, lamp and case for liquor ; the whole sitting very high on the axles so that through the side-windows he could survey the landscape over the tops of the hedges. But the " Bussell," as it was termed, possessed this disadvantage ; that going over a common in a high wind, it so swayed that it threatened to upset. I learned that when Mr. Bussell took his first drive in it, when it was surrendered to him by the coach-builders in London, he ventured into Hyde Park. I presume the result was not highly satisfactory, as he was uncommunicative as to the success of the experiment.

Another of his peculiarities was a passion for purchasing Donatives, that is to say, livings not under episcopal control. They have since been abolished ; but he possessed several, and still retains presentation to the livings, though they have been placed under the supervision of the bishops of the respective dioceses.

I shall never forget the shrieks and cries for help he emitted at Trewartha Marsh on the Bodmin moors, where he came to see the excavations I was making in a very ancient settlement. Incautiously he had trodden upon a quaking bog, which began to eat him up, beginning at his boots and ankles and proceeding to his knees, when my workmen and I succeeded in extricating him. From his waist to his knees his trousers were of a delicate lavender hue ; below, black as peat.

He was a thorough Greek scholar, and was specially acquainted with the writings of the neo-Platonists. Bussell was one morning invited with several other rising men to breakfast with Jowett. The Master of Balliol seeing Bussell dressed up to the top of the fashion, and his pink and white complexion and hairless face, turning to him said : " Mr. Bussell, what is your amusement ? Are you a boating man ? " " No, Professor, I do not boat." " Perhaps you are a cricketer ? " " No, sir, I have never held a bat." " Then you like lawn tennis ? " " I never play it." " Possibly, you hunt ? " " Never hunted in my life." " Then," said Jowett, " good heavens ! What *do* you do ? " Bussell made no answer. After a while conversation turned on philosophy. Then Bussell remarked, " I specially like Theon of Smyrna, for his treatise on music." " I have never read him," said the Master.

" You know how Alcinous tried to harmonize the views of Plato and Aristotle on ideas, and how he distinguished the ἰδέσι from the εἴδη." " I have not seen the book, much less read it," said Jowett. " Of course, Master, you are well up in Plotinus." " I cannot say that I am," colour rising into the Master's cheeks. " Then," exclaimed Bussell from the other end of the table, " Good heavens, Professor, what *have* you read ? "

I said in joke to Mrs. Bussell one day that I created her Baroness Rampenstein within the bounds of my estate. I found later that she had gone abroad with her son as Baroness Rampenstein and the Baron Frederick William von Rampenstein.

There lived in Lew in one of my cottages a very remarkable woman, a character. And characters were far more common in past times than they are at present, when education has ground down all asperities and angles, and made men and women as much alike as are marbles. I do not give her name further than her Christian appellation, as her great-grandchildren are with us to the present day. Marianne must have been handsome when young, she was strikingly picturesque when old. She was at bitter enmity with her own sister, Susan, who lived a mile off ; and the reason was that Susan, who had no children of her own, had adopted an orphan girl, Fanny, and had promised to leave her what little money she had hoarded. Susan was one of those old-fashioned people who kissed your hand, as well as curtsyed. When she died, not only did Marianne refuse to attend her sister's funeral as a mourner, but went into the middle of the road while the body was being carried to church, followed by the nearest relatives and friends, and there she danced and shouted opprobrious epithets at the dead.

Yet the woman was not without kindly feeling. When her sons fell ill as children with scarlet fever my mother carried her sheets for their beds. One of these she retained, and vowed that she would be buried in it. A son died, and she preserved his trousers, saying that she intended to be buried with them. She had a little farm, attended to the cattle, and tilled the land herself.

At one time her husband, who had been a cattle dealer, was returning from market at night, and was thrown from his horse, which shied in a dark place at something in the road. He was picked up by a neighbour and brought home. But his purse was missing. Marianne lit a lantern and searched the road where the accident had happened, but vainly. The search was continued next morning, but proved fruitless. Meanwhile the husband was left to recover as best he might. Thenceforth Marianne was filled with the fiercest rage against the neighbour who had assisted her husband home, and whom she accused of having robbed him. She filled the ears of the parishioners with her vituperations. She went to Tavistock market to tell the neighbourhood her story. Finally she made the position of the accused so intolerable that, on some excuse or other, the family moved to a distant part of the county. Not till after the husband's death, when the masons were whitewashing the house, was the purse found on a rafter above the bed in which the man had lain. He had put it there when in a condition of semi-consciousness after his fall and had forgotten all about it. Thenceforth the woman's rage and resentment were turned upon her deceased husband, because he had not informed her as to where he had deposited the purse.

Marianne was a notable brewer of metheglin, a liqueur distilled from honey. The sole occasion of my falling off my pony through tipsiness was after having imbibed metheglin at a farmhouse from the hospitable hostess. Marianne's liquor was not so strong as that ; one could not visit her without being forced to drink a glass of her brew.

I reproved her once for never coming to church. " Oh ! " said she, " I've got my Bible here," pointing to one on a side table. I looked at it, the cover was thick with dust, so with my finger I scribbled on it *Marianne's Bible*. " You may have a Bible," said I, " but it is never opened. If you read it you would find therein, ' Thou shalt not bear false witness against thy neighbour.' " " Oh ! " she said ; " I am so short of amusements. Men have horse races, fox hunting, shooting and cock-fighting. What are we poor women to do for a little entertainment ? To set a lot of women by the ears is rare sport."

I give an instance of the woman's energy and resolution. She had some fine apples growing in her garden. She filled a large basket with them to take to Germansweek, five miles off, where they were scarce. But she had one of her children, a babe, that could not be left at home, so she took it on one arm and the

S. BARING-GOULD

basket on the other. She had not gone very far before she discovered that this was beyond her strength ; so she set down the
child and carried the apples a few hundred yards, deposited the
apples, returned for the infant, and carried it forward beyond the
basket for about the same distance, set the child on the ground,
and went back for the apples. So, alternately carrying the fruit
and the babe, she arrived at Germansweek, where she sold the
apples and walked home with her offspring in the basket slung
round her neck at her back.

The impression in the village and the neighbourhood was that
Marianne was rich, and that she kept a large sum of money in
her bedroom, reached by what was rather a ladder than a stair.
As she lived entirely alone, I once spoke to her on the subject,
and advised her to get some one to live with her, so that should
she be ill in the night, she might send out and obtain assistance
and the doctor.

" Never was ill in my life," said she, " save when confined.
And I shan't be that again. That warn't illness, only a na'rel
infirmity you men don't suffer from, more's the pity."

Reverting to the matter of her solitary life, I said : " It is the
talk all round that you have a bag full of money upstairs. Some
tramp or evil-disposed fellow might attempt to rob you in the
night."

" I should like him to try. I can use a scythe as well as any
man. Mow him down, as soon as his head appeared above the
floor. I've cut off many a head of a sow-thistle in the marsh.
I should rather enjoy it."

The old woman was not regarded as a witch, but she was
accredited with a profound acquaintance with herbs and their
virtues. Neighbours feared lest they should be " ill-wished "
by her. In various sicknesses she was consulted, and she was
invariably liberal, even to foes, in prescribing and administering
teas and lotions. There were two plants that she grew, to which
she attributed marvellous powers. One was the mandrake ; what
the other was I do not know, but she called it " Christ's Hand."

The mandrake was a most baleful plant, and the possessor
of it was able to work incalculable evil against all such as the
owner " ill-wished." The other plant, " Christ's Hand," availed
to arrest the evil caused by the mandrake, when it was like to

proceed too far. Marianne would never show me the two plants, and since her death, I have been unable to find the mandrake and identify " Christ's Hand." It was not till some years ago when I was staying at Lapford that the daughters of the rector showed me the plant in the garden. It had been grown there by the former rector, Froude, who has been sketched by Mr. Blackmore as " Parson Chowne " in *The Maid of Sker.* He was an evil-minded and evil-living man, and the terror of the neighbourhood. I have given an account of him in my *Devonshire Characters and Strange Events.* Much of his power was attributed to the possession of the mandrake, more to his being in league with a gang of ruffians who, at his instigation, set fire to ricks and even to farmhouses of such as had defied him or had given him offence. The mandrake (*Atropa mandragora*) is not a native plant of England, but grows in the East and in Spain and Portugal. It is closely allied to the deadly nightshade, and has everywhere mysterious powers or properties attributed to it. This is probably due to the shape of the root, which divides or forks into a couple of carrot-like rootlets, so that the trunk with these appendages bears the form of a human being. It possesses a fetid corpse-like odour. The flower is white. According to Pliny (lib. xxv. c. 13) the mandrake is either male or female ; the former is white, the latter black. To raise it the operator must keep to windward, and with the point of his sword draw three circles round it. Columella (X. 19) calls the plant *semihomo mandragoras.*

The mediæval notion of lifting the mandrake was more elaborate than that proposed by Pliny. When it is being extracted from the earth it cries, groans and utters such piercing shrill screams that the operator is liable to die of fright. He must therefore stop his ears with wax or pitch and have in attendance a black dog without a white spot on its body. The operator makes three crosses above the plant, and then excavates the earth in a circle about the mandrake, so as not to cut and wound the root-fibres. He then attaches the dog to the head of the plant by its tail. The next procedure is to lure the dog away by the offer of a bit of meat or bread. The beast rushes after the food, and in so doing, rips the mandrake out of the soil. This is accomplished with such cries from the plant as to scare the dog to death. The mandrake is then washed in red wine and wrapped in red and white silk, is placed in a small chest, is bathed every Friday and clothed after the bath with a clean new smock. The possessor can ask what he will of the mandrake, and has secrets and mysteries revealed to him. Every night a coin is placed on the box and this is found doubled in the morning.

According to another receipt the Alraun, as it is also called must be dug up early on a Monday in spring. The fleshy, two-pronged root must then be buried in the grave of a recently interred man, and for a month must be watered daily before sunrise with whey in which three bats have been drowned. At the conclusion of this period the mandrake is dug up and found to have acquired a further resemblance to the body of a man than it possessed previously. It is then dried in an oven heated with sprigs of verbena, and laid aside wrapped in a piece of linen that has covered the face of a corpse. The possession of the Alraun entitles the owner to vast riches, and makes a barren woman to become a fruitful mother of children. It certainly had not the first effect with Marianne ; possibly she failed to obtain the requisite amount of verbena, but it may have had the second effect, as she became the mother of a large family.

When the possessor of the Gallowsman dies it passes into the possession of the youngest son, who in acknowledgment is bound to lay in his father's coffin a coin and a slice of bread.

Dragon's blood is still largely employed by herbalists, is in great vogue among ignorant love-lorn damsels in the poorer districts of London, and is sold in the country by gipsies. A twopenny packet of dragon's blood (which is really a gum used in wood-staining), burned at midnight on a Friday, will, it is thought, rekindle the affections of a lover who has jilted his sweetheart. Tormentil root and mandrake, which most herbalists stock, are used as love philtres, though not to the same extent as dragon's blood. A street seller of mandrake has a regular pitch near Petticoat Lane, his stock-in-trade consisting of roots selected because of a fancied resemblance to the human form. " I pulls 'em up at midnight," he tells his customers, " and they screams orfull as they comes out of the ground." The conviction, if ever possessed by the vendor, that they bring to riches must have died out of his heart, for he does not seem to be in prosperous circumstances. It was so with the alchemists of old ; they pretended to make gold and silver by their red and white tinctures, but they never succeeded in enriching themselves.

In the case of Marianne, if she did hand over the mandrake to one of her sons it must have been to the youngest, who alone of the large family of boys came to remarkable prosperity.

Naturalists in past days told strange stories of the plant and its properties, but modern botanists have discarded them all, especially since it was discovered that charlatans were wont artificially to fashion the roots, so as to surprise the credulity of the people and induce them to pay large sums to obtain specimens.

That it was deemed a means of curing barrenness we learn from Genesis (xxx. 14). Reuben, the son of Leah being in the field, lighted on some mandrakes, which he brought home to his mother. Rachel had a mind to them and purchased them of Leah by the surrender to her of Jacob for twelve hours.

In Germany the mandrake is called Alraun, or the Galgen-männchen, or little Gallowsman, and has been regarded as the Devil's own plant. The possession of one gives incontestable proof that the owner has sold himself to the Evil One.

On the 20th and 21st January, 1860, a case came before the criminal court of Zürich that revealed the astounding credulity still existing among the people relative to the virtues of the mandrake. The Canton of Zürich had for the previous thirty-five years possessed the best schools in all Switzerland, and the educational budget exceeded that for the army fivefold, and yet the superstition of the Protestant peasants had not been destroyed.

On August 31, 1859, a manufacturer named Heinrich Kurz, at Oetweil beside the lake died. He was a man who, by his energy and capacity, had created a business that made him to be regarded as the King of Spinners, and he left to his heirs the sum of over twenty million francs, beside the flourishing business. Popular opinion held that he was five times as rich as was given out ; that he had sold himself to the Devil, who had furnished him with an Alraun that bore every day a gold coin. It went even further than that ; it persisted in believing that, although dead and buried, he would rise out of his grave after a few weeks' rest and resume his place at the head of his factory, and would call his heirs to account for the way in which they had disposed of his inheritance. Heinrich Kurz had not only been a mighty manufacturer, but he had been as well colonel in the Swiss army. He had not married, had been a hard and harsh master, rough with all, and though esteemed for his money's sake, had never been beloved.

At the trial all this was disclosed, various frauds having been perpetrated upon people who believed Colonel Kurz to be in possession of the mandrake and therefore all-powerful to make those whom he favoured fabulously wealthy.

Superstition has far more vitality than religion. And repeatedly do we see, as we have had evidence in our own days, that those most prone to superstition are such as have lost their hold on true religion.

The real Devil's herb was rooted in Marianne's heart. She had at one time a granddaughter of thirteen or fourteen years old staying with her, and she employed this girl in writing attacks on the character of one of her neighbours with whom she had picked a quarrel, and these placards were posted up upon the walls. I tore them down whenever I saw them, and I charged Marianne with the origination of them. She stoutly denied the fact, and bade the girl deny that she had been her amanuensis. It came to such a pass that I threatened to have an action brought against her unless she at once sent the girl back to her parents. This answered ; and the libels ceased to be published.

Although Marianne was not thought to be a witch, or perhaps I should say, a white witch, yet we did have a woman on Lew Down who was held to be the latter. She was an old spinster, and had one eye and eyebrow higher than the other, which caused her to have an uncanny appearance. She protested that she had no intercourse with Satan, and that all her operations were honest and performed through the grace of God, and by justifiable charms. She was in great request in cases of wounds to stop bleeding. On one occasion, at hay harvest, a young man at Kelly, some eight miles off, cut his leg with his scythe. At once the farmer for whom he worked sent a handkerchief soaked in his blood to this woman, who on receiving it stroked the kerchief three times, muttered a charm, and the messenger returned to Kelly with the kerchief. Meanwhile the flow of blood had ceased.

It was by no means unusual to meet the postman for Bratton Clovelly coming to Lew Down or going back to Bratton, with his right hand extended to the uttermost holding a kerchief that was to be blessed, or which had been blessed by the witch.

I made a collection of the charms employed. They are harmless and silly. Here are specimens.

For Inflammation.—The Virgin Mary set the Babe on her lap, and there an Inflammation caught and a blister rose. She blew on it, and the Child also ; and the Blister left. So shall it leave . . . In the Name of the Father, and of the Son, and of the Holy Ghost. (To be repeated three times.)

For a Sprain.—As Christ was riding over Crolly Bridge, His horse slid and sprained its leg. He alighted and spake these words. " Bone to bone, and sinew to sinew." And He blessed it and it became well. And so shall . . . come well, in the Name, etc. (To be repeated thrice.)

For a Snake Bite.—

Let God arise and then the foe will turn to flight
And from fear would scatter out of sight,
The Fire that melts the wax. Wind blow this away,
Then in the presence of the Lord this wicked shall decay.
In the Name of, etc. (Thrice repeated.)

For Burns or Scalds.—

There were three angels came out of the North,
One bringing Fire, the other Frost, the third the Holy Ghost.
In Frost, out Fire, in the Name, etc.

For Stopping Blood.—Ezech. xvi. 6. With Invocation as above.

A Cure for Jaundice (not a Charm).—Take an old well-blackened clay tobacco pipe. Grind up the bowl, and take as much as will go on a sixpence, before each meal.

A Cure for Costiveness (not a Charm).—Take every 3 hours a dropping of a sheep, till relieved.

Here is a recipe given me by Marianne, for a sprain :

2 oz. oil of Turpentine.
2 ,, ,, Swiillowes (? squills).
2 ,, ,, Earthworms.
2 ,, ,, Nerve.
2 ,, ,, Spedilock (Opodildoc).
2 ,, ,, Spanish fleas (flies).

When my brother William, my sister and I had the whooping cough at Lew, my mother was strongly urged to cut some hair off the back of an ass at the cross, enclose it in a silk bag, and hang one round each of our necks. When my child Beatrice died of whooping cough, the coachman's wife told me that she could have saved her had she been allowed to employ this same remedy.

In cases of thrush with children, it was usual to pass them thrice under a bramble that had rerooted itself, after throwing out a long branch. I have seen hazel trees split to serve the same purpose, but this was in Cornwall.

Amongst the many remarkable characters in our Devonshire parishes was a man named Jordan, who did job work as a blacksmith. His wife more than once ran away from him and took with her a little daughter. Whereupon, Jordan, who lived at Chillaton, not in Lew parish, would go in quest of her ringing a bell, and would visit Kelly, Lew Down, Coombe Bow, and even Bratton, calling, after he had sounded his bell :

> " Lost, Stolen, or strayed
> A wife and a young maid.
> If they return, all I will pardon
> And give them onions and leeks out of my garden."

On at least one occasion he recovered his wife, and brought her back with a yoke about her neck. His grandsons are now with us.

My carpenter, named Dawe, had a first cousin, who had the inn at Merrivale Bridge on Dartmoor. I knew him well. He bought his wife at an auction for a jar of brandy. I was at the inn one day collecting folk melodies, when I saw that his " wife " had a black eye. I asked her the occasion. " The *Door* did it. I ran against it," she replied. There was a model wife.

CHAPTER XII

THE MONTAFUN THAL
1885

IN 1885 my friend Gatrill and I revisited the Montafun Thal.

We found that it had gone through greater changes in seven years than had the world in general. In 1878 there had been no proper road above Schruns, nothing but a track as lumpy as life, and the perambulator containing Julian had to jump over boulders. I do not think that he minded that. Almost the first words he learned to utter were " Go ! go ! " and go and get on is a very good maxim wherewith to start life.

At S. Gallenkirch we ascertained that Madalina, who had been supposed to run the little inn in which we had previously stayed, had blossomed out into the wife of the proprietor of the rival tavern, which itself had gone through a transformation from a Wirtschaft into an hotel. This had been effected by mechanically lifting the roof, much as though the inn were saluting coming guests by raising its hat, whilst an additional story had been erected on the old walls ; and a commodious and well-appointed Speise-Saal had been thrust out at the side. Berliners had discovered the Montafun, and a court-preacher of the Kaiser, with a greasy face, a dowdy wife and several pasty-faced children had settled there for the Sommerfrische.

When we were at S. Gallenkirch in 1878, the post came up from Schruns only twice a week, and with the letters brought such meat as the butcher at headquarters cared to let us have. Now the postman arrived daily, and the meat consigned was such as the Berliners exacted, and, not as before, such as the Schruns-dwellers had rejected. But perhaps as remarkable a change as any was that affected in the hostess. She had been a maiden, whose hooks never fitted into the eyes, whose collar was invariably on one side, and whose apron was mottled with grease stains. Now she had developed into something very like a town lady, with scarce a reminiscence of Montafun costume, and—she had *grown a bust*. I think I have already said that in this district the female breasts were suppressed under a board, and a young woman was considered as grossly wanting in delicacy, unless she were as flat-bosomed as a man. The Montafun women wear fur caps like the headgear of grenadiers, covering and enveloping the hair, but in the Walserthal the fur cap is round and flat. Madalina had now discarded this bear-skin muff for a coquettish cap from Vienna, and her abundant black hair was tastefully dressed and waved above her brow with hot tongs.

The Montafun women and maids smoke like the women in England who have renounced their claim to be regarded as ladies, but Madalina had discarded her pipe, as likely to give offence to the Berliners.

A malicious *Kellner* related that when, after a smoke, Madalina had presented the bill to a spruce young Prussian officer, he held his nose while inspecting it, and while paying his charge. After that, Madalina buried her pipe of peace in a drawer, and did not bring it out again till the tourist season was over.

The grub had become a butterfly. In all conscience it had been grubby enough before.

We made a deflexion from the Montafun, to visit Feldkirch, a cheerful town that once belonged to the Counts of Montfort, who had as their residence the Castle of Schattenburg. The Montforts were a well-estated family and had their dwellings throughout the Wellgau. But good nature was the cause of their ruin. Count Rudolf VII was a kindly, cheery noble, who devoted himself and his revenue to promote the happiness of his people. For the sake of the children he instituted festivals several times in the year, and hired mountebanks and puppet-showmen to come to Feldkirch to entertain the youngsters, fiddlers and pipers also to play, so that the young folk might dance, and he furnished hogsheads of beer or wine for the quenching of the all-but-unquenchable thirst of the aged. Thick vegetable soups, bread and cheese in slabs, and porridge were distributed to the children, who were as hungry as their grandsires were thirsty. The Count further instituted an annual shooting match, at which an ox was roasted whole, liquor again flowed, and the Count distributed the prizes. This went on till Count Rudolf was so overwhelmed with debt that he was constrained to sell his estates to Austria in 1471. " It is a blunder to be over-good," said the Count.

The late Gothic church is fine, and contains a fifteenth-century hammered iron pulpit by Hans Sturm, given after the annexation to Austria ; Count Rudolf's money had been expended on Morris dancers, puppet shows and fiddlers. The Montfort race went back to Carlovingian times, and disappeared altogether in exaggerated good nature.

In the church is also a " Descent from the Cross " by Holbein. In the Church of the Capuchins is a fine high altarpiece by an unknown master. When I was there, in a side chapel lay the body, or the representation of the body, of a lately deceased friar. No one was watching it. No candles burnt by it. I could not make up my mind to touch it and ascertain whether it were a wax image of the deceased, or the actual corpse. I have noticed in several Roman Catholic churches, that where they possess relics of saints, they embed the few bones in a wax ideal model. Possibly the wax image of Feldkirch had been substituted for the departed friar. The Romans have funny ways, such as we English do not understand. After a man is dead in England, the biographers write his life and represent him as a model of all the virtues. They build an insignificant man, very generally, of paper and ink, whereas the Romanist constructs a dubious saint out of beeswax.

As I did not care to ascertain the nature of the figure by touch, I watched the procedure of a blue-bottle that was enclosed in the same chapel. As the insect manifested no desire to be further acquainted with the departed, but exhibited impatience to reach the open air by dancing at the window-panes, I came to the conclusion that the friar before me was a make-believe.

To one who is fond of flowers the special interest at Feldkirch is the Botanical Garden, kept in admirable order, wherein most of the Alpine plants are cultivated, and have the names attached.

Feldkirch was menaced by the French under Massena, in 1799, at the head of an army of 18,000 men. He was encountered by the Austrian general Jellachich, at the head of 5000 regulars and an ill-disciplined crowd of loyal peasants. It was Easter Day ;

the bells of Feldkirch and of all the mountain village churches were ringing to welcome the Lord's Resurrection. And to the pealing of these bells the battle was engaged, in which the French army was totally routed. While their husbands and sons were fighting in the valley, the women gathered in the churches and prayed for their success.

It may be as well here to notice the little principality of Lichtenstein, because after the dissolution of the Empire in 1918, it passed through the melting-pot, and emerged intact. Lichtenstein, with Monaco, Andora and San Marino, were the tiny relics of a former condition of affairs, partly feudal and partly republican.

Lichtenstein was left after the Treaty of Vienna as an independent principality extending from the high Alps to the shores of the Lake of Constance ; it occupied three square miles and comprised a population of 8700. The government was monarchical, with a representative house that docilely registered the decrees of the sovereign.

Although the Prince had a palace at Vaduz, the capital, he rarely visited it, as he resided among the luxuries and distractions of Vienna. The taxes imposed on the Lichtensteiners were light, but the rates fell, and ever will fall, heavily on the mountain population (half of that of the principality) because the banks of the Swabian Sea and of Lake of Constance, so far as they pertain to Lichtenstein, have to be protected against the rollers driven before a north and a western gale that are disposed to eat into them.

The principality is made up of the ancient baronies of Vaduz and Schellenberg, which were united in 1328. In 1699 Schellenberg, and in 1712 Vaduz, were purchased by Prince John Adam von Lichtenstein, and in 1719 the combined baronies were raised into a free imperial principality with sovereign rights by the Emperor Charles VI, eight years after his coronation.

The houses of Liechtenstein or Lichtenstein, of Schwarzenberg, and of Esterhazy have been the largest estated among the Austrian nobility. What they will become when the upheaval after the great European war has subsided, God only knows. Among petty principalities that of Lichtenstein was the smallest. It owed its retention as a sovereign state, says Vehse, " To the gallantry of the Great Powers at the Congress of Vienna." The Lichtensteins can trace their pedigree back to the year 942, and they owed their importance and advance to the fact that they became *Ministrales* of the Empire, and hereditary Marshals of Carinthia. They did not, however, receive promotion to the ranks of the high nobility till the Thirty Years' War, when they were advanced from being *nobles* to become *illustres*. Their principal estates were in Moravia, which came to them in 1249. At the Reformation the Lichtenstein family became mordantly Protestant ; but they always looked on which side their bread was buttered before they bit into it ; and the sons of Hartmann IV, who died in 1585, rejoined the Church, more out of complacency towards the Emperor Rudolf II than out of conviction.

At present there is not to be found a Protestant, that is a native in the whole principality.

The highest peaks in Lichtenstein barely attain the line of eternal snow. The lower portions of the little land from the roots of the mountain spurs to the lake are fertile and consist of alluvial soil.

Returning to the Montafun Thal we made our way to the head of the valley, crossed the pass, which was still partially covered with snow, and entered and descended the long trough of the Patznauner Thal. Here the rich soil is so precious that it is begrudged to the dead, who are no more suffered to occupy their graves for an unreasonable length of time than is a peasant to lie abed in the morning when he ought to be up and ploughing. After a period the bones are dug up and cast into a heap ; but the skull is docketed and put in a wooden structure like a pigeon house, each in a private box.

Messrs. Churchill and Babington were the first English travellers to notice, and, in their book on the Dolomites, to record the fact that some of the inns in the villages of the Tyrol are kept by the descendants of the nobles who formerly occupied the castles that frown down upon the villages at their feet, and are now in ruins. This is the case. The castles were small and could not accommodate the servants of the guests invited to stay with the nobles in their towers. Nor was it always convenient for these latter to house travellers. Accordingly the Hochwohlgeborne Herr Baron erected a hostelry amidst the clustered dwellings of his peasants at the foot of the rock on which his eyrie was perched, and over the door suspended his shield as a sign.   Hence the Brown Bears, Golden Lions, Eagles, Crowns, etc., which were all feudal badges, and have now become the signs of many such inns.

In process of time, owing to three causes, the noble family itself descended from the *Burg* and took up its residence in the *Schenke*.   In the first place, the Ritter Herrschaft felt the inconvenience of having to carry up all the necessaries of life from the village to the high-perched castle ; in the second place, the high and well-born family had become impoverished ; and in the third place, the young folk and the mother as well desired to see more of life than soaring eagles and skimming swallows. Society in a village might not be very select, but it was society ; and society affords distraction.   The young people could see the travellers pass the door of the hostel, or, better still, enter the porch and invite themselves into the Gaststube.   Further, in the village, even in the smallest hamlet, there existed a free circulation of scandal, and that could not be acquired in the high-seated castle from the screaming eagles and the shrill swifts.   If the family did receive and entertain travellers, it could no longer afford to do so gratis.   The visitors were expected to pay an acknowledgment.

I saw something of the kind at the Oetz Thal, at Umhausen, where my friend Gatrill and I spent the night.   There was no tavern in the village, and it was the parish priest and not the lord of the manor who kept open house.   In the evening the peasants assembled at the parsonage to eat, drink and talk politics, and, upon leaving, put some money into the hand of the Pfarrer's sister.   We were lodged there, and on leaving next morning did the same, whilst his Reverence looked out of the window and hummed a Gregorian tune.

In course of time many of the inns bearing heraldic sign-boards have changed proprietors, but in a considerable number they remain in the hands of the descendants of the old knightly and noble families which had at one time possessed a considerable tract of territory over which they exercised lordly rights.

At Mals, both the village inn and the village store, at which were sold boots, sugar, spices, paper, coffee-berries and children's copy-books, were run by the lineal descendants of the old feudal lords ; and in the churchyard were to be seen the family tombstones emblazoned with their arms and coronets, down to that of the father of our landlord at the inn, whose final resting-place by this time, I doubt not, is indicated by a coronet of strawberry leaves, and a shield with supporters.

We visited the Oetz Thal, and were disappointed. It consists of a cleft between glacier heights, but we could see no snow. To obtain a view of these mighty Alps and their *Firner* one must ascend one of the sides.

We reached Oetz on a Saturday. The afternoon was oppressively hot, and as I was tired with walking, I cast myself on a bed to rest, but was roused by hearing children singing, and on running to my window I saw a procession of little boys and girls carrying bunches of forget-me-nots, on their way to the churchyard. Upon inquiry, I ascertained that the old parish priest had been a great favourite with the little ones, and that, since his death, they went every Saturday, so long as there were flowers to pick, to decorate his grave. When later I visited the churchyard, I found his grave covered with clusters of this pretty blue flower. It was as though each posy were an appeal from every one of the hearts of these innocents to their friend and pastor in Paradise : " Forget-me-not ! "

I remember when it was considered in England a shocking thing to decorate a coffin and a grave. Now it is shocking to neglect such a tribute to the memory of the deceased.

At Göflan, near Schlanders, are quarries of white marble, as white as that of Carrara. But Göflan is within the Italian frontier. As there was at the time cholera raging in Italy, all the loads of marble as they passed into Austrian territory were disinfected with carbolic acid, but not the workmen and the drivers of oxen. The country might really have been under an English bureaucracy for the imbecility exhibited by the Austrian sanitary authorities and police. Officialdom everywhere practises the Goose-step, making great pretence of exertion, but accomplishing nothing.

We ascended the Martel Thal, and saw the little church of Maria Schmeltz, with two massive blocks of white marble like enormous lumps of sugar which had fallen one on each side of it, without having disturbed a tile, and with another still wedged in a crevasse of the cliff above, threatening at every moment to descend with a bound and crush the house of God into the earth.

The two blocks fell in 1868, and one cannot be surprised at the peasants considering that Our Lady, to whom the little building is dedicated, had extended her protection to this sanctuary.

" It is like the Church of Christ," said Gatrill, " ever menaced, never destroyed."

" But by a mass of black basalt, and not, as here, of candid marble."

" The blackest basalt is painted white," said Gatrill.

The effect of the tower with its red spire, and the nave red-roofed, with the quoins painted green, couching between two massive blocks white as snow is singular enough.

From the Martel Thal we crossed by the Madritscher Joch to Sulden, and thence went on to Meran. It was not the season for visitors, and the town was empty.

We spent a week at Innsbrück. The weather was delightful. We saw the young Duke of Braganza and his brother, the sons of Michael Marie Charles Egidius Constantine Gabriel Raphael-Gonzaga François de S. Paul-Francis of Assisi-Janvier. It is customary to give to a child the names of its godparents, as also of its heavenly patrons. The mother of these handsome, lively boys was a daughter of Prince Maximilian of Thurn and Taxis. We get on very well in England without such strings of Christian names. The utmost we get from our sponsors is a silver rattle or a mug. As for the heavenly godparents, I am not aware that they have done more for the children they are invoked to aid than do the Percys, Leslies, Howards, and the like nobles, whose names are given to gutter children, for their namesakes.

In 1885, on September 29th, in the Embassy Chapel, Paris, I married my cousin, Alexander Baring, to Louise King Thorne, who was an American by birth. She was aged only nineteen, very sweet and graceful, and had been educated in England by Miss Sewell. I was not able to remain in Paris, as Mr. Morshead's lease was up and we had to shift quarters from the Rectory to Lew House.

At the wedding breakfast the bride looked towards me and nodded ; I understood it, as indeed it was meant to be under-stood, as a request that I should say grace. But my so doing appeared to puzzle the Americans present. I can quite under-stand a revulsion from the long and tedious graces said by the

I will conclude this chapter with an anecdote told me by Lady Young. She had been Lady Lawrence till the death of her first husband,[1] and then had married Sir George Young.

Lord Lawrence had been invited to Windsor to dine. When he arrived at the Castle, and was preparing for dinner, he found that he had not packed his dress trousers in his portmanteau, and had only a light dove-coloured pair on his legs. He rang and asked one of the servants if by any chance he could be provided with a pair ; but it was some time before he could be fitted. When he came down the Queen had already gone in to dinner. Lord Lawrence went into the dining-room, and slipped into his place at the left side of the Queen. He was the guest of the evening, but Her Majesty was offended at what she considered a gross breach of etiquette, and would not notice him. Lord Lawrence told his story in a low tone to the lady on the other side. She was vastly tickled, and repeated it to her neighbour, and so the story travelled round the table and reached the nobleman on the Queen's other side, and he told it to Her Majesty, who went into a fit of laughter, and turned to Lord Lawrence, all amiability, and ever after when she met him, could not forbear smiling at the recollection of his trouble.

[1] Lady Young's first husband was Sir Alexander Hutchinson Lawrence, Bart., who was a near relative of Lord Lawrence.

CHAPTER XIII

BOHEMIA
1886

IN the summer of 1886 my friend Gatrill and I went to Munich, taking Augsburg on our way. With this latter city we were grievously disappointed. Till comparatively recently it was a walled town, with sixteen picturesque towers forming a coronet. Its crown has been cast down, to reveal a shabby collection of houses.

The town consists mainly of one long, broad street, with the Cathedral at one end and the Church of S. Ulrich at the other. The former is an early Lombardic structure, having a low vault which rests on square piers, and interesting for its antiquity. The Church of S. Ulrich is in late Gothic style, and not good in that. Neither of these churches contributes to render Augsburg picturesque.

Augsburg was the cradle of the princely family of the Fuggers, just as Florence was of the Medici ; both risen from the loom, and both marrying into the best blood in their respective lands.

The founder of the princely and countly family of Fugger was a John Fugger, a humble hand-loom weaver in the village of Graben, near Augsburg. By his diligence and rectitude he earned sufficient money to enable his sons to settle in the city as burgher. John Fugger had eleven children, of whom the most notable were Ulrich, George and James, who lived under Frederick III and Maximilian I. These three amassed much wealth by becoming wholesale cloth merchants and bankers.

In 1473, when the phlegmatic Frederick III arrived in Augsburg on his way to meet Charles the Bold, Duke of Burgundy, at Trèves, Ulrich, with the assistance of his brothers, clothed the entire suite of the Emperor in gold, silver, silken and velvet

157

is empty. Take one or two plump hens or chickens, wring their necks, and whilst they are still fluttering immerse them in boiling water. Their plumes and skins come off immediately. Clean, cut into pieces, throw into a pot with water, butter, flour, cream, and abundance of red pepper. Very shortly after the dismembered fowls will be served up swimming in a dish of hot, greasy gravy, delightful to recollect, and a joy to consume. These hot dishes are or were making their way throughout Germany from Hungary, the land of their inception, where the red pepper grows abundantly. With the exception of the English with their curries, the Hungarians at one time were the only Europeans sufficiently civilized to know the value of that most indispensable article of culinary luxury—red pepper.

The Marienkirche is of red brick ; one vast roof covers nave, side aisles and chapels. A large number of monuments are affixed to the outside of the church. I noted one of interest, dated 1493, representing a musician, surrounded by harp, flute, one stringed sordine, and a lute. He himself is figured as playing a hand organ, as clumsy a contrivance as any employed in the thirteenth and fourteenth centuries. It could be played with one hand only, whilst the other worked the bellows.

Munich has always struck me as a remarkably ugly town. The kings Ludwig I and Maximilian II made it that. Not a structure raised by these princes is other than an eyesore. I was walking with Gatrill down the Ludwigstrasse, between rows of buildings in blocks, like bars of kitchen soap, yellow and white, scribbled over here and there with unmeaning ornaments, when he burst out with : " For Heaven's sake, let us get into a parallel side street. The houses there may be ugly enough, but are without pretence." It is a pity that instead of being ennobled, the architects Klenze and Gärtner were not hung in the openings of the Feldherrnhalle, which is a miserable copy of Orcagna's Loggie dei Lanzi at Florence. Such churches as S. Ludwig, the Allerheiligen, or Court church, and the Basilika, are beneath contempt. But on the other hand the new National Museum is admirable, and the church of S. Benno is delightful, as is also the new Rathhaus in the old German style.

The modern street buildings are now for the most part constructed of concrete made out of the clay and wash that underlies the city. It is a cheap material, and possibly if treated intelligently might prove effective. But as employed by the builders of to-day, is very ugly ; the mouldings are coarse and the buildings look as though shaped out of rhinoceros hide.

Gatrill and I had resolved to explore the Bairischer Wald, a chain of granite mountains that divides Bohemia and Bavaria. The highest peaks are the Arber, 4780 ft. ; the Rachel, 4765 ft. ; and the Osser, 4240 ft. On the eastern side the range goes by the name of the Böhmer Wald, and is occupied by the Czechs.

The chain is actually a continuation of the Erzgebirge, so valuable to Saxony for their metal deposits. The Erzgebirge themselves constitute a continuation of the Riesengebirge that separate Silesia from Bohemia, and which we proposed to visit after a brief stay at Prague. The Riesengebirge are themselves continued eastward and acquire the name of the Sudetten. Then the range loops round to the south, declines in height, is covered with forests, and forms the division between Bohemia and Moravia. The Bavarian Forest is not itself perhaps of conspicuous and startling beauty, but it is interesting on account of the glass works and of the peasantry ; these latter live in primitive simplicity, remote from towns, hemmed in to the east by the Czechs, whose language they do not understand, and with whom they are by tradition and prejudice at variance.

One Sunday I was at Mass in a village church in the forest ; and at what we are wont to call the offertory, all the men in the congregation rose and walked two and two up to the altar, promenaded solemnly round it, from the north side round the back to the south, where each laid on the altar his small contribution which the priest blessed by touching it with his stole. I put down a mark, and at the unwonted aspect of silver a smile broke out upon the face of the celebrant, and he laid his stole on my hand, which he tapped in friendly acknowledgment. When all the men had made their contributions, the women went up in pairs, passed round the back of the altar, and deposited their humble alms at the south end, enlarging the little heap. I saw the priest put his finger into the brown mound and turn up my mark, as a hint for the women to give silver ; but the hint proved ineffective.

I witnessed a pretty sight at another village. It was the funeral

M

of a little child. Every one present had brought a coil of wax taper, lighted, and all planted their coils around the grave, so that the little coffin was lowered through a belt of stars.

The Bairischer Wald's principal attraction are the lakelets distributed throughout it. These are rather tarns than lakes, and usually present the aspect of still pools of bottle-green water under a granite precipice on one side, but enveloped on all others by thick forest. No springs feed these tarns, nor do streams flow out of them. Some are black, owing to their depth. In all, the water is crystal clear. They generally have the aspect of ponds occupying volcanic craters, like the Maars in the Eifel district. But this appearance is misleading, for there has been no volcanic action in the range.

Gatrill and I walked over a pass in order to visit Eysenstein with its remarkable church, very oriental in appearance. At the summit of the pass was a divergence of paths, and I asked a peasantess whom we met which was the one to take so as to reach our destination. " To the right hand," said she promptly.

Accordingly we did turn *rechts*, and were led thereby some four or five miles out of our proper way.

Upon reaching our destination, hot and tired, I told mine host of the inn how we had been misdirected.

" Who told you to turn to the right ? " he inquired.

" A woman whom we met," I replied.

The landlord looked hard at me, and shook his head. " Inexperienced," said he. " Ever since the days of Eve woman has diverted the sons of Adam from the right road. Do you not know that a woman thinks of her left hand as if it were the left of anyone she meets. She is incapable of putting herself in the place of him she faces. In future, when you meet a woman and inquire of her your way and she bids you go to the left, then with positive conviction take the right hand direction. Mein lieber Herr, in coming to Eysenstein you have learned a lesson for life. I shall not charge you extra in the bill for this advice."

The church of Eysenstein with its red copper gigantic onion-like roof and its radiating chapels is curious enough, but cannot be set down as beautiful. Pleasant forest excursions may be made from the place. Enormous pines are to be seen in parts. They will not pay for cutting down because of the difficulties of carriage and transportation to a railway. Moreover, some of these forest giants are regarded by the natives with superstitious reverence.

A singular custom prevails in the Bavarian Forest, but is not absolutely peculiar to it. When a man or woman is dying, he or she is taken out of bed and laid on a Todten Brett, a plank provided for the occasion, with a shelf for the feet to rest against. The body lies on this till buried, and after the funeral the board is painted and furnished with a pent-house roof. Where the

DEATH BOARDS AT CHAM

head rested is a circular disc in which is a painting representing the deceased kneeling in the attitude of prayer, and in the sky are representations of the Trinity, or of the Virgin and Child. Sometimes instead of a picture, the circle is figured to represent a clock-face, with the hands pointing to the minute and hour of decease. Below the disc, where the back of the corpse rested, an inscription is painted, recording the name, date of death, age, dignities and virtues of the departed. Occasionally the record is placed on two tables, black lettered on white.

Then the board is erected by the side of the road, near a

crucifix, or at a cross-roads ; in the case of an accident, at the place where the person met with it, and perhaps died. As the bases of these Todten Bretter decay they lurch, and the effect as darkness descends is startling. One sees near the road ranges of apparently drunken men, waiting to waylay the traveller. As every man, woman and child who expires is thus furnished, there are literally crowds of these death-boards. At Neukirchen, in the Oberpfalz, under the Hohenbogen, where the church is a mile from the village, the whole way is lined on both sides with these staggering mementos. I can conceive of nothing more trying to the nerves than a walk along this avenue on a night when there is just sufficient light in the sky to show their outlines.

The eastern slope of this granite range is the Böhmer Wald, where glass manufacture is the principal industry. The district favours the manufacture, both here and on the southern slopes of the Riesengebirge, owing to the vast stores that exist of fuel and potash, with the quartz ready at hand and lime accessible. The Venetian glass manufacture was soon distanced by that of Bohemia, which maintained its supremacy till the beginning of the eighteenth century, when English manufacturers discovered the process for making flint-glass with oxide of lead as an ingredient ; but this caused a heaviness in English glass which the other did not possess. The Bohemians, finding their craft in danger, introduced ruby and blue glass, engraved with figures and landscapes, that delighted the public. To our eyes at the present day such decoration is in bad taste, and of late has been abandoned for painted or enamelled glass ; a recovery of an adornment common in the fifteenth and sixteenth centuries, and very charming.

When we were in Bohemia in 1843 the engraved glass was produced in great quantities and found a ready sale. There were views of Prague, Dresden, the Prebisch Thor, the Bastei in Switzerland as well as hunting scenes, pastoral groups and mythological subjects. Over white glass was laid a coat of ruby or azure enamel. The engraver sat at a lathe with a little rack before him which contained a score of sharp-edged copper discs, mounted on spindles and of various sizes. He inserted a disc in the mandril, touched it with a drop of sweet oil, set it spinning and held the glass against it from below. The little wheel eat its way through the outer film of coloured enamel, and exposed the

REV. J. M. GATRILL

white glass underneath. A succession of discs, smaller and ever smaller, completed the design to the finest touches, such as tree leaves, blades of grass, tips of antlers, human eye-brows, etc. We brought home specimens. I never liked them, and I believe they have gone the way of all glass where there are domestic servants in the house. I cannot say that I regret their disappearance. Some of our white engraved glass is pleasant enough, and a fashion has set in again for cut glass. I fear that the painted glass is already going out of request, but I am glad to say I had a whole set for the dinner table painted for me with mediæval foliage, crests and arms, before this took place.

The peasant in the Bairischer Wald employs a glass bottle as his snuff-box. It is corked with a flock of wool. When he wants to obtain a dose, he turns up his nose, unplugs the bottle, and pours as much powdered tobacco into his nostrils as they will hold. The Icelanders do much the same with powder flasks. How completely snuff-taking has gone out of fashion. Formerly ladies were great snuff takers. Queen Charlotte laid a train of tobacco-dust on her left arm, held horizontally, and ran her nose down over it, picking up the snuff on the way by her inhalation. It were well if cigarette smoking were also to go out of fashion. Ladies' breath now does not savour of milk and honey, but of stale tobacco pipes.

We were at Prague on the Emperor's Name-day, when the city was in gala, and the troops were paraded. Then and there I witnessed a touching incident, on which I wrote some lines in *The Silver Store*, entitled " The Secret of Life."

The cardinal, Prince Franz von Schwarzenberg, Primate of Bohemia, pontificated in the cathedral in the morning. The Schwarzenbergs exercise all but sovereign rights in their vast territories in Bohemia, and the reigning prince is believed to have a fabulously large rent roll. The Schwarzenbergs possess one-thirteenth of all the land of Bohemia, and the Prince is entitled *Durchlaucht* (Your Transparency).

Whilst at Prague Gatrill and I went to the opera to hear *Tannhäuser*. The music was superior to the decoration. In the act wherein the evening star is addressed, there was a hole in the back scene, and against this latter was planted, in rear, a pair of steps. By some negligence a light had been left burning behind

and drowned, as his resistance to the purpose of the king to con-
fiscate the emoluments of the abbey of Kladrau, wherewith to
endow another episcopal see in Bohemia ; a very reasonable proposal. The Bishop, in his appeal to the Pope against Winceslas,
mentions the tortures and murder of John of Nepomuk, but says
not a word of his refusal to reveal the queen's confession. Two
contemporary writers state that the canon was drowned because
he had ventured to remonstrate with the emperor for his crimes.
Thomas Ebendorfer, who died in 1460, was the first to state that
John of Nepomuk " was drowned in the Moldau, *as it is reported*,
because he refused to break the seal of confession." Paul Zidek,
writing in 1470, says that " the king having a bad opinion of his
wife . . . came to John of Nepomuk and asked him to tell him
with whom she had had forbidden relations . . . and as John
would not inform him, the king had him drowned." Not till
seventy-seven years after the death of John was the refusal to break
the seal of confession, stated to have caused John's execution.

Bohemia is one of the most Catholic countries in Europe, and
yet it was a cradle of a revolt against the Papacy and the scene of
furious religious wars between the Calixtines and the Catholics.
The demand of the former was the restoration of the cup to the
people in communion. Later Bohemia was honeycombed with
Protestantism. Yet here the Counter-Reformation was most
successful. It is true that the Council of Basle restored the
chalice to the Bohemian laity ; but this did not satisfy them, and
a revolution broke out which was only crushed by the victory of
the White Mountain. The battle destroyed the prospects of
Calvinism in Bohemia, when it was almost the master, and after
it the imperial troops occupied the capital, the heart of the whole
country. Ferdinand II, advised by Jesuits, subjected the people
to inquisitorial inspection, and in every house of every Czech
town, the heads of the families, their wives, work-people and
servants were required to return a categorical answer to the
questions : 1. Are you a Catholic ? 2. Have you been converted
to the Catholic faith ? 3. Do you promise to become or to remain a Catholic ? Whoever refused to embrace Romanism was
declared incompetent to exercise any corporate trade, was generally deprived of his property and expelled the country. These
summary proceedings proved successful. But one may well ask

whether such a procedure could have had a lasting effect. It is possible that, when the Czechs have shaken themselves free from the clutch of the Austrian eagle, there may ensue a religious revolt, and S. John Nepomuk may be tumbled into the Moldau once more, and his pedestal usurped by John Huss.

After the rout of the White Mountain and the flight of the Winter King, Germanization became the order of the day, and the noble families dropped their Czech names for titles derived from their castles. These castles had been built in the German fashion and by German architects on rocks, in place of being planted in marshes, as had been usual among the Czechs. The Vitkovy family called itself Rosenberg, the house of Dipolditz changed into that of Riesenburg, Ransko was metamorphosed into Waldstein, and Divishofzi into Sternberg. Even the family of John Nepomucen Germanized themselves from Hassil into Löschner.

There is a strong and growing patriotic feeling in Bohemia, and a waxing hostility to Austria. But just as the Welsh owe all their noble churches and castles to the Norman invaders, so in Bohemia all that is architecturally beautiful came from German architects. Their literature has been nothing but folk ballads, their music mostly imported from Vienna. Their language isolates them, and they are compelled to speak German if they want to become manufacturers, lawyers or physicians.

In Bohemia not only are the inns in the hands of the Jews, but so also are the factories. If an inn or a factory were carried on by a German, no Czechs would enter it, and so, on the other hand, would one possessed by a Bohemian be scouted by the Germans. In Prague there are two opera houses, one for each nationality, two book-sellers, two apothecaries, two confectioners, in fact, everything is duplicated. The Jews thrive and become wealthy through the mutual antipathies of Teutons and Czechs.

Artistically the Bohemians have only distinguished themselves, as did the Huguenots and the English Puritans, as destroyers of everything that was beautiful—churches, statuary, coloured glass and paintings. Wherever the Hussites swept, they made havoc of the houses of God. At the present day the proportion of Protestants to the Catholics in Bohemia is 2½ per cent. In Moldavia the proportion is double that.

arms, that she had but two with which to hold the infant, and that if the child had broken the mug it was the fault of her Graciousness for tickling its ribs. The Baroness, in no way pacified, declared that she would allow the nurses no more beer and rushed off to the " Restauration " to ascertain what she had to pay for the broken vessel.

During her absence the nurses drank the milk provided for the children. At a table hard by sat two young lieutenants, who commiserated with the pretty nurses and insisted on sharing with them their beer. The girls were cheerily sipping, when meine Gnädige emerged from the refreshment saloon, and the storm broke loose with renewed vigour. At this juncture my friend returned, rather downcast. " I have seen the range ; rather like the Malvern Hills but not so bold in outline. A storm is about to descend on us." This storm developed into three days of rain and cloud which enveloped the mountains and concealed them. We went on by train to Schmiedeberg, the engine ringing a bell that was attached to the funnel, to warn off cattle and men from the line.

At Schmiedeberg we were detained for three days by a heavy downpour, and I declared I would return to Prague, without having seen the Riesengebirge.

" You might have seen them," said Gatrill dryly, " had you not been attracted at Hirschberg by those pretty Polish nurses."

" It was not the nurses," I replied indignantly. " It was the babies that kept me at the station."

" Quite so," responded Gatrill, "and the babes were the attraction to the lieutenants, as well."

Happily, on the fourth morning the sky cleared, the sun came out, and we were able to prosecute our journey.

It is a saying in the neighbourhood of Tavistock :

> " O the glorious County Devon,
> Where it rains six days in seven ! "

Much the same might be said of the Riesengebirge. They condense the moisture gathered both by the North wind from the Baltic, and by the North-west wind from the German Ocean.

The story goes that a farmer of Schmiedeberg made seventeen several attempts to see the view from the Schnee Koppe, and on each expedition was driven back by the rain. He vowed that he would not renew the venture. However, an unwonted period of drought ensued, and the neighbouring farmers in a deputation besought him to reascend the Schnee Koppe.

" Go up the Schnee Koppe ! What for ? "

" To bring us rain," was the reply ; " you are Aquarius incarnate."

There really is snow on the Koppe, but only in its pockets, the *Schneegruben*. At the bottom of the largest of these the snow does not melt throughout the summer, for the sun cannot get at it. Beside it is a green patch of meadow, which the owner mows, sets up the hay on a rick of poles, and leaves there until the winter, when he can reach the spot by means of a sledge. During the warm weather the place is inaccessible by any vehicle, on account of fallen masses of rock.

The comic paper, *Kladderadatsch*, had an engraving representing some Berliners on the Riesengebirge, making believe that they were on the Alps. They had spread an umbrella over a patch of snow about the size of a door-mat to protect it from the solar rays. Above was a notice board inscribed *Verboten*, and severe penalties were provided by the police for such individuals as should approach so near as to threaten the sheet of snow with dissolution, either by their breath, or by their personal heat.

The *Veilchenmoos*, a grey lichen that grows on these bare mountains, exhales a faint odour of violets. It is sold to visitors as a rarity.

An object often visited is the Wanderstein, a granite block shaped somewhat like a die, weighing thirty tons, which is said to shift its quarters occasionally. This was first observed in 1807 ; it resumed its travels in 1810, when it descended the slope 300 feet ; in 1822 it advanced 200 feet, and in June in another year it progressed 72 feet. The block rests on moss and soft earth, and is not very firmly balanced on its base. Probably a slight earthquake shock, or even a furious blast of wind may cause it to move over the spongy soil.

Much *Krummholz* grows on the range. This is a dwarf pine that crawls along the ground, and never rises above one's knee. The natives carve out of it heads of Rübezahl, and cigarette holders. A favourite figure is that of a mother holding a babe in her arms. The babe is the holder for the cigarette, and to employ it, the babe has to be removed from the arms of the mother.

At the top of the Schnee Koppe is the Rhigi Hotel, much frequented by Germans from all the northern provinces. Visitors to this hotel are roused by a horn to get up and see the sun rise. I prefer that the sun should get up and see me rise. There is nothing of interest to be seen from the top of the Schnee Koppe save the vast Silesian plain to the north. What one does see in this hotel are the contrasts of faces of the Silesian, the Bohemian and the North German. The latter has a round visage, flat, broad, and usually ignoble in profile and feature, and eyes of a frosty blue. The Silesians have angular visages, with prominent chins. The faces of the Czechs are oval, often finely shaped in feature, and furnished with bright, intelligent, dark eyes.

If the granitic range proved disappointing, there were subsidiary objects of interest that well repaid our visit; and these were the stony labyrinths of Weckelsdorf and Adersbach, where the rock is sandstone. These are reached via Landshut, and are in Bohemia. The appearance of the country affords no idea of what lies hidden in the recesses of hill and forest. Indeed, the existence of a marvellous labyrinth of rocks at Weckelsdorf was unknown except to the neighbouring farmers, who held their tongues about it till the year 1824, when the forest caught fire, was burnt down, and disclosed the secret.

During the Thirty Years' War, on the approach of the Swedes, the inhabitants of the neighbouring villages disappeared along with their cattle and household goods. The mountain had swallowed them up. After the fire of 1824 a fresh forest arose above the charred stumps, and again drew a curtain over the district. In 1866, when the Prussians poured through the mountain gate above Friedland, on their way to Königgrätz, once more the entire population vanished; the earth had opened her mouth and they had gone down quick into the bowels of the hills, with all that appertained to them.

Let my reader imagine a huge mass of veined marble and suppose all the felspar washed out of the veins, leaving the block cleft in every direction. Such are the sandstone formations of Weckelsdorf and Adersbach. It takes three hours to thread the passages made accessible to the public. A path leads up a glen, on each side of which start up pinnacles of sandstone, till it contracts, and is partially closed by a wall of rock. The opening has been artificially closed with a door that opens only in answer to a silver key. High aloft is Rübezahl's axe extended over the head of the intruder. On passing through a door one is in a narrow

RÜBEZAHL'S TOOTH AND THE DEVIL'S BRIDGE, ADERSBACH

street between blank walls rising a hundred and twenty to two hundred feet, sheer and smooth. Between them the passage in places is so narrow that it can be trodden in single file alone. The rocks assume the strangest shapes. Here is the Rübezahl's Tooth, and the Devil's Bridge with pines growing above the arch, and there, squatted on top of a pedestal, is a monstrous stone toad. Further on we reach a colossal Virgin and Child. High aloft in a cavern, visible only in certain lights and wholly inaccessible, is a snow-white lamb ; of what composed one cannot say, since there is no stalagmitic deposit in sandstone.

The walls suddenly fall apart and we are in the Market Place ; before us rises the natural spire of Rübezahl's Cathedral. Through a narrow fissure one creeps into the Cathedral, all at once an organ begins to play, and then the guide is seen aloft in a natural pulpit, whence he holds forth on the virtues of charity, and exhorts his hearers to be liberal in the matter of tips of which his pocket will hold any amount.

Again we pass through lanes in the rocks, traverse a natural gateway and at once find ourselves on a vast stage with side scenes, each side scene being composed of sandstone precipices rising a hundred and thirty feet. We are now in sunlight, and look down on a vast amphitheatre covered with pine, a crater-like depression ; and at the distance of a mile is seen the hamlet of Zaboř. One lives to learn. In Bohemia the symbol ř has the sound of *rsch ;* consequently Zaboř is pronounced Zaborsch, and Jaromiř is pronounced Jaromirsch.

Recently fresh explorations have been made in this strange region, and fresh phenomena have been discovered. The sand-stone rock faces are glazed with moisture in summer and with ice in winter. This is due to the salt in the stone that exudes in warm weather.

About three miles from Weckelsdorf is the Adersbach laby-rinth, equally curious but with features peculiar to itself ; a lake in it and a waterfall in one of the chasms. The sandstone here is softer and more worn than at Weckelsdorf, and some of the pinnacles stand in the open like gigantic prehistoric monoliths. The Adersbach labyrinth has long been known. In 1772 a couple of Englishmen when exploring it, were struck by lightning. In 1820 a lightning flash fell into the chasm and split a rock.

It seems to me apparent that the upheaval of the Riesengebirge is one of comparatively recent geological times ; and that the granite was forced through an overlying bed of sandstone of vast thickness, cleaving it in half, leaving one-half on the north, as the so-called Saxon Switzerland, and on the south the formations of Adersbach and Weckelsdorf. All between splintered and crumbled, and has been washed away. As might have been anticipated, this region has long served as a haunt of bandits.

One evening in the autumn of 1839 at 5 p.m. a carriage drove up to a little inn at the fringe of the Dobrish forest. A couple of ladies were in it, and, when the Jewish landlady appeared at the door, they inquired if she could furnish them with a room and a supper. She assured them that she could supply them with both.

" We hardly like to drive into the forest at night," said one of the ladies, " because of Babinsky, but "—as she saw rough, wild faces peering at her out of the guest room—" what sort of fellows have you here ? "

" Oh ! respectable packmen," answered the hostess. "Babinsky has never visited this house ; in fact has not been seen in these parts."

The ladies were shown into a plain, tidy, scantily furnished apartment. The stove was lighted, and they were served with a creditable supper in their room.

Now there was, against one side of the chamber, a large old-fashioned wardrobe. Whether it were curiosity, or whether the ladies required the use of it, I cannot tell, but, though it was locked, before they retired to bed they managed with a knife to force back the bolt and throw open the doors. The wardrobe was empty, but they discovered a trap-door at the bottom. This they succeeded in raising, and to their dismay found that it revealed a well, from which an unpleasant odour was exhaled.

They lighted some sheets of newspaper, threw them down the pit, and, to their unspeakable horror, perceived by the flames a half-naked corpse lying at the bottom. The ladies closed the trap door and the wardrobe, and considered what was to be done. It was clear that they had stumbled into a den of murderers, probably one of the haunts of the notorious Babinsky.

The youngest lady, who had more presence of mind and was endowed with courage, at once descended the stairs, and opened the guest-room door. Seeing her coachman at the table, she said : " Hans ! it is now half-past nine o'clock. This is the time when my brother-in-law, Captain Feldegg, promised to leave Prague at the head of a military escort to conduct us through the depths of the forest." Then turning to the hostess, she said : " You seem to be too full to be able to accommodate a body of hussars, so we will drive back and meet them." Then, addressing the

N

coachman, she said : " Hans ! we will start as soon as you can
harness the horses, and meet the party on the road and not
compel them to come on here, where there is obviously no
accommodation for them."

Hans finished his glass of wine and rose. The men looked
at one another, but uttered not a word. The young lady put
money in the hostess' hand, apologized for the trouble she and
her mother had given, and left the room. In half an hour the
carriage rolled away, unmolested, and passed out of the fringe of
the Dobřish forest—pronounce the name Dobrschis. It is
like honey to the mouth, and music to the ear.

Next morning the police were informed of the discovery, but
the inn was not searched. It need hardly be said that the ladies
had met with no escort, and that the account of the arrangement
with Captain Feldegg was an invention on the part of the girl.

A few days later a ragged middle-aged fellow with a grinding
organ arrived at the inn, entered it, and called for a glass. In the
guest room were the same " honest packmen," and some equally
wild-looking wenches. The party were quite unsuspicious that
the ladies had detected what manner of men they were, and had
given notice to the police.

The grinding organ was put in requisition, and to its strains
the revellers danced till past midnight, when the door was flung
open, and a stalwart man, well armed, entered the room. A
whisper of " Babinsky " passed through the room, and the
dancing ceased.

The organ-grinder had so ingratiated himself into favour with
the robbers—for these were in fact some of Babinsky's band—
that they resolved on retaining him as their special musician. He
was conveyed across country, through deep forests, till the gang
reached such another rocky refuge as Weckelsdorf or Adersbach.
There the musician spent three weeks, and he was only suffered
to leave it when he was made to accompany the band for a frolic
and a dance at one of the Jewish taverns that they frequented.

To reach these rendezvous they went by twos and threes so as
not to arouse suspicion. One day, as the organ-grinder and two
of the bandits were passing along a road that was tolerably frequented, they saw a blind beggar sitting in the hedge, soliciting
alms with a dismal whine. Some coppers were thrown into his

cap by the robbers. The organ-grinder lagged behind to bestow a few kreutzers on the man, and at the same time slipped a scrap of paper into his hand.

That night, the tavern, which had been chosen as the scene for a revel, was surrounded by the military, and the whole band, along with their captain, was captured. This occurred on October 15, 1839. The organ-grinder was the Prague detective, Hoch.

The trial was conducted in the usual dilatory way that was customary on the Continent, and dragged on for several years. Finally, some of the robbers and murderers were executed, and some were condemned to ten, some to twenty years' imprisonment with hard labour. No sufficient evidence was producible to justify convicting Babinsky of murder, or of participation in the murders that had been committed, and he was sentenced to penal servitude for life.

Conceive of the state of my feelings on reaching England when I read in the letter of the Vienna correspondent of the *Standard*, that at the little town of Leitomischl in Bohemia, at the foot of the range of mountains Gatrill and I had been visiting, an innkeeper and his wife and son had been arrested on the charge of murdering their guests, during a succession of years.

Hirschberg we found to be a cheerful and pleasant place at which to stay for a few days. It is a starting-point whence Prussians, Berliners especially, make excursions to explore the Riesengebirge. A local guide-book says that " in this superb range one might well expect to meet with avalanches, like those that occur in the Alps, but so far few have occurred." In the nineteenth century only three were recorded, whereof one fell on a frozen pool, and cracked the ice ; a second knocked off a man's hat ; but on the 29th November, 1875, the third did actually overwhelm a tipsy individual. Further, the author remarks that in such a magnificent range one might anticipate meeting with waterfalls ; unhappily, however, there are no streams to precipitate themselves from heights, and no precipices over which they might plunge, did such streams exist. There are, however, in the neighbourhood numerous lakes, if that designation can be applied to the puddles.

Hirschberg is a little town of 14,400 inhabitants, of whom only 3070 are Catholics.

order succeeded, and with the wine and punch, songs were sung. Amongst these latter was one by the cox, so filthy that I writhed in my chair. Opposite me on the wall was an engraving of this very painting, and looking at it I saw the well-remembered eyes meeting mine. I started from my seat, and, disregarding the hootings and groans of several at table, left the room.

The modern picture that had delighted me as a child was one that represented a wealthy and noble boy showing his picture-book to one or two ragged children. The owner of the book was looking away, disregarding his possession, and rather despising the poor urchins for taking so much delight in the pictures. That subject has haunted me ever since.

It is singular how little matters affect the after life ; things at the time not of much apparent importance have gone to build up a character and to give direction to conduct. I learned and took to heart from that picture the duty of sharing such things that we possess with those to whom they have been denied. I do not know that I consciously thus moralized at the time ; but ever and anon that picture has recurred to me, and checked selfish enjoyment. My mother was ever ready to inculcate altruism as true Christianity ; but the teaching by mouth that enters the ears is not so effective as the silent teaching that comes from what one sees.

Some possess very beautiful houses, with gardens and grounds, and many strangers ask leave to see them. Some I know do not approve of this. They say, and there may be truth in it, that the sight of things possessed by others and unattainable by themselves may breed envy and class hatred. I do not think so. I allow that one's good-nature, as it is termed, is liable to be imposed upon. Lord Mount Edgcumbe throws open his grounds once or twice a week to the Plymothians, who picnic in the park and strew the sward with ginger-beer bottles, often broken, with cigarette cases and empty match-boxes, as also with discarded, crumpled and dirty newspapers. He has to employ men for a whole day after such invasions in clearing the grounds of this refuse.

Again, Mr. Rodd of Trebartha has a waterfall in his grounds, as well as pretty ponds. He is often solicited to suffer Sunday Schools, or the Salvation Army, or Clubs, to be allowed free run of his grounds on specified days. On one occasion lately he met a Sunday School teacher, heading his class, with his arms full of *Osmunda regalis* that he had dug up, and was carrying away.

" Are you aware," said Mr. Rodd, " that this fern was planted by me five years ago, and has only now attained to the size at which you have torn it up ? "

Nevertheless, I think that anyone who *has* must share with the *have nots*.

There was a fifth painting in the Dresden gallery that I remembered having impressed me as a child, but I cannot recall any more than these four.

The famous Mary Magdalen of Correggio is a beautiful painting, but I fancy that the principal reason why it interested me as a child was that outside Launceston Parish Church, in the east wall, is a recess cut in the granite, and in this recess S. Mary Magdalen is represented lying in the same attitude as in Correggio's painting, with her pot of ointment at her side. Thus, when at Dresden I looked at the picture, I contrasted it with the sculptured figure ; and whenever I am in Launceston and look at the granite figure, very clumsy and grotesque, of the patron saint, my memory spreads its wings and darts back to the Correggio in Dresden.

CHAPTER XV

FOLK SONGS
1887-88

IN 1888 I began to collect folk-songs and melodies in Devon; and later those in Cornwall as well. The occasion was as follows. I was dining at Mount Tavy, at the hospitable table of Mr. Daniel Radford, a man for whom I entertained the highest esteem, when the conversation turned upon Devonshire songs. Some of those present knew " Arscott of Tetcott," and some knew " Widecombe Fair," but none could recall others such as : " The Oxen Ploughing " and " Green Broom," in their entirety, though some remembered snatches of them. I remembered how, when I was a boy, I had ridden round Dartmoor, and had put up at little taverns. In them I had seen men sitting and smoking, and had heard them sing ballads. I mentioned this. My host said to me : " Come, you are the man to undertake the job of collecting these songs and airs. It must be done at once, or it cannot be done at all, for in a few years they will be lost."

I shall not forget my walk back next day from Mount Tavy to Lew. My mind was in a ferment. I considered that I was on the outstart of a great and important work ; and to this day I consider that the recovery of our West-country melodies has been the principal achievement of my life. I had a great friend, the Rev. H. Fleetwood Sheppard, rector of Thurnscoe in Yorkshire, an accomplished musician, and one who was not a formalist, but could throw himself into a ballad air, make it his own and surround it with a flood of dainty harmony. He had the poetic faculty in music, which is so wanting in many who can write an accompaniment that is scientifically correct, but is void of feeling.

So soon as I saw that the material was plentiful, I invited him to come to me and assist in gathering up the melodies. The words I could collect, but was able to recover the tunes only when I had the singer by me at the piano. But to work the country properly, it needed that we should visit the cottages and taverns, where no such adventitious aid was to be obtained. At that time the gramophone was not invented.

During the Christmas and the Long Vacations I could calculate on the assistance of Mr. F. W. Bussell of Brasenose College, Oxford, whose mother and sister had taken the Cottage on the Ramps that I had built. Later Mr. Bussell became a Mus. Doc. and Vice-Principal of his College.

At first I went to the farmers and yeomen ; but soon ascertained that no material of any value for my purpose was to be obtained from them. All the songs they knew were such as had been published early in the nineteenth century, and were to be found in sundry " Vocal Charmers," " Apollo's Cabinets " and the like. There was, however, one exception, Jimmy F—— of Chaddlehanger, a great fox-hunter, and a merry soul to boot. He was married to a stern, solemn, Puritanical wife, who regarded us with indignation for encouraging the frivolity of her husband. From him we did obtain some good hunting and drinking songs.

It was necessary to drop to a lower level if we were to tap the spring of traditional folk music. I speedily discovered that what I wanted was to be obtained mainly from such men as could neither read nor write. At the outset we did not attempt to extort songs from the old women ; in fact, we worked that field very little, and very inadequately, but it was one that Mr. Cecil Sharp found later to be fruitful in Somersetshire.

I soon learned to mistrust the words of the songs, which were often, but not always, corruptions of Broadside Ballads, transmitted orally. Thus " the Northern Knight " was changed into " the Northern Cat," and the expression "And she the laurel wore " had become "And she was lorriowere." In the ballad of " Death and the Lady," the former was described as " he was of the Branchy Tree," in place of " he was an Anatomy."

The printed ballads of Such, Fortey, Ryle, Catnash and others are not trustworthy. The Broadside Ballad publishers received the songs and ballads that they printed from itinerant singers, extremely illiterate, who had themselves received them orally, and had corrupted them unintentionally. They were paid a few shillings by the publishers for what they supplied and no attempt was made to verify or to edit them from earlier copies.

There were, however, a certain number of ballads that we received from our " song-men," that were obviously more correct in diction than those produced by the publishers who furnished the sheets that were hawked about at fairs.

That which became daily more evident was that the melodies were incomparably more valuable than the words. The latter might be borrowed, and be in common circulation over England, but the tunes were for the most part local. And, what was more, the melodies had a character of their own distinct from those of Somerset and Dorset.

Robert Bell, in his *Ballads of the Peasantry* (1857), gives " Sweet Nightingale," of which he informs us : " This curious ditty we first heard in Germany, at Marienbad (burg) on the Moselle. The singers were four Cornish miners, who were at that time (1854) employed at some lead mines near the town of Zell. The leader, or captain, John Stocker, said that the song was an established favourite with the miners of Cornwall and Devonshire, and was always sung on the pay-days and at the wakes ; and that his grandfather, who died thirty years before (1824) at the age of a hundred years, used to sing the song, and say that it was very old. The tune is plaintive and original."

I wrote to the *Western Morning News* to ask whether anyone in Cornwall could furnish me with the melody, and it was promptly sent to me by a gentleman of S. Ives, who wrote that " the melody had run in his head any time these thirty years." I have since had it as well from old miners.

Now the interesting feature about the song is that the words come from Bickerstaff's *Thomas and Sally*, 1760 : a ballad opera, the music by Dr. Arne. The words may have travelled down into Cornwall (where, by the way, there are no nightingales)[1] on a Broadside, but not the music, which was either an adaptation of an earlier traditional air, or was one composed by some local

[1] Baron Wrangel found in Northern Siberia, i.e. on the edge of the frozen sea, Russians who sang poems on the nightingale.

musical genius. If old Gaffer Stocker learned it in 1820, and then considered it an old tune, the new setting must have occurred very soon after the publication of *Thomas and Sally*.

From a lame road-maker at South Brent I got the song " 'Twas on a Sunday Morning." Now the words were by Charles Swan, and were set to music by Francis Mori and published in 1853. But the stone-breaker's tune was totally distinct from that by Mori, and in my opinion superior to it. In this instance also the words had come to the poor working man in South Devon and he had fitted them to a melody, whether original or traditional who can say ?

One day I asked a tanner at Launceston whether he recalled any song upon cyder. He replied that he would think the matter over. Next week he came to me with a cyder song. There was no merit in the words, which, on being pressed, he admitted that he had himself composed ; but there was an antique flavour in the air, and again, on being questioned, he told me that he had fitted his composition upon cyder to an old tune that he recalled, but what the words had been he could remember no more save in snatches.

At first I supposed that village organists and conductors of village choirs had originated these melodies, but I have come now to an entirely different opinion. A great many of the compositions of these worthies, mostly carols, exist in manuscript. Collections of them have been published, and not one of them is worth the paper on which printed ; what is more, not one of them has survived to be sung by any choir.

The real composers were either the ancient wandering minstrels, whose tunes live still, orally transmitted through many generations ; or else they were the spontaneous compositions of ignorant village song-men, who chirped, supping their cyder in the settle by the fire of the taverns. As these airs were unaccompanied, their vitality depended entirely on the quality, the originality, and the freshness of the melody. If a tune has lived and has been orally transmitted from one generation to another, it cannot be commonplace. It must have musical character, that is to say, must enshrine an original melodious idea.

In the West of England, and it was probably the same elsewhere, every village inn retained its Song-man who amused the company by his ballads and lyrics, and was repaid by the topers with free drinks.

Their *répertoire* was extensive. James Parsons, who went by the name of " the Singing Machine," was one evening at the tavern at Sourton with three other men, one of whom, named Voysey, worked for me. Parsons by profession was a hedger and thatcher. He told me that upon the occasion mentioned, a bet had been laid that he could not go on singing fresh songs all the night from sunset to daybreak. He did so, and won the bet. I found it difficult to credit the story, so I asked Voysey whether it were as Parsons had related.

" Ay ! it's true enough," said the man, shaking his head. " I reckon I shan't forget that in a hurry, as I had to empty my purse to pay the bet."

Some of the songs are of considerable antiquity, and may be discovered in Early Garlands, but not on Broadsides. One that I published in my *Songs of the West* as " Strawberry Fair," is actually " Kit hath lost her key (cow)" that was issued, words and melody, in 1561. But as it is an indecent ballad, I was fain to write fresh words to it. The tune had hung on from one generation to another, and it was adopted by Beuler, in or about 1835, for his comic song " Ben was a hackney coachman rare."

I got from Sam Fone, a workman on Black Down, the ballad of " The Death of Queen Jane," that relates to her having submitted to the Cæsarean operation for the birth of Edward, afterwards King of England. The circumstances are not true, as she survived the birth several days, but it was generally believed at the time in England. Dr. Alexander Barret also obtained the ballad from a gipsy woman in Somerset. The tune was a canon.

Hall in his *Chronicle* under 1511 gives an account of the piracies of Andrew Barton; and Percy, in his *Reliques*, printed a ballad relative to him and his achievements. But this is a recast made in the reign of James I, at which period many of our old English ballads were rewritten in the affected style and measure of the period. But this tune has gone past recall, and the recast ballad is unknown to our village singers. They do, however, retain the original words and melody, but have transformed Andrew Barton into Harry Martyn.

From Fone, the miner, I also recovered a lengthy ballad called

" The Duke's Hunt," concerning a chase by Villiers, Duke of Buckingham, in the reign of James I. This was printed in 1650, " to an excellent tune, much in request." The tune, however, was not published, nevertheless it has been retained in the memory of our peasantry for three hundred years. We obtained it not only from Fone, but also from singers at Launceston, Stoke Gabriel, and Menheniot. Consequently it is " much in request " still.

One song we recovered from a tanner at Liskeard, entitled " Ormond the Brave," relative to James Butler's attempted landing in 1714, in favour of James II. It is a stoutly expressed Jacobite song glorifying Ormond, who was a rather contemptible creature. This ditty must be of local origin. It is as vigorous as an air as it is in diction.

From an old woman at Kingswear, opposite Dartmouth, I acquired the early ballad of " King John and the Abbot of Canterbury."

I have transmitted to the Public Free Library at Plymouth copies of all those ballads and melodies we collected with the original words and the variations in the airs, as also the pages of music-paper on which the airs were taken down by Mr. Sheppard and Mr. Bussell. As a great part of the words was obscene or indelicate it became absolutely necessary for me to write fresh verses to such as were not fit to be sung in a drawing-room. Unhappily some of the most dainty airs were wedded to the most indecorous words. I had the example of Burns to justify me in this course, for he did precisely the same thing, and it is due to this procedure that so many charming Scottish melodies have been preserved.

A Plymouth dentist, Mr. Spence Bate, who had retired from business, had a house at South Brent. He wrote to me to inform me that there were living in the place a miller, John Helmore, ruined by the setting up of a steam-mill, and a crippled stone-breaker, named Robert Hard ; both notable song-men. He invited Mr. Sheppard and me to pay him a visit and gather up the fragments of folk music that remained to be discovered at South Brent. Accordingly we went. It was the depth of winter, and the weather was bitter. Mr. Bate's house was built over a stream from the moor, a so-called " leet," and it was like an ice-house.

After dinner we adjourned to the kitchen, where was a roaring fire, and the old men were set up with jugs and tankards of ale. But some neighbouring gentlemen and ladies, notably the latter, had been invited to be present at the performance. This I saw at once would never do. Tunes have to be repeated several times to be noted with accuracy, as peasant singers are disposed to embroider them with twirls and flourishes of their own device ; and further, I was not at all sure that the words of the ballads would in all cases be fit for ladies' ears. And so it proved. For after the singing of " The Mole-Catcher " by John Helmore, the aged miller, there ensued a rapid dissolution of the company. I inserted the song in the last edition of *Songs of the West*, but to very much chastened words.

On the following day Mr. Sheppard and I had the two old men to ourselves, and between us we recovered the words and airs of some very interesting pieces. In the summer I went to Mr. Bate's house along with Mr. Bussell, and gleaned more songs. Finally I went alone in the winter of 1890, and the Vicar of South Brent very kindly surrendered to me his drawing-room and piano, and gave me a good fire. I had in old Hard. Then and there I obtained from him a further crop of ballads. That was the last reaping, for in the ensuing bitter frost the aged man was found dead, frozen on a heap of stones by the roadside.

John Helmore, the miller, after his wife's death, ended his days in the Workhouse. I asked him one day when he began courting his " Missus." " I reckon," said he, " when I was a baby. Us growed up together, and us did ever love one another ; and now her's took, please God I be took soon too, for I want to be wi' her. Us till now have niver been apart, and I du feel queer and lone at present."

Fone told me that in former days, before the train ran from Exeter to London, he went up to town in a carrier's van, along with his little sister, and that all the way up, day by day and hour by hour she sang " Seventeen on Sunday," which is not quite such a song as one would expect from a child. One day I was at Belstone visiting a famous singer, Harry Westaway, when he sang a ballad to us, but dropped one of the verses, whereupon his daughter, a tall, handsome girl of about eighteen, shouted

ROBERT HARD

from the kitchen : " Fayther, you've left out someut," and she struck up and sang a most—to say the least—indelicate verse.

There was an old man named Masters at Bradstone. The rector of Lifton heard that he was a song-man and that he was bed-ridden. Accordingly, to do me a kindness, he drove over and visited the apple-faced old fellow, who was in bed, but quite well enough to sing. The rector, the Rev. W. W. Martyn, was a specially modest-minded man. He could not note the music, but he could take down the words ; so placing himself on a chair by the bed, he pulled out a copy-book, and pencil, and settled him-self to write what Masters sang. The ballad selected by the sick man was " Polly Oliver," and it relates how that Polly fell in love with a gay cavalier, and, so as to be with him, dressed herself as a page boy and accompanied her beloved. The *dénouement* of the tale is what might have been anticipated. Mr. Martyn, later, gave me the manuscript. It was begun in a firm hand, but after a few verses, the writing became shaky, and the final stanzas were quite illegible.

Of course, it is only some, and they not very numerous among the popular lyrics, that are objectionable, and the singers have no thought that they are offending ears polite, when they mention in their songs and ballads matters not generally talked about, and when they call a spade " a spade " and not " an agricultural implement employed by gardeners." The relation of the sexes is the basis of most poetical compositions that circulate among the peasantry. " Its very intimacy," wrote Mr. C. J. Sharp, " and mystery cause many minds to shrink from expressing themselves openly on the subject, as they would shrink from desecrating a shrine. The ballad-maker has no such feeling. He has none of that delicacy, which, as often as not, degenerates into pruriency. Consequently, he treats ' the way of a man with a maid ' simply and directly, just as he treats every other subject." It is there-fore necessary for the editor to modify words, expressions, even statements of events recorded, so as to make the ballads and songs tolerable to men and women of culture. Burns, as already said, undertook this task for the Scottish songs. Sir Walter Scott did the same for the Border Ballads. The task had—and has—to be undertaken so as to rescue exquisite melodies from being killed by the words to which they are wedded. To do this, an editor must be imbued with the feeling of the folk-poet, and must divest himself of literary tricks. In a word, he must reverse the process of the early Stuart rhymers, who tricked out the ancient ballads with gew-gaws of their own fancy, and made them trip to unaccustomed measures.

Occasionally, but only rarely, do we obtain traces of early superstitious beliefs. There is a song sung throughout the South of England, entitled " At the Setting of the Sun." It tells how a young maiden went out one showery day, and, when the rain came on, threw a white apron over her head and hid behind some bushes. Her sweetheart happened to be out poaching, and seeing something white behind the hedge which he believed to be a swan, fired " and shot his true-love, at the setting of the sun." The lover was tried at the Assizes for the murder :

> " In six weeks' time when the 'sizes came on
> Young Polly appeared *in the form of a swan*,
> Crying, Jimmy, young Jimmy, young Jimmy is clear,
> He never shall be hung for the shooting of his dear."

But the ballad has in some cases undergone modification, and in place of the apparition of the dead girl in court in the form of a swan, she appears in that transformation in dream to her lover and foretells his acquittal.

A very popular ballad, often recovered in a fragmentary condition only, is " The Unquiet Grave." I have related in an earlier chapter the story of Joanna Worden, to whom a former lover appeared and demanded the love pledge he had given to her. The ballad evidently turns on the same conviction that when an engagement between a lad and a lass has been sealed by the gift of a token, or by a kiss, there is no release for the survivor till the pledge has been restored. The idea of the living appertaining to the dead is the foundation of Bürger's ballad of " Leonore."

The complete form of " The Unquiet Grave " is as follows : The eighth and last verses are my addition :

> " Cold blows the wind of night, sweet-heart
> Cold are the drops of rain ;
> The very first love that ever I had,
> In green-wood he was slain.

I'll do as much for my true love
   As any fair maiden may ;
I'll sit and mourn upon his grave,
   A twelvemonth and a day."

A twelvemonth and a day being up,
   The ghost began to speak :
' Why sit you here upon my grave,
   From dusk till dawning break ? '

' O think upon the garden, love,
   Where you and I did walk,
The fairest flower that blossomed there
   Is withered on its stalk.'

' What is it that you want of me
   And will not let me sleep ?
Your salt, salt tears they trickle down
   My winding sheet to steep.'

' Oh I will now redeem the pledge,
   The pledge that once I gave ;
A kiss from off thy lily-white lips
   Is all of you I crave.'

' Cold are my lips in death, sweet-heart,
   My breath is earthy strong.
If you do touch my clay-cold lips,
   Your time will not be long.' "

(Then through the mould he heaved his head
   And through the herbage green
There fell a frosted bramble leaf,
   It came their lips between.)

" Oh ! if you were not true in word,
   As now I know you be,
I'd tear you as the withered leaves
   Are torn from off the tree.

(And well for you that bramble leaf
   Betwixt our lips was flung.)
The living to the living hold ;
   Dead to the dead belong."

o

a May carol in France, whose melody had been adopted by the Church for an Easter hymn. The story of this melody is accordingly very instructive. It is a song to the coming of Spring of remote antiquity. Somewhere about the eleventh century it was adopted by the Church, and was sung as a sequence at Easter wherever the Latin Church prevailed, in England as in France. But although appropriated by the Church, it had not been discarded as a secular air, either in France or England. Then came the Reformation, and *O Filii et Filiæ* was no longer heard in church or minster. But the air as a secular melody lingered on for four centuries, till the publication of *Hymns Ancient and Modern*, in 1861, when once more the sequence was revived as *O, Sons and Daughters let us sing*, with its old tune as chanted in our churches before the Reformation.

When a new edition of *Songs of the West* was issued by Mr. Cecil Sharpe and myself in 1905, it was deemed by us advisable to omit " The Mallard " as a dance tune.

What an example of continued vitality in a good melody !

A man from whom we collected a great many songs, and whom I have already quoted, was Samuel Fone, of Black Down, in Mary Tavy parish. I cannot but think that he had gipsy blood in him. When he came to see me, he wore white trousers tied below the knee and a scarlet handkerchief about his neck. His father had deserted wife and children. One day the cottage door was partially opened, and a hand appeared holding it ; apparently the owner of the hand was doubtful whether to come in or retire without showing himself. Sam exclaimed to his mother : " This is father's hand ! " Instantly the hand was withdrawn, and when Sam and his mother ran to the door, its owner had disappeared. They ascertained that the father had been seen in the neighbourhood, and had made inquiries about his family ; but was now gone, none knew whither, and no tidings of him ever after reached the family.

For some time before his death Fone was bed-ridden, and to his great delight, I lent him a thick folio of Broadside Ballads I had collected. His daughter said to me : " Oh dear, we wish you had not let him have that book. He sings all night long. As he turns a page and comes on words he knows, he shouts them with the tune, and mother and I can get no sleep."

Mr. Bussell and I went to Prince Town on one occasion and visited a bed-ridden, or partly bed-ridden man, who was well known as a singer. He was, however, up and dressed when we visited him and came downstairs and sang to us, among other songs, " John Barleycorn." After a while we left, and I forgot my pencil, which remained on the table. Next day I returned to the cottage and asked for the man. A grim woman scowled at me : " What do you mean coming here and getting my 'usband to zing his old drashy songs, when he ought to be preparing to meet his Saviour ? No, you shan't zee him. He's in bed and shail remain there. I've took away his trousers and burnt 'em so he must remain abed till he dies, and as to thicky pencil you axes about, I've chucked him into the vire after his trousers. I don't want nother you, nor nothin' of yours here." I suspect the poor old fellow had enjoyed his afternoon singing to us, as he had not enjoyed one for many years. It was happy for us that we caught him when we did, when his wife had gone marketing to Tavistock.

One New Year's Eve, Mr. Bussell and I were at the " Saracen's Head," an inn at Two Bridges, on Dartmoor. It has since become an important hotel. Then it was but a modest tavern. We sat in the kitchen in the evening, where a number of moor-men were gathered to drink in and welcome the New Year. One of the singers gave us " Barbara "—or, as he called her, Barbaroo-Allen, with some additional verses to those in print. This was capped by another, who sang " The Brown Girl," of a somewhat similar character, which I sent to Professor Child for his great work on the Ballad Songs of England and Scotland, and which he inserted therein. But the most delightful melody we then obtained was " The Bell-ringers." We learned something from the singers ; not to press these men to give more, at a time, than a limited number of songs, for they are inclined to mix the tunes.

At Post Bridge, in a rude cottage of granite blocks put together without mortar, and in the midst of a marsh, lived an old blind man, Jonas Coaker, who died in the spring of 1890. When Mr. Sheppard and I saw him he was aged eighty-three, and came downstairs for a few hours only in the day. He called himself " The Poet of the Moor," but there was not a glint of poetry in his compositions. They were bad jingles, void of ideas. From

There was a handsome old man named Hannaford, on the east side of the Moor, from whom we had several songs. He had two daughters of really extraordinary beauty. One was married to the lodge-keeper of the Hon. Richard Dawson at Holne ; the other came to us as parlour-maid, and she was a great attraction to the hunters whenever we had a meet in front of Lew House. But as she began to spread her toils about our groom, who was a married man, I found it advisable to send her away.

At Dartmouth I made the acquaintance of Miss Bidder of Stoke Fleming, daughter of the " Calculating Boy." She introduced me to a number of old women who had their songs, and as she was an accomplished musician, she was able to take down their melodies.

There was a song I was particularly anxious to recover, " The Oxen Ploughing." I could get the chorus in many places, but not the main part of the song. At last I heard that there was a man at Liskeard who knew it, so Mr. Sheppard and I went thither, and called at his house, to learn that he was dying, and could not be seen. However, I heard of a singer near Trebartha, in Cornwall, and drove there to see him. I found him cutting ferns in a field. I asked him if he knew " The Oxen Ploughing." He did. So I sat on a heap of cut fern and he on another and he sang it, and I after him, till I had got it by heart. All the way home, a drive of eighteen miles, I continued singing it till I reached Lew, and was able to note it down with the aid of my piano.

Mr. Bussell and I went to Fowey, in Cornwall, and put up at the quaint old inn of the " Lugger," kept by Mr. Varcoe. We heard that there were some singers among the navvies engaged on the line up to Lostwithiel. But the difficulty was to get them. I went to the station-master. " I will do all I can for you," said he, " you were so good to my brother-in-law." That same brother-in-law had come to Lew as schoolmaster, but had gone off his head and had run away. I rode after him and found him in Launceston where he was smashing his watch in the street. I got him back to Lifton and wired to his relations, and he was removed. Before the magistrates he behaved most strangely ; he assured us that a hole was bored through him, and that if we stooped and looked through his stomach we would be able to see the sun on the further side. I had done all I could for him, and his brother-in-law was willing to assist me ; and so Mr. Bussell and I had the navvies and got from them some songs, but they were not of much value. We had better luck with the harbour-master of Charlestown, who had been an old smuggler. He told us many yarns of old smuggling days and also sang us some good songs.

At Chagford, Mr. Bussell and I put up with the Perrots, well-known guides to the Moor. They kept a boarding-house, but some of the family were wheelwrights. They claimed descent from Sir John Perrot, natural son of King Henry VIII by Mary Berkley, who was afterwards wife of Thomas Perrot. She was a beautiful woman, and Perrot was old. Sir John was the living image of his father. He was one of the four appointed to uphold the canopy over Queen Elizabeth at her Coronation. He was made Lord-deputy of Ireland in 1584, but having uttered a gross and insulting remark relative to the Queen, was recalled in disgrace and committed to the Tower under a charge of high treason, and there he died in 1592. The Perrots of Chagford have their coat-of-arms emblazoned, and their pedigree framed and hung up in the house.

The organist of Chagford parish church was a blind man. We invited him and several others who were said to be singers to dine with us, and after the meal, with a bowl of punch on the table, the singing began. We here obtained a good haul. Mr. Hurrell, the organist, sang to us " Barley Straw," which he had learned from a carpenter, William Beare, fifteen years before. The air is fine and robust, but Mr. Sheppard was obliged to rewrite the words, softening down what was indecorous. Another capital song was " In Bibberly Town,"[1] sung by John Bennett, a day labourer, aged sixty-eight. The words were vulgar, the point being that a tinker goes round the country and kisses all the girls he meets who pay him with " guineas of gold " for these kisses, and he drinks the guineas away in the tavern. There was a spice of impropriety in the song, and for publication Mr. Sheppard had to re-write it. We were fortunate as well to get a correct version of " I Rode my Little Horse," from John Bennett. We had obtained the words before from Edmund Fry, of Lydford, but his tune was faulty. So also we got " Tobacco is an Indian

---

[1] By Bibberly Town no doubt Beverley was meant.

remote part of the Southern Appalachians. " The region is poor, and owing to its inaccessibility a very secluded one. There are but few roads—most of them little better than mountain tracks— and practically no railroads. Indeed, so remote and shut off from outside influence were, until quite recently, these sequestered mountain valleys that the inhabitants have for a hundred years or more been completely isolated and cut off from all traffic with the rest of the world. Their speech is English, not American." Now from among these colonists, Mr. Sharp and his fellow-worker, Mrs. Campbell, have collected 122 different sets of words and 450 tunes. And the words are almost all familiar ballads and songs that have been sung by our English peasantry. And the tunes possess the same musical peculiarities that do most of ours.[1]

In 1907 Mr. Cecil J. Sharp wrote : " The subject of English folk-song has recently been very prominently before the public. Twenty years ago, however, it was only by a very few people that folk-songs were known to exist in this country ; and even they, probably, were quite unprepared for the developments that have since taken place. At that time, and for several years afterwards, it was generally assumed that we had no folk-songs of our own, and that the English peasant was the only one of his class in all Europe who was unable to express himself in terms of dance and song. How, in the face of facts as we now know them, such an amazing misconception could have originated, obtained credence, and escaped disproof for so many years, is an enigma which we will not here attempt to explain. . . . Folk-songs, genuinely and demonstrably English, have already been gathered in their hundreds, and of a quality at least as remarkable as their number. The work of collection, too, on any comprehensive scale, has only just begun. The larger part of rural England is still virgin soil, while, of those districts that have already been visited, very few have, as yet, been explored with any degree of thoroughness."[2]

When I began collecting I wrote to a rector who was musical, to learn whether he had any song-men in his parish. He replied to me : " None whatever. Never was there a parish where was less music to be found." In spite of this deterrent opinion, I went there

---

[1] Campbell (O. D.) and Sharp (C. J.) : English Folk-songs from the Southern Appalachians, New York, 1917.
[2] Sharp (C J.) : *English Folk-song : Some Conclusions*, Novello and Co., 1907.

and opened in it a most profitable mine. As already intimated, folk-songs are not to be collected from the farmers ; and what is more, they are unaware that their labourers possess any ballads and songs. One young farmer in Chagford, to whom I applied for directions to the cottage of a couple of old brothers-in-law who worked for him, and who, I had been told, possessed a treasure of song, burst out laughing, and said : " Stoneman and his brother-in-law, singers ! Nothing of the sort. Know naught." However, Mr. Bussell and I went to their cottage. A cauldron over the fire contained their dinner : a bit of fat bacon, potatoes, and carrots and turnips galore. Whilst that was cooking, the old fellows sang to us a dozen valuable ancient pieces with their ripe melodies.

There are two kinds of airs, those which have been composed by individual musicians, and which can be traced to them, and the folk melodies, which cannot be traced ; like Topsy, " they have growed." They are the expression of the minds, artistic sense, and feelings of the people, just as truly as are the songs of thrush, blackbird and nightingale. This is largely Mr. Sharp's doctrine. He says : " Once establish the fact that the folk-song has not been made by the one but evolved by the many, and its national character and its fitness to serve a national purpose follow as a natural consequence. Musicians would then no longer place ' Tom Bowling ' and ' The Seeds of Love ' in the same category, but perceive that they typify, respectively, two distinct species of music, that differ not in degree but in kind."

I have already mentioned how that so many of the folk-airs are in the Gregorian modes. Those of Parsons were so for the most part. I will quote Mr. Cecil J. Sharp, as he is a musician and I am not.

" English folk-tunes are cast in the Dorian, Phrygian, Mixo-lydian, Æolian and Ionian (major) modes and occasionally in the minor. Personally, I have never recovered an English folk-tune in the minor mode, and very few have been recorded by other collectors. Minor folk-airs, are no doubt, Æolian airs that have been modernized by the addition of a leading note.

" The majority of our English folk-tunes, say two-thirds, are in the major or Ionian mode. The remaining third is fairly evenly divided between the Mixolydian, Dorian and Æolian modes.

" With many folk-singers the proportion of modal songs is

What Dryden says of the faculty of appreciating true wit and poetry applies as well to the power of relishing good music. He remarks how that the rabble at a play prefer " the husk and rind of wit," prefer a quibble, a conceit, a vulgar *double entendre* to solid sense and elegant expression. " They are but a sort of French Huguenots, or Dutch boors, brought over in herds, but not naturalized ; who have not lands of two pounds *per annum* in Parnassus, and therefore are not privileged to poll. And those who curry favour with them, and are most admired by them, are as truly fine actors, artists and men of genius as mountebanks or the masters of the ceremonies in a bear garden. But it often happens, to their mortification, that as their admirers improve their stock of sense they soon forget them."

Happily, at the present hour there are musicians of real freshness and merit among us who are diving into the old cisterns of Elizabethan and Stuart music, and of folk-music as well, for inspiration. The latter furnish them with a well-spring of purest melody, the former supply superb examples of harmony. Perhaps the first to lead the way of exploration was Sullivan. At the time when I was working on the folk-music of Devon and Cornwall, I spent days in the British Museum, examining the old published music there, as well as the printed garlands of words, to discover if possible the origin of the tunes and the ballads circulating among our people. One of the librarians told me : " Sullivan is often here, doing much the same as you. But he is searching for musical *ideas*, whereas you are in quest of relationships of melodies and words."

But Sullivan, though he picked up a certain number of ideas for modern use, did not go back far enough. The sources he went to were too late, Hanoverian, or of Queen Anne's date at the earliest. That was too recent. The finest period of English music was in the Tudor and Stuart reigns ; and, alas ! much of what was then produced was scattered and lost in the time of Puritan supremacy. Nevertheless a certain amount remains. And, as in architecture we have quitted Palladian design and have reverted to Gothic and early Renaissance, so it must be with regard to our music if it is to become national and precious.

To produce a melody, that has in it life, is a creative art. It may, however, be crude, and demand expansion, refinement and

development. It is the same with poetry. An idea is a falling
star, but a star that is not necessarily quenched in its fall. The
poetic idea may not always be perfect in form and emphatic in
expression, and this must serve as my excuse for the manner in
which I have dealt with some of the lyrics I have obtained from
illiterate country folk. We must strive to catch the thought and
to divest it of such vulgarisms as it has acquired in its passage
through many minds and mouths. The stream of water is there,
but choked with dead and decaying leaves and with weeds. Surely
it is justifiable to clear the channel and let the limpid and original
idea flow unobstructed. I was specially impressed with this idea
when I was at South Zeal collecting traditional songs and music.
From two old men I obtained " The Flowery Land of Canaan."
Both set the words to the same melody, but the words did not
agree, although the main thought was perceptible through sundry
and strange accretions, through misconceptions and local inser-
tions, due to forgetfulness of the original, and to clumsy repairs.

I took the leading idea, and recast the song as follows, pre-
serving the uncouth and irregular rhyme :

" I'll sing you a little song, as we trudge the way along,
  Tho' the darkness on the daylight's gainin' ;
The wind is in my face, and though flaggin' is my pace,
  Yet I'm walkin' to the flow'ry land of Canaan.

The darkness and the rain, in the narrow miry lane,
  Are a trouble. There's no profit in complainin',
For the lane will be o'er past, and the sky no more o'ercast,
  When we come out in the flow'ry land of Canaan.

There's little Jim and Joe, and Baby Pol, I know,
  At the end their hands to me are strainin',
Sayin', ' Never mind, old dad, tho' the way be foul and bad,
  All is smoothness in the flow'ry land of Canaan.'

So I will not look behind, but will face the beatin' wind,
  Never dream of here in darkness remainin',
But will stagger wi' my pack full o' troubles on my back,
  To shake it off in the flow'ry land of Canaan.
        So, mates, cheerily on,
    Jolly thro' the days that are wanin',
        Never mind the weather
        As we jog along together,
    Looking forward to the flow'ry land of Canaan."

uninteresting : the inside is Lombardic with old frescoes and much exquisite white marble Italian Gothic sculpture-tombs, altar-pieces, etc. I had not much time, so could not see all ; but it is very fascinating.   Yours truly,

S. BARING GOULD.

GENOA,

MY DEAR G.,   *Feb.* 17, 1889.

Here, as in France, the linings of the almuces worn by the clergy in choir vary according to the church to which they belong. In the church of S. Maria della Vergine here they are of white rabbit skin lined with carnation : at the cathedral of S. Lorenzo the lining is purple. In both churches the minor canons wear grey fur (Belgian hare ?). In the cathedral the canons' cassocks are carnation-coloured and of silk : the seminarists wear purple cloth cassocks with scarlet cuffs and collars.

The services at S. Lorenzo are dignified, but unmusical, that is, sung with merely the accompaniment of a small organ. About half the seminarists lead the singing which is Plain-song, without instruments or paid singers. There is nothing operatic either at Mass or Vespers. The seminarists occupy the structural choir.

It is very delightful to take a walk round the old walls of Genoa that crown the heights above the town and command glorious views. The towers are in ruins, with tufts of wall-flowers and stocks sprouting out between the stones : of course these are not in flower just now.

There are places in the Gulf of Genoa where well up streams of fresh water, so that vessels needing a supply can furnish themselves with any amount without coming to the shore. This is due to the rain that falls on the huge tract of limestone on the French and Italian Riviera. The rain drains down into vast subterranean reservoirs, finds its way by channels underground and under the sea, and bursts at the first outlet in great volume, which the sailors recognize by the colour of the water. How many sweet springs there are in the human soul, as well as in the great sea of humanity, welling up amidst much that is bitter and salt with tears !   I remain,

Yours truly,   S. BARING-GOULD.

JAMES GOULD
From an Oil Painting

My dear G.,   *Feb.* 28, 1889.

I cannot quite understand their ways here. Septuagesima
Sunday was observed with great pomp at the cathedral, with
purple frontals and vestments. Tuesday was a high day with
pontifical mass and white vestments. On Sexagesima Sunday
the High Mass was quite mean and without even decent singing.

The Sunday Schools in Genoa are on their last legs. In the
cathedral there are but two classes, composed of children under
twelve years old, ten little girls in one class, eight boys in the
other. The Sunday Schools are no better attended in the parish
churches. The classes in the cathedral on Septuagesima Sunday
were conducted by a seminarist and a canon. Last Sunday the
girls' class was taught by a layman ; and, as no teacher turned up
for the boys, they played for an hour, pinching each other, kicking
one another's shins, and then straggled out of the church regardless of Vespers, that were being sung with incense fuming in the
choir, at the back of the high altar. There is certainly slackness
here, and a lack of zeal. I trust that the presence of the
Waldensian heretics will be the means of prodding the clergy into
activity.

Genoa itself is not a beautiful town, as far as buildings go. Its
glory is in its surroundings. There is grand scenery when one
gets out of the half-crater in which the place lies. But to get outside means a scramble of near 2000 feet, unless one takes the
tram to San Pier d'Arena and the Campo Santo. Along the
two valleys in which these lie is one continuous street five miles
long. Beauty is found in keeping to the heights around, and there
the views are superb.

The Campo Santo is crowded with monuments in Carrara
marble, all execrable in taste, showing that Italian art, at all
events as far as sculpture is concerned, is beneath contempt.
There is one representing the departed husband with the widow
standing by with a parasol over her head, all delicately cut out of
the beautiful white stone. I do not think I saw one tolerable
monument in the whole cemetery.

Ruskin complained of Italian modern painting as utterly
debased. The music is not much better.

We have now cold weather but bright sun : the wind is from

the north-east, not strong but cold, and there has been frost at
night so that icicles were formed along the edges of the fountains.

I had a lovely walk to Madonna della Guardia on Friday.
There was a glorious view there over the Apennines, a splendid
scene of tumbled mountain peaks, some of the heights well bedded
in snow. Away to the north-west were the glittering glaciers
and white peaks of the Savoy Alps.

This inn is fair, only fair. It is clean, which is something, but
the feeding is monotonous, no outbreak of fresh ideas ; and
imagination is as needful in a cook as in a poet. The beds are
good, comfortable and clean. The *pension* price is 8 francs a
day : enough for what one gets.

I do not see much beauty in the Genoese women ; there is a
good deal of brown hair, very little of the special Italian type of
feature.

In the fish shops octopus are offered for sale, ghastly pink
objects, with staring eyes—no soul speaking out of them, any
more than out of the orbs of certain in the human order—and
with tentacles stretching and groping and coiling about whatever
comes in their way, and can be hoped to be edible. Only the legs
are eaten, not the sepia bag. They are leathery and tasteless.

S. BARING-GOULD.

CONVENT DE STA. CROCE, ROME,

March 13*th*, 1889.

MY DEAR G.,

I came on to Rome, and where do you think I am lodged ?
In a convent. When at Genoa I wrote to a friend in Freiburg to
ask if she could recommend where to go in the Eternal City ;
where, in fact, in the event of a return of influenza I might be
cared for, she replied by return of post : " Go to the Third
Order Sisters of S. Francis in the Via di San Basilio." I wrote to
the Superior (Sister Fabiola) and she expressed her readiness to
take me in at 7 lira per diem. On arriving I found an iron gate
with beggars swarming outside, waiting for soup and broken
viands. It seems that the Sisterhood possessed land and vineyards and with the proceeds kept up an orphanage and school.
But the Government has seized their estates and they are compelled to keep a *pension* for their own maintenance and that of the

orphanage. I was kindly received and given a very clean and cheerful room. There is a considerable number of guests lodging here of all nations and languages, except English. I am the sole representative of Britain.

I have made the acquaintance of a Baron Bentinck, who is a Dutchman, a Catholic and residing permanently at the convent. He is a man of about seventy. I asked him if he belonged to the Duke of Portland's family. "Excuse me," he replied, "he belongs to mine."

The sisters wait on us at table, but otherwise we see nothing of them. The wine is good—or fairly so—and not charged extra ; but Baron Bentinck knows at what osterias the best Asti is to be found, and as we go walks together daily he takes me to them.

I have been on Sunday to the Uniat Armenian Church. The service is most striking. There are two veils hiding the altar : the outer one of green baize, the inner one of muslin. The choir stands without facing east, clad in remarkable coloured dresses, and singing very fast tunes, that seem to me to partake of the character of music-hall melodies. Presently the thick veil is sharply drawn aside and one sees the lights on or about the altar. Then after a while the muslin veil is withdrawn and the priest is revealed in purple and gold cope, with a crown on his head, running towards us to give benediction. He was a singularly handsome man, much like the traditional representations of our Lord. With the exception of the sacristan I was the only one in the congregation. Actually the church belongs to the Armenian college, and the attendants are students who stand in the choir.

At S. Peter's the service is performed in a side chapel behind glass doors. One may enter and stand against the door and listen to the squalling of the eunuchs, gross creatures. I do not, I cannot appreciate S. Peter's. To my mind it is immeasurably inferior to our S. Paul's, not only in dignity and religious feeling, but in its architectural features. To think how in order to meet the vast cost of the erection, a sum of ten million pounds, Popes Julius XI and Leo X were obliged to hawk indulgences about Europe, thereby leading in a great measure to the Reformation ! I detest the church ; every stone in it has cost a human soul. Frederika Bremer was quite right when she said : "The exterior and the interior of the building appear to me more like an apotheosis of the Popedom than a glorification of Christianity and its doctrine." "As to the beauty of the temple," wrote Mr. W. D. Howells, "I could not find it without or within."

I have been out to the villa of Livia at Tre Torre, in the atrium of which was found one of the very finest statues of Augustus. The palace has been excavated and reveals what is most delightful, the painting of the walls of the atrium representing a wood with a railing in front of it and flowers peeping through the bars, red anemones and narcissi. But what is most striking is the atmosphere of the painting, the delicate tints of the distant foliage as contrasted with the brighter hues of the trees near at hand.

I remain,

Yours truly,

S. BARING-GOULD.

One Wednesday morning I visited the Campo de' Fiori, a busy scene on that day, when it is crowded with peasants selling vegetables, also antiquities. I there bought at a very reasonable price a roll of lovely old Italian silk brocade, which I gave to my wife and she had made of it a gown for a dinner-party. This piazza was the scene of the most terrible *autos-da-fé* instituted by the Dominicans, in which Jews and Christian heretics were burnt alive.

I paid several visits to S. Peter's and came to dislike it more and more. The great church itself is like an opera house and makes on me no religious impression. Undoubtedly the portico, that is a later addition, spoils the effect from the East ; but from a distance S. Peter's is without dignity. As to the interior : that of S. Paul's is religious, that of S. Peter's smacks of the world. But what else could have been expected of the Pope and cardinals at its inception.

The most striking object in S. Peter's is the ring of ever-burning lamps about the *Confession* of SS. Peter and Paul, where are supposed to lie their bodies. But this is probably not the case. In August, 1846, the Saracens forced their way into the Borgo quarter of the Vatican and rifled the Vatican Church, and an annalist tells us that they violated the tomb of S. Peter, and that, though they could not carry away the great bronze sarcophagus, they scattered abroad all its contents. "Painful indeed," wrote

Mrs. Hemans, " would be the admission, whilst we contemplate the superb Confessional, amidst its crown of ever-burning lamps, under the high altar, that not even the dust of the Apostle can be supposed to remain at this day entombed under that pyramid of splendours."

Probably the relics there adored are no more than substitutes. The Church of Rome could not afford to be without the tombs of the Apostles, which draw crowds of pilgrims from all quarters of Europe to spend their money in Rome, and pour it into the treasury of the Church ; and Pope and cardinals without scruple would replace the dispersed ashes with any bones they could find.

The Court of Rome has always allowed the lowest fraud and imposture in the working system of the Church, and has suffered reason and faith to be shocked. The Reformers, on the other hand, were in deadly earnest ; and none of the " Churches " they founded, Lutheran or Calvinist, were ever guilty of the falsehoods and frauds at which Rome connived. They, at all events, had clean hands. The human mind at the Renaissance was entering on a new stage in its history ; and that great movement which has been steadily advancing ever since began then.

I went naturally to see Pasquino, and brought a little book containing his witty sayings. Pasquino was a tailor who kept a shop at a corner of the Braschi Palace. He was noted for his caustic and satirical sayings. He does not seem himself to have come to harm through them. After his death the name was transferred to a mutilated statue opposite his shop, and the wags of the day affixed to it their witticisms on passing events, and on prominent personages. Another statue at the foot of the Capitol went by the name of Marforio, and the two were supposed to dispute with one another.

It was not safe to comment on the Popes and their misdeeds when Rome was under the rule of the Church.

One morning, when Sixtus V was Pope, Pasquino was found to have donned a very dirty shirt. Whereupon Marforio inquired the reason. Pasquino next morning bore the answer : " Because my washerwoman has been created a princess." The allusion was to Camilla, sister of Pope Sixtus, who had done washing before her brother was raised to the purple. Thereupon Sixtus V published a proclamation that, on his faith as Pope, he

Q

would not only grant the writer his life, but also accord him two thousand pistoles. The author of the Pasquinade was fool enough to give himself up. Sixtus said to him : " I will keep my promise. I give you your life and the assured sum, but I will have both your hands cut off and your tongue transfixed with a red hot iron, to prevent your writing or uttering similar insolences for the future." And this sentence was executed.

On Alexander VI appeared the lines of Pasquino :

> " Vendit Alexander claves, altaria, Christum.
> Emerat ille prius, vendere jure potest."

When Julius II threw the keys of S. Peter into the Tiber, declaring that the sword of S. Paul was of more avail to him, the Pasquinade appeared :

> " Cum Petri nihil efficiant ad prœlia claves,
> Auxilio Pauli forsitan ensis erit."

One of the last was affixed during the stay of the French in Rome, by Marforio :

> " I Francesi son tutti ladri."

To which Pasquino answered :

> " Non tutti—Ma Buona parte."

I often visited the museum of ancient sculpture in the Vatican. One of the quaintest objects therein is the Family Tree. Of such there are three or four specimens. In the period of the decline of the Republic and the beginning of the Imperial government the families of the Roman nobles and senatorial houses were so small as to cause alarm, and, by order of Augustus, Carrara marble trees with nests in the boughs were required to be erected in the palaces of those nobles whose families numbered over three children. In the nests are perched little children. I give a sketch of one of them. The *paterfamilias* had been twice married. By his first wife, who was dead, he had two children ; by the second, who was alive, he had three.

The occasion was as follows, according to Eckhard's *Roman History*. Augustus, upon his return to Rome at the conclusion of a war, received complaints that too great a number of the young men of quality were unmarried. The Emperor thereupon assembled the whole Equestrian Order, and, having separated the married from the single, gave particular honours to the former, and told the bachelors " that their lives and actions had been so peculiar, that he could find no name by which to designate them ; not that of Men, for they performed nothing that was manly ; nor that of Citizens, for the city might perish for all they cared ; nor that of Romans, for their procedure was such as to extirpate the Roman name."

Interesting as well are bas-relief representations of various mechanical contrivances for hoisting the cargo into ships, and of elevators for building purposes. I was also struck with the bust of a Latin contadino in the classic period ; it might have been modelled from a peasant of the present day.

I was walking one day with the tutor in the palace of Prince Borghese, and I asked him to tell me frankly what would be the result were the temporal power restored to the Pope, or, at least, if Rome itself were made over to him. " Revolution on the morrow," was his answer, " and unless the Holy Father managed to escape, he would be tarred and feathered. Romans are not so short of memory as to have forgotten the condition of affairs in the States of the Church till the Papal rule was abolished." I asked the same question of Baron Bentinck, and of him received, sorrowfully confessed, the same reply. I questioned on the same matter a German Catholic priest, long resident in the Eternal City. He admitted that the restoration was absolutely impossible.

One of the saddest pictures presented in the history of the Church is that of the condition of the States of the Church under Papal rule. It exhibited systematic and purposeful degradation of the people, intellectually, socially, politically and morally. To stultify his subjects appears to have been the aim of the successor of S. Peter.

What excuse can be made for the encouragement of gambling by the Popes, whose tiara and cross keys surmount the stalls for the sale of lottery tickets ? What exculpation can be afforded for the sale of a monopoly to a barber in the Via Papale enabling him to set up over his door : Qui si castrono li cantori della Cappelle Papali ? The Albano princes purchased the right to make pins, and whosoever ventured to import papers of pins was punished by fines and a flogging.

Nothing could be more rotten to the core than the government of the States of the Church. The highest offices were filled by prelates ; but these prelates needed not to be in priest's orders. They were under no ecclesiastical disabilities, except only that they were forbidden to marry. The consequence was that they had mistresses, and some were known to maintain harems. In most of the great families there was a provision, called the *Prelatura*, set apart for the second son, whose destination was a well-paid office under the Pope. The cardinals were selected from the prelates, but were not necessarily priests. Consalvi was not, nor was Antonelli. Such men filled all offices only to mismanage them, and were not called to give an account of their stewardship.

When Pio Nono was restored by French bayonets, he promised an amnesty to the Republicans ; but a Papal promise is like pie-crust. He crowded the prisons with those who had risen against his misrule, and would have sent them by hundreds to the scaffold had not the French prevented the executions by providing those doomed to death with passports from the English resident, Mr. Freeborn.

In June, 1846, Mr. Whiteside wrote : " It is a painful reflexion how different the political rule of the Popes has been from what we might expect. The Pope, chosen from the College of the Cardinals, is generally a man advanced in life, supposed to possess learning and virtue, to be free from pride and adverse to profligate and corrupting pursuits. One might suppose such a sovereign, selected on the score of personal merits, peculiarly fitted to promote the happiness of his subjects.

" The reverse has unfortunately proved to be the fact. The dominions of the Papacy have been notoriously ill-governed ; the inhabitants are miserable. The vice of the system seems to consist in the personal character of the government. The sovereign being elective has no connexion with his predecessor, nor care for his successor ; nor can he guess who that successor may be. The whole administration changes with the Pope. A new set of ministers and officials comes into power, whose chief business it is to grasp all that is possible during the brief tenure of political existence. Love of country or disinterested patriotism is not even pretended. Profound dissimulation and unbounded selfishness characterize the Papal Court. No man's real disposition becomes known till he has clutched his prize : then his true nature becomes manifest. A political government of this description is fraught with incalculable evils. The people's interests, liberties and happiness become the sport of scheming adventurers, hypocrites and bigots ; and if occasionally a statesman of capacity and honesty appears, he is beset with difficulties and ultimately overthrown. Such a political system could not be reformed ; it must be radically changed."

Sir Edward Dicey's *Rome in 1860* fully confirms the above.

Every Roman, except the few whose interest binds them to the Vatican, feels precisely as did Mr. Whiteside and Sir Edward Dicey. I have seen the pupils of the various ecclesiastical colleges at Rome, walking two and two, under the guidance of their priestly tutors in the street when the royal carriage drove by. Every Roman and foreigner raised his hat, save these cubs, who studiously ignored the King and the Queen, or else insultingly thrust out their tongues from their mouths at them.

One can understand a feeling of dissatisfaction entertained at the change of government and of hostility felt towards the House of Savoy, but these ill-conditioned youths chose to exhibit their anti-national sentiments before the eyes of the Roman people and feed their hostility against " the black army."

Under the new regime some great mistakes have been made, but not such as affect the welfare of the people. For the first time in history real efforts have been made to ameliorate their condition, to educate their minds, to give them a desire to work and to quicken their self-respect. A mighty change such as the regeneration of a degraded people cannot be achieved in a score of years. The result of centuries of debasement and stultification, deliberately and remorselessly pursued, cannot be obliterated in a couple of generations, but a beginning has been made, and the dawn is brightening. One can see it in the faces of the people. A new, honest, and free world is opened to them. At first they are dazed, as was the prisoner of the Bastille when he was brought into the sunshine and the fetters were struck off his feet, but in time there will be recovery, for there is much elasticity and recuperative power in the Italian character. The basest of all is the Neapolitan, but even there some germs of a better life are showing.

The visitor to the English cemetery outside the gate of S. Paolo will doubtless be struck by the fact that the inscriptions on the monuments of the dead, before the fall of the Papacy, fail to express any Christian hope for the departed. This was due to the Papal censor, to whom the inscriptions had to be submitted before the monuments were erected. There could be no hope of salvation, and no prospect of Resurrection to Eternal Life for a Protestant, so argued the censor.

An English lady of some position died during the pontificate of Gregory, and her husband submitted the epitaph to the Papal censor. It expressed a hope through Christ for the departed. He drew his pen through it and forbade its reproduction. On the accession of Pius IX the bereaved husband made application to have the desired inscription added. The application was made to the *Liberal* Pope, and was presented by Archdeacon Beresford. The petition was refused. It was declared to be impossible to comply with a request that implied a hope, a possibility of acceptance by the Saviour, of one who had died out of communion with the Roman Church.

As to the religious condition of the people, I heard a good deal about it. Now that the Papal despotism was at an end, and the populace were not divided into the two classes of the spies and the spied upon, priests as well as laymen were not reluctant to express their opinions. All gave the result of their observations and experience with singular unanimity. The popular religion, according to them, is mere superstition, in no way conducing to morality, honesty, truth. The faith of the people consists of a jumble of ideas in which promiscuously are mixed S. Peter, some local saint, the Almighty and, above all, the Blessed Virgin. As Madre di Deo she is supreme, and if the Almighty refuses her requests, she will not give Him the breast. The priests make no attempts to raise the people morally and spiritually. They are content to get them to hear Mass on Sundays and Festivals, to fast in Lent, to go periodically to Confession, and to buy Masses for their dead parents. This, however, only applies to the States of the Church and to Naples. It seems to be the general opinion that the further from Rome, the better is the quality of religion, and the more zealous and pious are the clergy. This is certainly true to the north. In Piedmont, Savoy and Tuscany there is a much purer and more moral Christianity taught and practised, and the parish priests on the whole are men of blameless lives, earnest and devout.

The observance and the attraction of the Holy Week services in Rome have been vastly overrated. The cardinals, bishops, clergy and laity take little interest in them. They are tedious, and consist more in the glorification of the Pope by undressing him, dressing him, kneeling to him and fanning him, than in the worship of Christ.

The Tenebræ service on Maundy Thursday is very tedious. It is rattled through as quickly as the choir can chant, and during the *Miserere* a couple of hundred of little mops are distributed to the priests and singers. The psalm ended, the mop-bearers march up in procession, two and two, to the High Altar, and wipe the bare slab with their mops.

The washing of the Apostles' feet is equally unedifying. Instead of there being twelve representatives, there are thirteen, due to a foolish legend relative to S. Gregory the Great. The Pope nominates two, the others receive their appointment from the various ambassadors. The sole requisite for these men is the possession of a flowing beard.

Formerly, on Good Friday, a huge illuminated cross was suspended from the dome in S. Peter's, but this was discontinued by Leo XII because of the rowdy element that filled the church, more intent on picking pockets than on attending to the service.

I have given with some fullness an account of my stay in Florence in the introductory chapter of my book *In Troubadour Land*, 1890.

On leaving Florence I went to Bologna, from which town I wrote the following letter to Gatrill :

ALBERGO TRÉ RE.,

My dear G.,   *March* 21, 1889.

I have got as far as Bologna on my way home, and hope to be back in England on All Fool's Day. I am charmed with this city : such an interesting pile of churches clustered into one lump is San Stephano—seven in all, of which one, SS. Peter and Paul is an early basilica, originally Byzantine, then enlarged in Lombard times to include the tomb of S. Vitalis. Adjoining is a Lombardic San Sepulcro, and two series of cloistered courts of the quaintest and most picturesque description, also an old crypt ; the other churches have been more or less modernised. The museum also is interesting with its Etruscan tombs and a very good collection of old musical instruments, theorobo, psaltery, lute, viol de gamba, sordine, etc., which I have been sketching this afternoon. The leaning towers here are very strange : one is 10 feet out of the perpendicular, but the other only 4 feet : they adjoin and lean in different directions. I got a little tired of Florence. The exterior of the Cathedral is lovely and the galleries are intensely interesting, but that is all. I like Bologna better by far, more to see in it, and more early work. I go on to-morrow to Chiasso, and on Saturday to Faido, where I think of spending a week. I am tired of towns and want to get into the country for Alpine flowers and hills. In Italy all roads are walled up on both sides, and you go through miles of walls before you get clear of the town. This is wearying.

Yours truly,

S. BARING-GOULD.

CHAPTER XVII

ROME REVISITED
1890

WHEN I had been at Rome previously I had worked at the Catacombs, and on this occasion I had made a resolve to study the portrait-busts of the Emperors, for I had in my head a scheme for writing a book on the Cæsars from Julius to Nero.

I left England on January 21, 1890, and made my way direct to Rome. If I had reckoned on seeing the Carnival with the horse-races in the Corso, I would have been disappointed. The Carnival at Rome at present is very different from what it was in the times of Papal misgovernment, and the Corso races have been abolished.

These races, by the way, had a remarkable origin. They were instituted by Pope Paul II in 1468, as he thought to combine outrage to the Jews with amusement to the Christians. He ordered that a procession should open the Carnival, led by a body of Jewish elders in shirt and doublet, followed by a cavalcade of Roman senators. Then these Jews were to race on foot along the Corso from the tomb of Domitian, by the Porta del Popolo, to the church of S. Marco in the Piazza di Venetia ; Jews, asses, buffaloes and horses running in a promiscuous crowd, helter-skelter, to the laughter and howls of the Italians lining the street, and pelting the runners, men and beasts, with opprobrious epithets. This degrading spectacle was witnessed by noble ladies and purple-robed cardinals, whilst the Pope himself looked on from his decorated balcony, applauding and shaking his sides with laughter. To add to the enjoyment, later Popes devised additional humiliations to which the Hebrews were to be subjected. They were ordered to run stark naked, save for a narrow loin-cloth, with a rope round their necks. Thus was it continued for

233

being eaters, talkers and nothing more. Signora Sopranzé is always on the brink of bankruptcy, and anon recovering from it, as the guests pay their bills. We know when that takes place, because at the ensuing meal, meringues are served up. The instant that the dish of these sweets is seen to enter the *salle*, the whisper runs down the table : " Who has paid his bill ? "

The main difficulty with our good hostess is that she has settled on her a Piedmontese marquis and his wife and two grown-up daughters. They have been here since the beginning of January and have not paid one lira. They came from Florence, where they had also lived in an impecunious condition at a *pension*, and had ruined the proprietor. Our kindly hostess was afraid to turn them out, lest, by so doing, she might offend the Roman nobility, and thus lose their recommendation. So the English guests in the *pension* have to pay in advance weekly. Sometimes Signora Sopranzé has not enough money in her purse to supply the dinner, unless helped. I would go elsewhere but that the company amuses me vastly.

The Marchesa is a big, uproarious woman with fine Italian dark eyes and hair ; she is ever on the shout ; and her daughters are equally vociferous and smoke cigarettes in the *salon*, flirting with a young South Italian marquis and a Neapolitan count. This latter, curiously enough, is a Conte Sabini.

In the evening they dance, or play cards, but none cares to take a pack with the Lombardy marchioness, as, if she loses, she cannot pay, and, if she wins, she exacts payment to the last *soldo*. The marquis has a heavy, depressed countenance, but with a flexibility in the muscles that shows he can put on an insinuating smile upon occasion. He is usually out of the *pension* during the day " on business," as the Marchioness tells us. On his return at meal-time she raises her eyebrows and puts on a questioning look that is answered by a slight shake of the head and a droop of the corners of his mouth. I have no doubt in my mind that he has been visiting sundry noble Roman families soliciting loans, and has met with refusals. Once I saw him approach the Jew, with the most urgent expression on his face. The Hebrew's quick eye noted this. At once he put his thumbs through the arm-holes of his waistcoat and extending his palms and fingers flapped them much as a fish works its fins. The

Marchese saw the action and backed, much as a subject would from the face of a king, with fallen jowl.

The French Abbé is plump and by no means ascetic. He had been a soldier and had visited Japan and Ceylon. What induced him to take Holy Orders is a puzzle to me. At table he tells stories, not always very delicate, whereat the young Italian counts and the two girls explode with laughter, and the Benedictine monk looks scandalized. I find that the Abbé has got into trouble with his Bishop, and that he has come to Rome to try to get the Bishop's sentence reversed by the Pope. He has some acquaintance with one of the cardinals and was invited to dine with His Eminence one evening. He returned to the *pension* in the cardinal's carriage, accompanied by His Eminence's brother, who, as the Abbé told me, throughout the drive had been endeavouring to worm facts out of him relative to himself and his deprivation.

"Now," said the Abbé to me, "I want you to give me your candid opinion. Do you think I had better return to France and patch up my difference with the Bishop, or should I remain here awhile? You see, the Pope is getting on in years and is very infirm. Who can say that my cardinal may not be elected as his successor? And then I am a made man."

"My dear friend," replied I, "from what I have seen of you, I feel convinced that you, with your poetic, conversational and anecdotal gifts, would be utterly thrown away upon the peasants in a remote village of Provence; whereas, in my opinion, you are cut out to shine in a brilliant circle in such a city as this."

"That is precisely my own opinion," shouted he, slapping my knee. "I shall stay in Rome."

Yesterday the Abbé told us that he had been crying all the morning, and when asked the reason of his sorrow, answered that he had had nothing to do and no one to go out for a walk with.

The young Benedictine monk has a face like an angel. He is in deacon's orders only. His name in religion is Notker. I asked him after which Notker he was named, Notker Labeo or Notker Balbulus? He stared and said: "What do you know about the Notkers?" "I know much, especially about Balbulus, for I have read the delightful life of him by Eckhardt. Why," I went on, "was it not he as he was watching the erection of a bridge over the chasm of the Martinstobel and saw the peril to which the workmen were exposed, who composed the famous sequence *Media vita in morte sumus?* and do we not have it recited at every funeral in England ? " (In the midst of life we are in death ; of whom then may we seek for succour but of Thee, O Lord ?) " Well ! " exclaimed Brother Notker, " when I gave my name to the Professor of Ecclesiastical History here, who is examining me for priest's orders, he asked me where I had picked up such an outlandish name. The saying is quite true that is current beyond the Rhine : ' Ein Esel in Deutschland ist ein Professor in Rom.' " (An ass in Germany is a professor in Rome.)

We soon became intimate friends and went daily walks together. Not only so, but he insisted on my forestalling his examination from the text-books in history and theology, upon which he would be questioned by the examiners.

He purposed saying his first Mass at Subiaco, and wanted me to go there with him, after his ordination, and assist at it. This I would gladly do, but that I must get home early to work away at my *Lives of the Saints*.

He cannot abide the French Abbé, and when he sees the fellow dancing in the *salle* with his scapular flying behind him, he retires in haste to his own room and to his studies.

I am working diligently at the portraits of the Emperors. They deserve attentive study. I suspect that casts were taken of their faces. All the early Cæsarean family have the left eye not as near the nose as is the right eye. Had the portraits been idealized this would have not been so.

One of the loveliest and most engaging of all the faces is that of the youthful Caligula. Poor boy ! he was stunted in his intellectual growth, and had no moral growth whatever. He was epileptic and probably scrofulous. There are indications of glandular swellings in the necks of several of the family.

PENSION SOPRANZÈ,
VIA CAMPO MARZIO, 69, ROMA,
April 15, 1890.
MY DEAR GATRILL,

There has been a fracas here. Poor Signora Sopranzé was no longer able to house and feed all the family of the Lombard marquis, so she announced that they must turn out. Whereupon the Marchesa spilt a cup of scalding coffee over her foot, blistering it. And the tender-hearted Signora could not possibly show her out of the door in this condition, and the Marquis and the Signorinas could not tear themselves away from the suffering wife and madre, so a compromise has been reached. The Signora will give them leave to lodge beneath her roof, but will no longer feed any save the lamed duck. So now for breakfast and dinner the lawyer who is managing the affairs of the Marquis comes to the door of the *pension* and rings. Whereupon the Marquis and his two daughters sally forth with the solicitor to a restaurazione to be there fed at his expense.

An additional sensation connected with this family has cropped up. It appears that the Conte Sabini has for long been engaged to a cousin at Naples. Her family got wind of how he was carrying on with the two girls of the Marchesa here, and accordingly the brother of the intended came plump in upon us when we were at breakfast, and with much bluster called on the Conte to give him satisfaction. The Conte replied that he would talk the matter over when he had done his veal cutlet. Accordingly, having demolished this, all but the bone, he wiped his mouth, rose and retired to the *salon* with the intended bride's brother, where they arranged to fight a duel on the same evening with swords.

When the encounter occurred, the Conte received a scratch and shed ten drops of blood, and then promised to leave the *pension* and see no more of the two girls. He, moreover, confided to his intended brother-in-law, that he really did not care for either, as both were scrofulous, and neither of them more than passable in looks. But this has been a cruel blow to the Marchesa, who had calculated on marrying one of her daughters to the Conte, who is reported to be rich, and the lady has been pacifying her creditors with promises of payment "so soon as my daughter marries the Conte, which will be shortly." The lawyer is turning restive. The feeding of the family is costly, and where is he to look for a return, now that the chance with the Neapolitan Count is gone ?

I have been interested this winter in following the excavations at the church of SS. John and Paul. The Clivus Scauri runs up rather steeply, and is a narrow lane. On the left side is a huge

wall, that of the church, which was built by Pope Adrian IV,
the only English Pope there has been. It is served by the
Passionist fathers. Now the Padre Germano, one of them,
looking often and hard at this great windowless, blank wall,
thought he perceived traces of blocked up windows in stories
one above the other, very much as if the front had been that
of a modern factory. Then the idea shot up in his head that
here was actually the face of an ancient Roman house, unique,
for no other exists entire in Rome or in Pompeii. Thereupon
he obtained leave, and collected money to dig under the existing
church, where appeared indications of a bricked-up doorway.
He very soon discovered that he had unearthed the ground
floor of an ancient Roman mansion. Through this, when the
upper church was built, had been driven substructures to
sustain the mass above ; but by circumventing these supports,
by degrees the whole of the plan was revealed.

Now John and Paul had been chamberlains to Constantia,
daughter of Constantine the Great. For some reason not very
clear, they had incurred the anger of Julian the Apostate, who
ordered their murder, to be executed secretly in the bath or
cellar of their own house. This was done, but it leaked out
that they had been put to death by Julian's order, and a wild
legend grew up about their story, so wild and grotesque was it
that doubts arose whether any such martyrs had actually existed.
Their deaths took place in 362 ; the next year Julian himself
died. For some reason he had been most unwilling that publicity
should be given to their murder, or that they should be recognized
as martyrs. Forty-eight years after, a basilica was erected over
the place of martyrdom. All doubts, however, as to the occur-
rence have now been dispelled by this excavation. The fact
of the house having belonged to Christians, and of its having
been regarded as the scene of their martyrdom has been
thoroughly proved. The paintings on the vault and walls of
the chambers are of sacred subjects. In the cellar are amphoræ
for wine marked with the Christian symbol. Also the very box
of white marble has been found in which the bones of the
martyrs lay till their removal to the upper church in the twelfth
century. Hard by this still stands the Carrara marble three-
cornered table with a bowl for a lamp to burn perpetually at

their tomb. And it was oil from this very lamp that Gregory the Great sent to Queen Theodolinda a century later, in response to her request for relics ; at the same time he reminded her that the worth of a relic depended more on the disposition of the recipient than on the intrinsic value of the object. This flask of oil is still preserved in the treasury at Monza, where Queen Theodolinda's gold hen and chicken are duly kept. By the way, what a satisfaction it was to popes and prelates to be able to make presents that cost them nothing. Now, one cannot give a wedding gift even to a servant girl or a farmer's daughter that costs less than a pound ; *then* a bit of tow dipped in lamp oil, or a scraping of a bone, or an Agnus Dei in wax not worth sixpence was gratefully received. But of course all depended on *where* the oil had been stored and to *whom* the bone belonged.

As in one place in the house there seemed to be a blister in the plaster, it was picked away and disclosed that the mason had put a little lead seal marked with the symbol of Christ against the wall, and then had passed a whitewash brush over it, so as to preserve it as a token that the work had been done by a Christian. When Adrian IV rebuilt the church, which had fallen into ruin, he crammed the house of John and Paul with earth and stones, and used it as a foundation for his super-structure. Till then, pilgrims had visited the old house and had scribbled their *graffiti* on the plaster, as high as they could reach. There had also been constructed for their convenience a stair-case leading to a little window, the *fenestrella confessionis*, through which they could look down on the tomb below lighted by the lamp, and could also lower ribbons so as to touch the marble chest.

I made the acquaintance of Padre Germano, who was most kind, and delighted to find an Englishman enthusiastic in such researches. At the request of the English colony in Rome I gave an address to visitors, on the spot, and took them round, explaining everything.

A further discovery was the old marble altar at which the Holy Sacrifice had been offered from A.D. 363 to 1158. The conversion of the house to a church was due to Byzantius, the father of Pammachius, the correspondent of Jerome. Pammachius somewhat later built a basilica over the place of martyrdom

R

View House on Lew Down and the stable, the snow was massed so that those in the dwelling for a day were employed in cutting through the drift so as to reach the coals that were stored there. At Lifton, as well as other places, parties were formed to carry food to outlying cottages, where the inhabitants were snowed in. The wind was from the northeast. For three or four days all main communications were stopped, no letters went out or arrived, and every village had to depend, in many cases every house, on its own resources. The passengers snowed up in the train at Meldon could not be rescued till the next day, and were found drowsy and stupefied by the cold. Some had not moved or spoken for eighteen hours, and were so torpid that they were unconscious that they were in the hands of helpers to life and activity. The wreckage of trees was prodigious. At Cotehele all the magnificent oaks were prostrated. Great havoc was wrought in the plantations made by my grandfather the year before his death, on the eastern range of the Lime Quarry Ramps. The great cedar west of the ball-room would have been completely broken down under the weight of snow lodged on the branches, had not men with poles been employed repeatedly to relieve it.

The *Tavistock Gazette* was issued on the Friday printed on crimson paper, such as is used generally for advertising placards, as the supply of white paper had run short, and none could be procured from Plymouth or Exeter, on account of the cessation of traffic.

The Rev. Dr. Bryant had been at Lamerton when the storm came on. Nothing daunted, he set off to walk to Brentor vicarage, but on reaching Heathfield he found the roads blocked with snow in which he sank to his waist. He was constrained to proceed on the tops of the hedges, till, reaching a cottage at the junction of several roads, he was so exhausted that he had to beg to be taken in for the night, and he slept on a chair before the fire.

Next day the air was still, and the sun shone brightly. He proceeded on his way, still stumbling along on the tops of hedges, till, coming to a gap where was a gate, he fell into a drift so deep that he sank above his head, and found it impossible to extricate himself. He had to remain buried in snow, shouting for aid, till a farmer, who was out looking for his buried sheep, discovered his parson deep in the snow and managed to pull him out. In this case it was not the pastor who sought and rescued the lost sheep, but the sheep that found and rescued the lost pastor. It was not, however, till the evening that he was able to reach his home, and then only by toilsome travelling on the tops of hedges, and groping for the top-bar, through the snow when he came to a gate. He reached his parsonage famished and exhausted, with his garments torn to shreds by the thorns.

Some of the sheep on Dartmoor were not rescued for over a fortnight. Happily, by their breath they thawed the snow about them and made their way forward so as to obtain grass. There were cases of men who were lost on the moor and were not found till many weeks later, and then, of course, were dead.

The birds suffered severely; many were starved, and lay about dead. The rooks for the nonce became birds of prey and attacked the sparrows, finches and thrushes on the wing, tore them to pieces and devoured them. Their own nests had been choked with snow, and very few young rooks were hatched out that year.

The spring and summer after the blizzard were exceptionally rainy. During the summer I was much engaged in excavating a most puzzling settlement on the slopes above Trewartha Marsh. This marsh occupied the bed of a lake, but miners had lowered the lip by which it decanted from the moor in the direction of Trebartha, and had streamed the basin. Not only was tin, but gold as well was found there, and the old squires of Trebartha were wont to present their daughters, when they married, with gold rings made of the precious metal from the " streamings."

Presumedly the settlement had been occupied by miners, but it must have been at a very early date, judging from the pottery found. We did find one flint tool, but that may well have belonged to earlier settlers. We unearthed a good many hones. One curious feature was the number of baking-ovens built up of granite that remained. All the huts were oblong and we could discover no foundations or remains of chimneys, only hearths on the floor. One long hut was divided into stalls by upright slabs of granite, and before each stall was a hearth stone. The colonists apparently had a stannary court, for one long hut had granite seats ranged down both the long sides, and at the head on one bench, on the left upon entering, was a presidential chair made of granite with granite slabs for arms. Most unfortunately we did not re-bury the remains after excavation, and a farmer carried off the presidential chair and most of the seats in the hall, wherewith to construct a pigsty.

We found no signs anywhere of smelting.

An instance here of corruption of names. A little stream runs down the moor slope to feed the marsh. On the brow of the hill is a gate, which is a well-known place of meeting for the hounds for a hunt. The notice, when such an assembly is to take place, is that it will take place at Rushaford Gate. Now Mr. Rodd of Trebartha informed me that in deeds this is *Thrusleford*, i.e. the ford or way over the Thrustle, Dur-isl, the shallow water; it is a Cornish name.

As the remains on the slopes of Trewartha were so interesting, and had not been noticed on the Ordnance Survey, I wrote to headquarters and requested their insertion. They sent down a man in November. I went with him on November 5 to Trewartha, and was engaged with him all day over the plans. The days in November are short, and we were many miles from any road and any houses. Nevertheless, I had been so often to the spot that I considered myself qualified to find my way back over the moors to Altarnun, where we were to put up at the little inn of Five Lanes. A watershed had to be passed, a backbone of moor with several elevations and depressions. In fact, the horizon to the north had much the appearance of a long Atlantic roller coming in, gathered into knots in places. But there was a point I had forgotten. In taking one's bearings it was necessary to see the five-horned head of Brown Willy to the north-west, and to make for that awhile, then bear away steadily in a more northerly direction. Naturally, with dusk, *dimmets* is the local term, the distant prospect became no longer visible. At last, when we had completed our measurements, my companion closed his book, wound up his chain, and we started for our comfortable little inn, where we knew that a pair of roast ducks, stuffed with onions, was awaiting us. We had been hard at work on the moor at an elevation of something over a thousand feet, since half-past eight, with only a small packet of sandwiches to sustain us, and we looked forward to those ducks.

"You are sure you know the way?" said my companion. "We took an hour and three-quarters reaching here this morning, and in an hour it will be pitch dark."

"In an hour we shall be off the moor and between hedges, with the smell of roast duck wafted down the lane into our noses, to meet us."

My companion was satisfied.

"I only made the remark," said he, "because I did not relish the notion of spending the night on the moor—and in November too. I suppose folks do lose their way sometimes."

"Rather so. Our host at Five Lanes told me of one last night, a native of the moors, who lives somewhere about this section. He went out to the Cheesewring to see some quarryman he knew, and came homewards at dusk—knowing every stone—lost his way, and wandered in a drizzling north-east rain all night, round and round in spirals, and did not reach his home till next day."

"And he knew every stone?"

"Yes, but there was a drizzling rain."

We had mounted a sufficient height to see Brown Willy, if visible, and so take our bearings. I halted and scanned the distance.

"Mr. Thomas," said I in a less confident tone than I had previously assumed, "can you see that five-horned beast, Brown Willy, in the distance against the sky? I am short-sighted."

My companion looked and shook his head.

"Never mind," said I, "Brown Willy is there, but he has drawn on his night-cap. He usually does so at sunset. We will steer our course as if he were visible. We cannot go wrong, I know every inch of the way."

"That is all very fine," said Mr. Thomas. "But it seems to me on this moor that one inch is precisely like every other inch—the same lichens, grasses, water, peat, granite, gravel."

"There are landmarks."

"Which draw on their night-caps when wanted."

" Trust me. We can't go wrong. I have been this way just two dozen times this summer."

" Exactly, but always by day."

I was annoyed.

" You simply *cannot* lose your way wholly on these moors," said I. " When you wish, you can always get off by following the course of a running stream."

" No doubt whatever about that," said my companion, " but as far as my observation has gone to-day, every running stream we have touched has been making as hard as it could in precisely the opposite direction to the roast ducks. Then, in the next place, we are above the region of running streams. We are on a moor where there are sloppy holes, but no streams at all. And, in the third place, that theory of yours of following running streams is uninviting. It means floundering through bogs, leaping confluent streams, tumbling down rocky slopes, where they brawl in cascades—dangerous to bones at night. No, I don't doubt that following running streams will land you somewhere, a maimed, starved wreck, but many, many miles from where you want to be ; from where are dry socks, ducks and bottled stout."

Thomas was hungry, and hunger makes some people querulous. Moreover, he was a Welshman. I was hungry also, but hunger made me incapable of sustaining the effort of controversy. So I let the argument lie.

Presently, to my unbounded surprise, I saw before me, cutting the sky-line, some rude granite upright stones, undoubtedly erected by the hands of men.

" Why, here is a prehistoric monument ! " I exclaimed.

" What of that ? You surely do not propose measuring and planning it now ? "

" No. But this is very extraordinary. I have never seen it before. It is a sacred circle."

" Sacred circle be hanged ! I thought you knew every inch of the way."

" Yes—but——" I said faintly, " we have lost our direction, I have no idea where we are."

Mr. Thomas was aghast. We had been walking for an hour, and it was all but black night. Had there been clouds in the sky, we could have seen nothing. Happily, the heavens were perfectly clear, a halo of departed day filled the region where the sun had set, but that was not the region we were aiming at. My companion was, I believe, too uneasy at the unpleasant discovery to say a word. I stood still to consider. Such a circle of stones as this must have a name, and must be indicated in the large Ordnance. The unsatisfactory conviction came on me that we had got into another section altogether, of which I knew nothing. On one point I was certain ; we had borne away too much to the East.

" Well," said I, " there is nothing for it but to get along as best we may."

" Whither ? "

" Towards the ducks."

" We have got there now, it seems," said Thomas testily, as he splashed into water.

There were tufts of coarse grass and reed, and we strode as best we could from one to another ; then came moss, thick as a sponge, and lanes of water, tracts which faintly reflected the steely sky, with scratches across the plate where a few long fibres of reed had rooted themselves.

" I say," exclaimed Mr. Thomas, " this is serious. How much is there of this ? "

" I cannot tell. I have never been here before. Let us keep apart and keep moving. The moss will not sustain two of us."

" No, nor one of us, if he stands still for a moment to look around."

It was even so. It was absolutely necessary to be on the move. One skipped from treacherous watery places to what seemed solid, but was mere moss, felted together, and which would sustain the weight of a man for a moment, but no more. Whether there were another piece of moss or tuft of reed to leap to or not, it mattered nothing. Go forward we must, or sink.

" It is rolling under me like waves," shouted my companion.

" Yes—it is a quaking bog," I replied. " Keep right forward. I will try to the left and he who reaches firm ground must shout to the other."

We pushed on, but to go in a bee-line was not possible ; one must go where one could, where a chance lay of finding momentary support. Time passed. How long I cannot tell, it seemed an hour, and there was not a token under foot of improvement. We were both exhausted, the effort to extract a foot when it sank was considerable, and the attention had to be on the strain the whole time. I had a long bamboo cane with me, a sort of alpen-stock, that had been picked up on the beach at Bude and which Mr. Radford had given me. It availed nothing for probing the ground ahead, where all was watery and no bottom could be reached. The bog at night exhaled a death-like sickly odour. Not a sound could be heard. No bird was roused, not an insect hummed. It was night now ; not even a spark, not a Jack-o'-Lantern. We could no longer see each other, and had ceased to call to each other. Then all at once a fear came over me that we had got into Crowdy Marsh. I had seen quite enough of that. It is not composed of peat ; it is simply water which is slimy with decomposing vegetable matter. It is dangerous to man and fatal to beasts. Our host at Five Lanes had told us of the severe loss to one farmer that same year of five bullocks that had gone in one after another, and had disappeared. They had been tracked to the edge of the bog, and there they had gone down.

But surely we could not be in Crowdy ; to reach that we must have crossed the main road from Launceston to Bodmin.

All at once I uttered a cry of " Help me ! " and sank to my arm-pits. It was instantaneous. I was in water, not on moss ; and, in sinking all I could do was to catch at some particles of floating moss, slime, half-rotten reed and water-weed, and rake myself forward with strokes like those of a swimmer till I could lay hold of the sponge-like surface of moss that formed the skin over the quaking bog. This moss was a foot thick, very porous, but light, so that it floated till saturated with water. In my struggles, I drew much of this moss towards me, but, as I pressed on it it sank under my weight, became water-logged, and surrounded me, helping to suck me down. Against the wan sky I could see the moss as a mound black as ink, which wavered and rolled as I clung to and dragged at it.

Finding that my efforts were unavailing, and that by this means I could never extricate myself, I extended the bamboo I held horizontally, a hand at each extremity, and pressed this down on the surface of the moss. By this means I managed to heave myself up, and I had just enough power to throw my head and neck for-

HUT CIRCLES ON DARTMOOR

ward on the moss, with arms extended like a spider. I can describe the suction I had to contend against in no more real manner than by saying that I felt as if I were striving against a gigantic octopus that was endeavouring with boneless, fleshy arms to drag me under water. So great indeed was the suction that the leather gaiters that extended to the knee were torn off my legs. There in Red Mire Marsh they remain.

Having thus reached the surface, and spread myself upon it, I worked myself along till I arrived at a hassock of coarse grass or reed, and on that I planted myself to breathe. There could be no growth of reed or grass unless there were soil, so that I trusted I was nearing solid ground.

After awhile I was aware of the shouts of my companion, who was in the greatest alarm. He could neither see me, nor did he know in which direction to look for me. Whether I were alive or dead he could not tell. He himself was in danger, and never able for above a moment to remain in one position.

I had no breath to answer him, and for some minutes he had to endure an agony of apprehension.

At length, however, my breath returned. I was quivering in every muscle after the supreme strain of wrenching myself out of the mire. I called to Thomas to go forward, I would follow, but received no answer. I called again and again, but met with no response.

There was still a long tract of moss very similar in nature to that through part of which I had struggled, and I was fain to go through it in the same manner as before, writhing along like a lizard.

At length I came to firm land, exhausted, panting, my brow beaded with sweat, yet at the same time conscious of extreme cold from immersion. I called again and now received an answer, and soon came up with Thomas. The stench of the decomposing matter in my nostrils sickened me. However, a sense of relief and exhilaration came over me, and we made our way on till we struck a road, and finally reached our inn. I found my purse in my pocket sodden, my watch in my waistcoat pocket stopped.

I have ever entertained a repugnance to wobbly ground. I like to have firm soil under my feet, theologically, morally, socially— and financially.

I do not suppose that Red Mire can in ordinary times be dangerous, certainly not in daylight. It occupies a basin on the summit of a ridge, and therefore cannot be of any depth. However, I found moss on my left shoulder, so that I had sunk so far, and, as I had said, the suction tore the gaiters off my legs. Possibly enough I may have fancied Red Mire worse than it was ; but we were in the pitch darkness of a November night, and we were quite unconscious in which direction to steer to escape out of this Slough of Despond. Never did roast ducks receive a more hearty welcome.

At Christmas I received a letter from the Editor of the *Graphic* asking me to go to Teck, at once, and write an article thereon, as the Duke of Clarence was engaged to marry the Princess Mary of Teck. As the Duke died shortly afterwards, she married the Duke of York.

I started for Teck on December 27 ; and on my return to England went to the Fens of Ely, to work up the material for my novel of *Zita*.

CHAPTER XIX

LES EYZIES
1892

I DECIDED in the winter of 1892 to visit *Les Causses de Languedoc*. Taking the night train from London, I was in Paris at 6 a.m. the next morning. Crossing the Seine for my station to the south, and starting for Brive at 7.40 a.m., I reached this land of marvels in time for dinner that evening. The cost of a ticket from Paris to Pèrigucux or Brive was 25 francs. I made but a short stay at Brive on my first visit, and then by a branch line crossed into the valley of the Vézère, and was deposited at Les Eyzies, a long, straggling village built under overhanging hard chalk cliffs, with an interesting Merovingian church at one end, and a ruined castle at the other. The distance from the station to the very humble inn was somewhat trying. On reaching the cabaret, I found that it consisted of a *salle-à-manger* adjoining the kitchen. As the chimney in the former was persistent in smoking, I usually sat in the kitchen by the fire and superintended the cooking. The inn was run by a dear old woman, who possessed a husband who did nothing but smoke and sip wine, and a son, Gaston, whose sole function consisted in attending to the stable.

The Vézère flows for some three or four miles between over-hanging cliffs of hard chalk that has been gnawed into by the weather, and the cottages are constructed partly against the rock and partly in it by excavation.

Since that first excursion I have made many more, and have recorded my acquaintance with the district in *The Deserts of Central France*, in *Cliff Castles and Cave Dwellings*, and also in my novel *Noémi*.

It is no intention of mine again to describe the topics of interest in the region. But I shall give a few instances of my experience among a specially pleasant and hospitable people.

My first cursory, and necessarily brief visit, revealed to me a region that teemed with interest, and that demanded exploration.

1. The country abounds in remains of primeval man of the age of the rhinoceros, the reindeer and the woolly elephant. This had been disclosed by Christy and Lartet, but in their time, as in that of my first visits, there had not been detected the rock-paintings which were to be found in the caves inhabited at a vastly remote period by our savage, yet artistically gifted ancestors.

2. The land abounds as well in megalithic monuments of the men of the Polished Stone and Early Bronze Period, hitherto principally studied in Brittany.

3. A speciality of the country is the rock dwelling and cave castle. The former the refuge of the peasantry during the miserable period of the Hundred Years' War, the latter the stronghold of the free companies that terrorized Aquitaine.

4. Another object of study are the domed churches, in a style borrowed from Byzantium.

At Brive I called on M. Massénat, a veteran digger in the Périgord caves, and he introduced me to the great deposits of the reindeer hunters at Les Eyzies. Conceive beds for some miles of relics of their feasts, to the depth of over 30 feet, dense with the remains of animals, the reindeer, the mammoth, the woolly elephant, antelopes, cave lions and hyænas, mixed up with flint scrapers and borers. There were also present bone arrows and spear heads, and pieces of ivory bearing rude yet skilful sketches on the bone. M. Massénat had been engaged here for thirty years, and there is enough of the deposit left for exhumation for many more.[1]

At the depth of from 30 to 40 feet are the earliest relics found around hearths, which had been built when the glacial period had come to an end and the country was habitable. I extracted from one hearth a reindeer's lower jaw. The back tooth had been knocked out so that the marrow might be sucked. Above the remains of this race came those of the Flint Age. Above those again were the hearths and deposits of a more

[1] On my last visit to Les Eyzies I found that a road was being driven through these beds, for what object I could not conjecture. No proper supervision was given to the road-makers to secure any find.

civilized race that employed polished weapons, and that built the rude stone circles and dolmens that have excited the wonder of later ages. Above, once more, are the relics of the Bronze Age, then those of the men of the Iron Age, the Gauls, with an occasional Roman coin, and then mediæval scraps. Finally the *sous* dropped by the peasant men who live in these caves with merely a face of masonry to serve as a screen against wind and rain.

What a Book of Chronicles the earth is ! Beneath the soil is the record of Creation, written in indelible lines ; the soil itself gives the history of man, to be read with pick and shovel.

When I was last at Les Eyzies the remarkable wall-paintings of primitive man had been recently discovered. In the depths of the caves, by artificial light, man had made his first pictorial experiments with red, brown and yellow ochres as pigments. Before this discovery all that had been known of man's first essays in art had been his sculptures and scratchings on reindeer bones and the pelvis of slain beasts. What was now revealed was of supreme interest. One stood at the bifurcation of two distinct schools of art ; the Oriental, synthetical, adaptive, and the European, analytical, originative ; that of Prometheus on one side and of Epimetheus upon the other.

The school-boy who has spilled a drop of ink on his copy-book, and with his pen seeks to shape it into a black-beetle, a horse or a human head, by adding here and cancelling there, is Epimetheus. But the lad who with a bit of chalk sketches his schoolmaster on the blackboard, represents the school of art that in sculpture reached its acme in Athens, and in painting its highest development in the works of the great Italian and Flemish artists. The branch of art to which the adaptation of the blot extended found its most exquisite representation in Japan. Beginning with a dab of paint, the Oriental artist went on by trimming and moulding, by the addition of other blots to represent a spray of syringa, a branch of flowering cherry, a shoal of rainbow fish, or a posse of dragons and dæmons. The Epimethean artist could never reach the point attained by the Promethean. The latter had studied what he had observed ; the former had only thought of conforming his blot to whatsoever beautiful representation it would lend itself. The former was led by fancy, not by intelligence.

It must be noticed that in Nature there is no such a thing as an outline. The outline is as distinctly an artificial creation as is the hedge around a field. No one has ever seen an outline in Nature ; only masses, bulks, substances. Consequently the discovery of the outline by primeval man was a distinct effort of intellect, the exercise of analysis.

At Donaueschingen, in the park of Prince Fürstenberg burst out numerous springs of water. One can stride from such sources as flow east and go to form the Danube, to such as well up to feed the Rhine, flowing west. And here, at Les Eyzies, the visitor stands with one foot on the spring of Oriental art and the other on that of Art Occidental ; poor little trickles each, yet each having a determinate course, and capable of indefinite expansion.

Art is found in every early race, the Hottentot, the North American Indian, the New Zealander and the Hindu weaver and metal worker ; only the English builder in towns seems to be devoid of the faculty. The first attempts of the artist are to copy Nature. The matured artist learns to discriminate, to select, to discard certain features and to heighten certain other. Nature is so complex, one portion balancing another, that the artist can produce a harmonious whole on his canvas only by limiting the objects he depicts and bringing them into accord. He has to pack all within range of sight into a space of a few feet or inches.

I am like a grasshopper in literature, I leap from one leaf to another. I must quit the prehistoric for the present.

On a subsequent visit I was told by my friend De Bosredon of three old ladies in the department, the Demoiselles Perrault, or as they called themselves De Perrault. They were descended from Charles Perrault, the French writer who died in Paris, May 16, 1703. His great efforts were directed towards showing how vastly superior were the modern authors to those of antiquity, and he wrote a piece of buffoonery on " The Walls of Troy." In the poem *Le Siècle de Louis le Grand* he declared that—

" Les Regniers, les Maynards, les Gomboulds, les Melherbes,
 Les Godeaux, les Rancans, . . .
 Les galants Sarrazins, et les tendres Voitures,
 Les Molières naïfs, les Rotrous, les Tristans,
 Et cent autres encore, délices de leur temps,"

far excelled Homer, Herodotus, Plato, Aristotle, Virgil and the rest of the classic authors.

It would have surprised Perrault beyond measure had he known that of all his writings that alone which would confer immortality on him would be his *Contes des Fées*, the first edition of which appeared in 1697. This speedily won for the author a fame that will never perish.

Does my reader know or possess the *Cabinet des Fées* in thirty-seven volumes, 1785–86? Perrault was the author of *Little Red Ridinghood, Puss in Boots, Cinderella, Hop-o'-my-Thumb*, etc. He set the fashion and was followed by the Countess d'Aulnoy, with *Beauty and the Beast, The Fair Maid with Golden Locks, The Blue Bird*, etc. Counts and countesses rivalled each other in their collections of fairy tales. These were not all original. Many, especially those of Perrault, were old French nursery tales rescued from oblivion.

How I have loved those thirty-seven volumes! How I have read and reread them; and could read them again had I not other matters to occupy my mind!

But to return to the Demoiselles. They were the last of the descendants of one of the sons or brothers of Charles Perrault. On their father's death his inheritance fell to the three sisters, and they divided it among them; one retained the château; the second the plate; and the third as her share had the family portraits, chief in value among which was that of Charles Perrault. As to the family linen and the furniture, it was parted among the sisters.

It so fell out that annually one or other of the Mesdemoiselles Perrault proposed giving an entertainment to the neighbours on the anniversary of Charles Perrault's birth (Jan. 12). Thereupon Julie, the eldest, yielded her château to receive the guests, Charlotte contributed the ancestral porcelaine and plate, and Babette, the third, sent the portrait of the great author of *Peau d'Ane* and *Petit Poucet* to be hung up in the *salle-à-manger*, there to be solemnly toasted by the guests, standing, and clinking glasses all the way round the table, at which the dear old ladies would burst into tears and wipe the floods away with their white handkerchiefs.

What would I not have given to have been present and to have

s

conveyed one across to La Laugerie, the great resort of geologists, and where most of the houses were excavated in the rock.

The boatman at the upper ferry had been in the army, had served in China, and had taken part in the pillage of the Winter Palace in Pekin. He had a little cabaret on the further side of the river but did a poor business with the cave dwellers, who were not numerous and were very poor. I went into his house to share a bottle of wine with him, whereupon he told me that of the spoils of the Pekin palace he had secured a gorgeous waistcoat, "which," said he, " I wear on high days and holidays when I go to church. Then I make my wife walk behind me."

" In that," said I, " you make an error in judgment."

" How so ? "

" As you go up the lane and along the street, the people obtain but a partial glimpse of your finery, what they see most of is the back of your coat and the seat of your trousers. Now, were you to provide your wife with your little boy's penny trumpet, and bid her precede you, blow a blast, and proclaim that The Waistcoat was on its way to Mass, the people would line up on each side of the road so as to obtain a good and satisfying sight of your glories."

" There is something in what you say," observed the man meditatively. " I will give the matter full consideration."

" Do you go often to church ? " I asked.

" Only when the waistcoat goes on great festivals. Beautiful and splendid things should not be made too common."

" One of our great poets said something of the same kind."

" Ah ! " he observed. " Great minds often hit on the same ideas, independently of each other."

I asked Gaston, the son of my landlady, whether he ever went to church. " Never," he replied.

" A bad look-out for you," I remarked, " when you enter Heaven, where it is church-going every day and all day long."

" I'll take my chance," he replied. " When I get a new suit of clothes, and a fresh pair of boots, I am in a state of discomfort for a fortnight. But I accommodate myself to my pantaloons and boots, or else they accommodate themselves to me. It will be much the same, I take it, hereafter."

Alas ! Gaston had caught a fever and was dead when last I

visited Les Eyzies. So he has gone to accommodate himself, or to be accommodated, in his new situation. I think the former will have to be the case, and not be got over in a fortnight.

I did not by any means confine myself to the Vézère valley, but widely explored the great elevated plateau about Gramat. I also wandered up and down the Dordogne and the Lot, and visited the numerous cliff castles to be found there.

I take but a single incident out of many occurrences, as illustrative of the Gascon character.

At Souillac one day a nice-looking girl, the daughter of our host, waited at table. She had very fair golden hair, large blue eyes and a clear and rosy complexion. She looked like a typical English girl : surely a trace of our domination over Aquitaine that we exercised for over a hundred years.

A bagman was one of the guests, and he sat by me. A dish of mushrooms was handed round. " How do you know," said the *commis voyageur*, " that these are not toadstools and poisonous ? " " I have eaten some myself," the waitress replied, so as to allay his scruples. " Pass me the dish ! " exclaimed the commercial traveller, " it will be so sweet for us to die together."

During the dinner I talked with the man, and chanced to mention Sarlat, as a place I had visited.

" Ah ! " he exclaimed, " you stayed at Sarlat—surely at the Hôtel de la Madeleine ? "

" Certainly I did."

" And you found the hostess a charming woman, and so sympathetic."

At once the young waitress interposed. Swinging herself round in face of the bagman, she said : " Just now, monsieur ! you wanted to die with me, and now you are praising the beauty and belauding the sympathy of Madame la propriétaire de l'hôtel de la Madeleine à Sarlat."

" Mademoiselle," rejoined he, with great composure. " I am so constituted by Nature that to see, even to think of, a woman overpowers me. You, at the moment, were behind my back, so my mind reverted to Sarlat. Now that I see you in full face, I feel sure that, not to die with you, but to live with you, would be supreme felicity."

There was a bagman for you, and a true Gascon !

The Swiss were a poor people, mainly peasants cultivating their little farms, and the only rich folk were the hotel-keepers who entertained tourists, English, American and German, and the hotel-keepers as a class were not disposed to give much to the Church. Accordingly, as he devoted himself to painting religious pictures only, he sold them *um einen Spottpreis*, as the Germans say. He never received more than a most modest sum for his paintings, and consequently died a comparatively poor man, leaving his savings to hospitals and orphanages.

The resolution he had formed condemned him to become only a second, or third-rate artist, for it debarred him from devoting time, study and pains to execute great works of art. There ensued such a demand for sacred pictures for the Swiss Churches, that in one year, 1870, he painted fifty-three; in 1871, that in which he did our altar-piece, he disposed of forty-nine. Such rapidity of execution, about a week over a large painting, was fatal to advancement in his art. He knew that well, and knew that it was one of the sacrifices he must make if he held to his resolution to do all for the glory of God, and not so as to make for himself a name as a first-class painter.

At Stans he has left a lasting memorial of himself. For the cemetery where his family had been laid from generation to generation, and where he himself now reposes, he painted a picture to adorn the graveyard chapel. It represents Moses on Mount Nebo, kneeling with outstretched arms towards the Promised Land, which he might see, and to which during forty years he had journeyed, but into which he was not suffered to enter. The scene is evening, and the setting sun is on the dying man's face. It was an expression of the longing of Paul's heart throughout his pilgrimage from the day that he stood before Milan Cathedral and devoted all his powers to the service of God. But, unlike Moses, he was destined to pass over and to enter into the land flowing with milk and honey.

In his last will, he characteristically commended his soul to God, " in Whom is supreme Beauty and perfect Love."

What Samuel Butler has said in his *Alps and Sanctuaries* of the poet is true also of the painter : " The poet is not known by knowledge alone—not by *gnosis* only—but also, and in greater

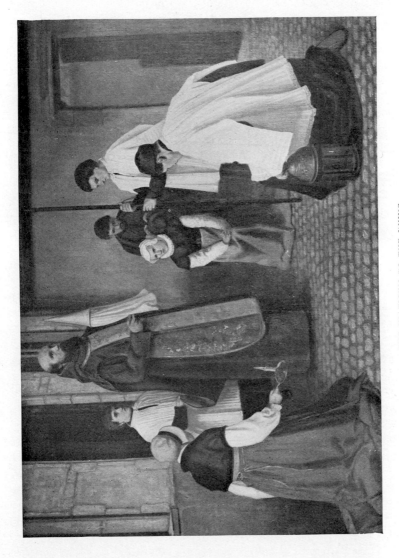

THE VIATICUM TO THE DYING
Painting by Ed. Tyck

part, by the *agape* which makes him wish to steal men's hearts, and prompts him so to apply his knowledge that he shall succeed." This applies to Deschwanden. His whole life was spent in appealing to the human heart to love God, and to draw nigh to Him ; he chose to know no more of the technicalities—the *gnosis*, of high art than sufficed for his purpose.

Another artist of whom I possess several paintings is Lavidière. When I visited Rheims on my wedding tour I was struck by a "Crucifixion" hung in the vestry. It showed the dying Saviour on the cross, in the light of the setting sun dipping under the western horizon among dark clouds dyed red. The sacristan told me that it was for sale ; it was painted by a local artist, named Lavidière. I purchased it, and it now hangs in Lew Church over the screen. At my request he painted a duplicate, which was much inferior to the original. This I gave to one of the Southwark churches.

The artist afterwards moved to Paris, where I visited him. He also painted for me a full-sized Entombment ; but this suffered through being hung against a damp wall. He did me a duplicate, which I gave to a church in the East End of London. He also painted for me an Ecce Homo, a landscape in the Bois de Boulogne, with in it two couchant white goats, and, as a present, a plucked fowl. Lavidière's great power was in painting flesh : and as a technical artist he stands far higher than Deschwanden.

Another foreign artist who has done work for me was Edouard Tyck, of Antwerp, of whom I have already made mention. He belonged to the new and rising school of Flemish artists. One of the best works of that school is the series of Stations of the Cross in Antwerp Cathedral. Tyck painted for me the Visit to the Dying, a friar carrying the Viaticum ; also a Flemish girl in the dress of the sixteenth century, leaving her house for the market.

Tyck came to visit me at East Mersea, and I took him to London and to Windsor. He was almost stunned by the ugliness of English street architecture as he looked at the house fronts about Russell Square. When he exclaimed at it I reminded him of the houses in the new part of Antwerp near the citadel. " It is true," said he, " the disease of the unsightly has manifested itself in my country, but in yours it has taken possession of the whole of your towns, like leprosy that masters the whole man." I took him to S. Alban's Church, Holborn, and he was much pleased with the service, and the picturesqueness of the precentor at a lectern in the midst of the choir, with his rod and habited in a cloth of gold cope. He pulled out a pocket-book and made a sketch.

Whilst I was at Hurstpierpoint I made great friends with one Lawless, an Irishman, and a charming artist. He was much bitten with the new Flemish school, but objected to a defect, as he esteemed it, in the shading. I possess no complete work of his ; only the head-piece and bust of a French peasant girl at the well with her *cruche*. I completed the painting as best I could. His last work exhibited in the Royal Academy represented a canal in a Belgian town, a priest carrying the Blessed Sacrament to the dying, and men, women and children on the bank kneeling.

Another artist I have employed has been Luigi Ghedina of Cortina d'Ampezzo. He had studied in Venice. He painted for me and for Lord Iddesleigh my great-aunt Lady Northcote.

When we were at Cortina he did the portrait of my wife. This, however, proved unsatisfactory, as he had made her look upwards to heaven, attracted, may be, by her sweet and spiritual expression. But as it happened, her eyes were invariably cast modestly down. The portrait was so unnatural to me that I got Head to alter the direction of the eyes. Alas ! that was a fatal blunder, for it threw all the muscles of the brow and cheek wrong. The painting is consigned to a dark corner, because the portrait, thus tampered with, proved a caricature.

In the course of my middle and later life I have had the happiness of being acquainted with two of the noblest men I could anywhere have met—Mr. Daniel Radford and Mr. W. J. Harris, of Halwill.

Mr. Radford was he who started me upon my labour of over ten years collecting the folk-melodies of Devon and Cornwall. His residence, when I first knew him, was the Bridge House, Lydford. Later he purchased Mount Tavy above Tavistock. He had begun life in a humble position, and with infirm health. He told me that he never knew a day without being in pain, yet by his integrity, assiduity and intelligence, he acquired a large fortune. One of the most simple yet beautiful memoirs I have ever read has been that which he wrote towards the close of his days. I thoroughly appreciated the loftiness of his character and his stirling qualities. Further acquaintance caused me to value him ever more and more, and to love him. In fact I do not know of any man who, in my middle life, exercised a stronger influence over me.

The Radford family exhibits a notable instance of the mutability of family fortunes. It was anciently seated at Okeford, also at Cheynstone in Chawleigh, North Devon, and in the church are several monuments to the family. But the last there estated died in 1703. By a succession of misadventures it did not rise to activity and position again till it was lifted to its present honourable state by Mr. Daniel Radford.

A curious instance of sudden expansion and subsequent contraction in a family is instanced in my own. John Prince, Vicar of Berry Pomeroy in 1681, published his *Worthies of Devon* in 1701. In that he said of the Gould family : " Edward Gould of Combe (in Staverton) was as memorably blessed in his issue as most we have ever met with ; for of his six sons, five lived to be men of great estates, and left them to their posterity ; in which they still flourish in very creditable fashion. . . . If ill-will, in defiance to the truth, shall deny antiquity to this family, yet this cannot be denied, that, however it sate out later than some others, it hath grown faster and spread wider than those who started long before it."

Note this. The whole family has but one single male representative at the present date, 1920, and he is very aged and unmarried. The family is now continued through the female line, and does not exhibit much token of further shrinking, for I have ten grandsons, and five male cousins.

The second friend to whom I have referred was Mr. W. J. Harris, of Halwill. He had been a corn-merchant in London, who had amassed a fortune. He purchased Halwill manor and settled there. A more desolate and intractable piece of country can hardly be conceived ; all stiff clay, growing only rushes and coarse grass, and oozing with water from its many swamps. Cottages of cob were few, and the inhabitants ignorant and poor. Mr. Harris spent thousands of pounds in draining land that would not repay the outlay. Then he broke up the estate into small holdings, built cottages, unhappily as ugly as ugliness could well be, and

I entertained a great affection for the jackdaws, audacious and clever birds. One in particular became very intimate with us at Lew House, and lost all shyness; in fact, became somewhat too forward. In a word, the jackdaw is a vulgar bird, devoid of breeding. Give him an inch and he will take an ell.

One day my favourite jackdaw entered the best bedroom. On the dressing-table was my christening pincushion, large and ornamental, of white silk and lace, with my name and the date of my baptism inscribed on it by means of pin-heads. Jack deliberately extracted all the pins, strewed the floor with them and tore the lace. I forgave Jack.

We had a young lady staying at the house. He entered her window, during the breakfast hour, and carried off a diamond ring that inadvertently had been left on the table. Happily it was recovered from the gutter between the roofs. Again, I forgave Jack.

The next bit of mischief that he perpetrated was the getting hold of an inkstand and spilling the contents over the sheets and counterpane of a bed. This was carrying his fun a little too far. A few mornings after that, seeing the window of the room in which the governess slept open, he perched on the sill, and stood consulting what mischief he would next commit. But she, observant and suspicious, caught up the candlestick which stood by the bedside and flung it at the bird. It hit him on the head. I was in the room below, and, seeing candlestick and bird fall past the window, I darted out into the court, put my foot on the prostrate daw and proceeded to wring his neck. So that was the end of Poor Jack.

The crow also is an enemy that has to be fought. I had at one time nineteen peafowl; I have now only three. I cannot rear the young. The crows possess a great partiality for young pea-fowl, and every year, so soon as the young have ripened into tasty morsels, the crows carry them off deliberately and without shame.

For " mice and rats and such small deer " I have no pity. They are mischievous and destructive creatures and must be exterminated.

When I was in Essex, the incumbent of Layer Marney, a converted Jew, advertised a pigeon-shooting match for the benefit of his church that needed restoration. Happily the bishop heard of this outrageous proposal and put a stop to it. Pigeon-shooting is cruel sport. Sport, indeed! Some men think that the best of sport consists in the torturing and slaying of innocent creatures.

It has always been a matter of interest to me at Lew to supervise the work of my masons, and it has been advantageous to me as cultivating patience, and preventing petulance.

The Devonshire man is an inveterate talker, and when he has something to say he downs his tools and cannot be induced to resume them till he has exhausted the subject.

The watches of these men have the peculiarity of construction, that they permit their owners to arrive half an hour late in the morning, and announce to them the time for leaving their work half an hour before my watch and all the clocks in the house declare that time of day. Another peculiarity of their watches is that they prolong the dinner-hour from noon to a quarter past one, or even half-past one. The masons have to be watched, for they are liable to commit blunders unless supervised. I was writing in my library one morning when I heard much thumping with a crow-bar. I went out to ascertain what was being broken up and discovered that my head mason was smashing up a granite doorway that had been ejected from its place by my grandfather and used for garden steps.

I have been informed by naval men that though Devonians make capital sailors they are dreaded for their loquacity. So do they make capital masons, capable of turning their hands to many descriptions of work, but you must not attempt to bridle their tongues.

The squab-pie is completed, and is ready to be covered up with the pastry.

INDEX

ADAM and Eve, and the Baker, 60
Addison, Joseph, on Folk-songs and ballads, 209
Adersbach, labyrinth of, 174, 176
Adrian IV, Pope, 240, 241, 242
Aggett, William, song from, 206
Algäu Alps, 67 *sqq.*
All Saints' customs, Freiburg, 89–91
Almuces at Genoa, 220
Alt-Catholic Church and Sect, Freiburg, 99
Amusements of our forefathers, 271 *sqq.*
Angell, Mr., 116
Animal sacrifice in Devon, 127
Anne, Queen of Bohemia, embroidery by, 167
Anwyll, Rev. —, 119
" Arscott of Tetcott," song, 184
Art, two schools of, development of, 255–6
Arts, the, in modern Italy, 221
Ashburton family and the Goulds, 77–8
" At the Setting of the Sun," song, 192
Augsburg and the Fuggers, 157–9
Augustus, Emperor, and the bachelors, 227 ; statue of, 224
Avenues, indicative of political views, 104

BABINSKY, the bandit, 177, 179
Baden, population of, 93

Bairischer Wald, burial customs, 161–2, 165 ; peaks of, 161
Baker, Mathew, 43–4 ; song from, 212
Mrs., 39, 42, 43–4
Baldersby, 18, 19
Church, 20
Park, 19, 20, 21
Ballads, printed, untrustworthy, 185–6
" Barbara Allen," 201, 209
Baring, Alexander, 154, 155 ; wedding of, 153–4
Baring, Charles, marriage of, with Margaret Gould, 77
Baring, Charles (II), wives and son of, 154–5
Baring, Mrs. Charles, portrait of, 154–5
Baring-Gould family
Barbara (Mrs. L. Burnard), 270
Beatrice, 145
Julian, 84, 146
Margaret (Mrs. P. D. Rowe), 37, 85
Mrs. Sabine (*née* Taylor), 28 ; Ghedina's portrait of, 268
Rev. Charles, 83, 106–7 ; death of, 100–1
Baring-Gould, Rev. —, half-brother, 112
" Barley Straw," song, 205
Barton, Andrew, ballad on, 188
Basle, Council of, 57
Bate, Spence, and Folk-song collecting, 189–90

Bath Abbey, E. Gould buried in, 77–8
Bear-baiting, 271
Beare family and the Rectory of Lew Trenchard, 103
Beef, a round of, 24–5
Belgian school of painting, 51–2
Belgium, holidays in, 51 *sqq.*; racial differences in, 53
"Bell-ringers, The," song, 201
Bennett, John, songs from, 205
Bentinck, Baron, 223
Bickersteth, E. H., Bishop of Exeter, 118–9
Bickersteth, Robt., Bishop of Ripon, 1
Bidder, Miss, 204
Birch-Pfeiffer, Frau, 86
Birth customs, Yorks., 22
Bishops, 13, 120
Bismarck, Prince, and his sons, 87–8
Black Forest, autumnal glory of, 85
Blood, flow of, charm to stop, 143, 144
Blundell's school, 115, 117
Bodmin Moor
  Gold, 245
  Lost on, 247 *sqq.*
Bohemia, Germanization of, 169; Jews of, 169; religious wars in, 168–9; tours in, 164 *sqq.*
Bohemian glass industry, 164–5
Böhmer Wald, 161, 164–5
"Bold Dragoon, The," song, 202
Bologna, visited, 231–2
Bovey Tracey altar lights, 117
Braganza, Duke of, and his brother; names of their father, 153
Bramwell, Baron, 34
Bread and wine, oblation of, Milan, 218
Brive, 253, 254
Brixham, 112
"Brixham Town," song, 202

Brixlegg, Passion Play at, 61–2
Broadom, hut circles of, 270
Broadwood and other churches, ghosts at, 125
Broadwoodwidger, Jack o' Lantern stories at, 122
"Brown Girl, The," song, 201
Brown Willy, 246–7
"Bryan o' Lyn," song, 198
Bryant, Rev. Dr., 271; adventures of, in the blizzard, 244–5
Buddle, ghost at, 124
Bulbs, wise and unwise, 243
Bull-baiting, 271
Burgoyne, Sir M., 108
Burial customs: Bairischer Wald, 161–2; Oetz Thal, 152; Patznauner Thal, 150; Yorks., 7
Burnard, Laurence, 270
  Robert, 113, 270
Burns or scalds, charm for, 144
Bussell, Miss, 185, 212
  Mrs., 135, 137, 185, and the owls, 273
  Rev. Dr. F. W., Mus.Bac., 135, 273, and Jowett, 136–7, and Folk-song collecting, 185 *sqq.*
Butterfield, the architect, 19
Byshop, John, Rector of Lew Trenchard, 103
Byzantius and Pammachius, 241, 242

CALDER River and Dale, 1 *sqq.*
Caligula, 238
Calmady-Hamlyn, Mrs., on Ploughing oxen, 208
Campbell, Mrs., songs collected by, with C. J. Sharp, 210
Campo de' Fiori, Rome, *autos-da-fé* in, 224
Camps, prehistoric, on Dartmoor, 270

Candlesticks, candles, and snuffers, 131 *sqq.*
as weapons, 134
Capitoline Museum, Rome, 234
Carrousel, the, Wurzburg, 55
Cass, Rev. A., 11–12
Catechizing of males in S. Ambroggio, Milan, 218
Catholic spirit diffused but suppressed, 106
Catholicism in Bohemia, 168
Causses de Languedoc, Les, visited, 253
Cave-dwellings, Les Eyzies, 253–5 ; wall-paintings in, 255
Chagford singers, songs from, 205–6, 211
Charles I, 80
Charles II, 81
Charles V, and the Fuggers, 158
Cheese, Rev. Mr., 23
Cheesewring, Dartmoor, 247
Child, Professor, 201
" Childe, the Hunter," ballad of, and its tune, 202
" Children in the Wood, The," ballad, 209 *n.*
Christian, E., architect, 84
Christmas Day at Lew, 1862, 109–10
" Christ's Hand " plant, 139–40
Church-going at Les Eyzies, 260
Compulsory, 108, 109
Church-grims or Bahr-ghests, 125–6
Church Revival, beginning of, 102, 107
Church screens, Earle's destruction of, 119
Church towers and spires, 72
Churches, domed, Les Eyzies district, 254
Cinnamon, ginger, and owls, 274, 275
Clarence, Duke of, death of, 252
Clementi-Smith, Rev. A., 18–19

Clerical drinkers, Swiss, 30–1
Reading, 22
Cleve, Moses, song from, 202
Cliff castles of the Dordogne, 261
Cloaks, Italian way of wearing, 217–18
Cloud-scapes in Essex, 48–9
Coaker, Jonas, songs from, 201–2
Cockerell, Mr. and Mrs., 48–9
Cockfighting, 271–2
Colchester, siege of, 40–1
" Cold Blows the Wind To-night, Sweetheart," ballad, 202
Cole, King, 63
Collins, Rev. R., 19–20
Colliers, 1
Cologne Cathedral, 68, 71
Como, cold at, 216–17
Confessional, the, and women, 262
Connaught, Duke of, courtesy of ; a contrast to, 67
Constantia, daughter of Constantine the Great, 240
Contes des Fées (Perrault), 257
Copper boot for heating spiced ale, 135
Coquilicot, M., and Mlle Jeanetton, 258–9
Cornish Folk-songs, collecting, 186, 204–5
Corregio's " Magdalen," 181, 183
Corso races, Rome, 233–4
Coryton black dog, 126
Courtship, a life-long, 190
Cranstown, Lord, 78
Cromwell, Oliver, 40, 80
Crowdy Marsh, 250
Crows, 276
Cunninghame, Anne Selby, Lady Ashburton, 78
Curates at Lew, 105, 112–13
Cures for costiveness, jaundice, and sprains, 144
Cyder song, evolution of, 187
Czechs, the, 161

T *